Advance Praise for *The Marketing Playbook*

"High-tech marketing—hell, any marketing—frequently hovers in the clouds, about forty thousand feet above real customers. At best, it's a costly effort . . . whose effectiveness is difficult to gauge. *The Marketing Playbook* . . . is not fodder for consultants but fuel for sales. Better get a copy before your next board meeting—and before your competition does!"

—Bob Stearns, founder and managing director, Sternhill Partners, and
former chief technical and strategy officer, Compaq Computer Corp.

"At last, an easy-to-use marketing book with all the value of a business textbook but without the heft and heavy theory. . . . Save your business from any Monday-morning quarterbacking by studying and following *The Marketing Playbook*."

—Doug MacKay, president, MacKay Media

"You can beat your competition and *The Marketing Playbook* will show you how. Written in the language of real business people who know what it takes—and have the battle scars to prove it!"

—Tod Nielsen, chief marketing officer, BEA Systems

"We live in a world of cultured messages. You often only get one chance to do it right and be successful. Any businessperson entering a market, launching a product, or kicking off a campaign would be well advised to read and heed *The Marketing Playbook*. Use it to test-drive your strategy and hone your message, and come back to it to stay on track as the results come in."

—Pam Edstrom, founder and executive vice president,
Waggener Edstrom, 2004 *PR Week* Agency of the Year award

"John and Rich have had ringside seats to the launch and development of some of the most powerful brands in the world, and they've packaged that experience into strategies that you can put into motion the moment you finish the book. Obviously, tech marketers can benefit from this team's insights, but any company looking for a simple, powerful marketing system will find value here."

—Christopher Ireland, principal and CEO, Cheskin

"*The Marketing Playbook* is like a 'Best-of-Both Play' cross between Michael Porter's *Competitive Strategy* and Adrian Slywotzky's *Art of Profitability*. Its powerful metaphors and insightful strategy tools make it a great addition to any business leader's arsenal."

—Dr. Mohanbir Sawhney, McCormick Tribune Professor of Technology and director of the Center for Research in Technology & Innovation, Kellogg School of Management, Northwestern University

The
Marketing
Playbook

The Marketing Playbook

Five Battle-Tested Plays
for Capturing and Keeping
the Lead in Any Market

John Zagula and Richard Tong

Portfolio

PORTFOLIO
Published by the Penguin Group
Penguin Group (USA) Inc., 375 Hudson Street, New York, New York 10014, U.S.A.
Penguin Group (Canada), 10 Alcorn Avenue, Toronto, Ontario, Canada M4V 3B2
  (a division of Pearson Penguin Canada Inc.)
Penguin Books Ltd, 80 Strand, London WC2R 0RL, England
Penguin Ireland, 25 St. Stephen's Green, Dublin 2, Ireland (a division of Pearson Books Ltd)
Penguin Books Australia Ltd, 250 Camberwell Road, Camberwell, Victoria 3124, Australia
  (a division of Pearson Australia Group Pty Ltd)
Penguin Books India Pvt Ltd, 11 Community Centre, Panchsheel Park, New Delhi – 110 017, India
Penguin Group (NZ), Cnr Airborne and Rosedale Roads, Albany, Auckland, New Zealand
  (a division of Pearson New Zealand Ltd)
Penguin Books (South Africa) (Pty) Ltd, 24 Sturdee Avenue, Rosebank, Johannesburg 2196,
  South Africa

Penguin Books Ltd, Registered Offices: 80 Strand, London WC2R 0RL, England

First published in 2004 by Portfolio, a member of Penguin Group (USA) Inc.

10 9 8 7 6 5 4 3 2 1

PUBLISHER'S NOTE: This publication is designed to provide accurate and authoritative information in regard to the subject matter covered. It is sold with the understanding that the publisher is not engaged in rendering legal, accounting, or other professional services. If you require legal advice or other expert assistance, you should seek the services of a competent professional.

LIBRARY OF CONGRESS CATALOGING-IN-PUBLICATION DATA
Zagula, John.
    The marketing playbook : five battle-tested plays for capturing and keeping the lead in
any market / John Zagula and Richard Tong.
        p.   cm.
    Includes index.
    ISBN 1-59184-038-4
    1. Marketing.   2. Marketing research.   3. Strategic planning.   I. Tong, Rich, 1961-
II. Title.
    HF5415.Z24 2004
    658.8'02—dc22   2004048540

This book is printed on acid-free paper. ∞

Printed in the United States of America

To Terri, for your unfailing perspective, judgment, and partnership

—JZ

To Connie, for your love and support

—RT

Strategy without tactics is the slowest route to victory.
Tactics without strategy is the noise before defeat.

—SUN TZU, CHINESE GENERAL, CIRCA 500 B.C.

Contents

Foreword

By Steve Hooper, former CEO of McCaw Cellular, AT&T Wireless, Nextlink, and Teledesic, and partner/founder of Ignition Partners

When I first met Rich and John, I wondered about these loud, opinionated Microsoft types who were communicating more by e-mail than face-to-face, and who didn't believe anything they heard unless it was presented in PowerPoint slides. They seemed like alien creatures.

They also spoke in an alien language, continuously saying things like "Let's start with the ABCs of this business," or "That company needs a clearer set of XYZs," or "The last thing this company needs to do is a High–Lo Double Drag Race." Made all the worse by their exchanging of knowing nods and under-the-table Blackberry™ messages every time.

Regardless of the company, industry, or topic we were discussing, they were always ready with lots of opinions about how to make the most out of marketing and business situations of widely varying kinds, and surprisingly enough they were usually right on target.

They were able to quickly simplify complicated technology discussions and presentations into short assessments and conclusions that just about everyone understood.

Maybe, I thought to myself, there might be something to all these secret code words after all.

I asked Rich and John to explain their curious phrases and mysterious methodologies, and the responses I got were simple, clear, and immediately valuable. I quickly understood the A, B, Cs, the X, Y, Zs, and the five plays. They had also developed a great toolkit for company and product positioning and for refining these into communications and hard-hitting in-market campaigns. And all of the tools in this system were really straightforward and easy to apply.

Over four years and thousands of business plans later, I and all of the companies I work with are using these tools and methods as if we had been using them all our lives.

The simple approaches laid out in this book are truly powerful. They have made it a heck of a lot easier for countless companies, mine included, to get to the heart of issues, define value, address priorities and strategies more quickly, and communicate all of these more succinctly and convincingly to all of their target audiences.

I'm confident you will find them as useful as I have.

Acknowledgments

As we have said throughout these chapters, whatever the play, you can't execute it yourself, you need a team to make it happen. In nothing has this been more true than in the development of these ideas and in the writing of this book. We have worked with a terrific team of people all the way and we owe them all a huge debt of gratitude. We do scant justice to their efforts and contributions by acknowledging them here.

Our deep and abiding thanks to three groups without whom this book would not and could not have been written:

- our longtime friends and colleagues from Microsoft, together with whom we laid the groundwork of the core concepts and components of the Playbook system;
- the entrepreneurs and company leaders with whom we have had the more recent privilege to work as part of our jobs at Ignition Partners—as well as the terrific Ignition team itself, who have tested, hardened, applied, refined, and expanded the relevance of the Playbook as a whole in the high-intensity forge of start-up capitalism;

• and finally, the brilliant, dedicated, immensely tolerant, encouraging, and supportive group of people who helped us pull this book together over so many months of twists, turns, and just plain hard work.

We owe a special debt of gratitude to longtime colleague Jonathan Roberts for his pioneering work on the plays themselves. He has been a true friend and teammate from the early days at Microsoft to our current endeavors at Ignition Partners.

At Microsoft, we both learned so much from great bosses who believed in us and gave us the greatest experiences we could hope for. Thanks to Jim Allchin, Pete Higgins, Paul Maritz, Bob Muglia, Jeff Raikes, Paul Shoemaker, Brad Silverberg, and Dawn Trudeau for all your faith in us. And of course lasting thanks to Bill Gates and Steve Ballmer for making Microsoft such a unique place. We will always remember the late John Neilson for showing us what "being upbeat" can do for any problem.

Our experience with PC Excel, then an underdog and now a market leader, formed the basis of our first Playbook. Thanks to Mike Conte, Joe Krawczak, Dave Malcolm, Dawn Trudeau, Hank Vigil, Liz Welch, Phil Welt, and the other early PC Excel product managers for blazing the trail. The Office marketing team, as they developed a whole new software category, helped evolve this Playbook significantly. Thanks to Robbie Bach, Reed Koch, Mark Kroese, Lewis Levin, Ruthann Lorentzen, Jon Reingold, John Sage, and Dennis Tennis for showing us the way.

From Windows marketing, we learned how an ecosystem gets created. Thanks to Ty Carlson, Brad Chase, Jim Ewel, Betsy Johnson, Jon Lazarus, Greg Lobdell, Yusuf Mehta, Cam Myhrvold, Mike Nash, Russ Stockdale, Jeff Thiel, Tanya Van Dam Vail, Gary Voth, Rogers Weed, and many others for teaching us this terrific play and the discipline and wherewithal that goes with it.

Thanks to Jim Minervino, Mike Negrin, and Alee Spencer, who broke new ground in how to research the playing field, simply, clearly, and with maximum practical insight.

When it comes to turning a play into killer campaigns on a playing field, we could not have asked for a better group of marketing professionals to work with or a better group of teachers to learn from: Ted Bremer, Midori Chan, Don Hall, Eric Koivisto, Tony Liano, Lorraine Nay, Dave Perry, Carol Philips, and Rob Schoeben—to name but a few—translating sound marketing plays into truly successful in-market campaigns.

In support of Microsoft, the outstanding team at Waggener-Edstrom—Pam Edstrom, Catherine Allchin, Marianne Allison, Connie Ballmer, Erin Holland, Claire Lematta, and Linda O'Neill—showed us how PR really works. The inimitable Jerry Weissman, of Power Presentations, taught us the power of Point B and so many other keys to presenting our ideas compellingly. Thanks to all of you for all you taught.

Beyond Microsoft, the Playbook grew immensely as we worked with new start-ups in an incredible array of circumstances. Particular thanks to the CEOs and companies mentioned in this book, including Vani Kola of nth Orbit, Tim Dowling of Pure Networks, Ed Schaeffer of Extend America, Jeff Brown of RadioFrame Networks, Thomas Reardon (formerly of Avogadro), Kelly Pennock of Intelligent Results, Paul Johnston of Entellium, and Joel Gendelman of N'site Solutions.

The team at Ignition Partners has helped us to understand how to work with every size business. Thanks to the general partners Jon Anderson, John Ludwig, Cameron Myhrvold, Steve Hooper, Jonathan Roberts, and Brad Silverberg, to the principals Carolyn Duffy, Michelle Goldberg, Robert Headley, and Adrian Smith, and to the other dedicated professionals there for including us in such an amazing group. Thanks also to marketing comrade and venture partner Bill Malloy. What we've learned from you all could not be contained in a shelf full of books. Also, many thanks to Mauread Bray and Stacey Pistole for all of your help keeping us organized and making every day a little easier.

Finally, converting a set of experiences into a book is a big undertaking, one that we could never have achieved alone. Thanks to Kelli Jerome, our literary agent, without whose guidance this text would still be only a dream. We also deeply appreciate Adrian Zackheim, Stephanie Land, and Will Weisser at Portfolio for their terrific support and expertise. Thanks also go to James Dugan for his help on contracts; to Susan Giordano, Lance Keerfoot, and Marc Pottier for their masterful artwork assistance; and to our discerning yet friendly readers David Schlesinger and Harry Samkange for their valuable input.

Thanks to Bill Simon for being the master of the literary Playbook and partner all along the way. Bill has been a best-selling book author and film writer for more than twenty-five years with over eight hundred published and produced works, from screenplays to award-winning documentaries to best-selling business books. We can only hope this work will be as well received.

We owe our most profound debt of gratitude to our families for all the support over the years and over the many months we worked on this project. To Alex, Calvin, Grace—you are the real stars of the Tong Team. To Sam and Louis—your good humor, tolerance, and understanding kept the Zagula Team going. Profound appreciation and love to Connie for humoring us and supporting us all the way as we embarked on yet another crazy project. Finally, deepest thanks and love to Terri for being there always, reading every word, and putting us back on the right track over and over again.

There are not more than five musical notes, yet the combinations of these five give rise to more melodies than can ever be heard.

There are not more than five primary colors (blue, yellow, red, white, and black), yet in combination they produce more hues than can ever be seen.

There are not more than five cardinal tastes (sour, acrid, salt, sweet, bitter), yet combinations of them yield more flavors than can ever be tasted.

—SUN TZU

Introduction

What do a rural telecom service provider, a fifty-person call center, a high-end computer manufacturer, a three-PhDs-in-a-garage start-up, the world's largest software company, and *you* all have in common?

Probably lots of things. But certainly one of the most surprising is that, for any given product and at any given time, each of them follows one of only five marketing strategies—or plays, as we like to call them—to win in their marketplace. Just five. Seriously.

Consciously or unwittingly, rightly or wrongly selected, well or poorly executed, these plays have been and are being used by companies as diverse as those above, each placing its bet on one of only five strategy alternatives to gain or defend its position in its market. And that includes you, whether you know it or not.

The Marketing Playbook has been over seventeen tough years in the making. Even before we knew we were following an actual system that could be articulated, we were continuously testing, retesting, and refining this book's methods, tools, and guidelines in the rigors of the real marketplace.

The core concepts at the heart of this book were first forged in the furnace of Microsoft's highly competitive market situations in the late 1980s and 1990s, when the two co-authors of this book were in the thick of the company's crucial marketing efforts. Whether you're facing large, entrenched competition, numerous smaller players, or an as yet undefined market landscape, finding the right path to market leadership is a hard thing to do. But across all these situations, through repeated trial and error, we found a common thread, a basic logic that lay behind all the moves that ultimately succeeded.

It wasn't until we were asked to share our methods and techniques to help train other marketing and business folks that it actually dawned on us we were following a discrete, focused system.

When we sat down to plan out the lessons we wanted to share with other Microsoft businesspeople and reviewed all the strategies that we had in fact deployed across our various product launches, competitive battles, and customer targets, we were surprised to find that, no matter how hard we tried to come up with more, we discovered that in each case, one of only five basic approaches had provided the path to victory. And this was not because our imaginations were limited; it was because these five really covered all the situations we faced. These are the five plays, the heart of the Playbook system.

The people with whom we shared these plays were struck by their clarity and simplicity, and how well they fit every type of situation. Many were seasoned marketing and business professionals, but time and time again, they consistently found the plays one of the easiest ways to understand and effectively guide their own plans.

The five plays really seemed universally applicable. But maybe we were just biased by our experience; maybe these strategies would not apply beyond the scope of our current jobs. After all, very few companies have the market position or financial wherewithal of a Microsoft. And indeed, after we left Microsoft and started a venture capital firm, we found ourselves confronting a whole new set of challenges.

The companies we worked with boasted fewer resources, had less-tested products than their rivals, and often faced competitors much larger than themselves. Further, they were under the gun, knowing that one significant misstep and they could easily go under. So there wasn't a lot of room for error. These companies needed to find a simple, reliable way to map out an effective marketing strategy that fit their unique goals and means. And it turned out that no matter what the company, product, or challenge they faced, one of the five plays worked for them, too.

All five are great plays. That said, it became clear that no matter what the play, if you're running it on the wrong playing field or with the wrong resources, it just won't work. Our experiences with small companies in different industries underscored how important it is to do your homework on these conditions before you bet your resources, reputation, and future on any given strategy. How well you do this homework can mean the difference between roaring success or auguring into the earth, fast.

And so, in addition to the five plays, we developed, tested, and applied a simple method for understanding your market and the conditions you face. This shorthand for plotting conditions as a map of your playing field has become a standard, both for how we as venture capitalists assess our investments and also for how our companies chart their course and choose their own play.

Finally, across all these companies and throughout our own careers, we have learned over and over that no matter how well you plan, execution is what ultimately determines the winner. Whatever your objective or strategy, you need a great, hard-hitting marketing and sales campaign to actually bring you across the goal line. And this is one of the hardest things in the world to pull off.

Through our work on multiple product launches of Microsoft Office, Windows, and related products, and in our work with portfolio and partner companies, we have accumulated a very tight set of skills, rules of thumb, and basic principles for pulling off great campaigns and ultimately capturing the lead position even in the most intense contests. These methods have also proven consistently easy to adopt and effective to apply no matter what the company, industry, or situation.

Another thing that this wide ranging set of companies and businesspeople we have worked with (and you) have in common is that they don't have a lot of time to spend reading marketing or business strategy books. They're too busy working their butts off trying to grab or hold on to the leadership slot in their market.

Why We Wrote This Book

It's because of the same group of businesspeople that we decided to write this book. These colleagues have repeatedly let us know that what they want is a more helpful, straightforward marketing guide than the hype, buzzwords, or academic theory they typically see. They told us that they would like to read a book that not only shows them how to gain and hold on to their rightful leadership position but also helps them repeat the process over and over, a book they could believe, a book whose methods and suggestions have been tested and proven in the heat of battle, a book written by people who knew from experience how to attain and retain the lead in a market but who also knew how to make the process easy to follow and implement.

And they told us that the method we had developed, tested, and shared with them really worked. They were convinced that others would benefit as well from reading and learning how to use this system.

In addition to our own accumulated experience, our interactions with these businesses and businesspeople have taught us huge, consistent, and enduring lessons. It is these lessons that we share with you here.

The will to win is important, but the will to prepare is vital.

—JOE PATERNO, FOOTBALL COACH, PENN STATE

1. Getting Started

What exactly is a "Marketing Playbook" and how do you use one?

Everyone thinks marketing is the fun and glamorous part of business, where you get to play around with creative stuff, brainstorm clever headlines, go to photo shoots, do press interviews, see yourself in print, and finally get a chance to toot your own horn. Marketing as imagination, art, and magic.

Sure, there is some of that. But marketing is deadly serious. Whether you're a stodgy financial services firm or a whimsical children's brand, winning companies with effective marketing derive even their most creative, off-the-wall efforts not simply from creative thinking but from sound strategy. Why?

Because winning matters—and it usually takes a strategy to win.

OK—so how do you go about deriving a winning strategy in a way that makes sense?

You can hire a consulting firm, spend man-months educating them about your business, and hope that, besides regurgitating a lot of what you told them, they might also give you some valuable input that justifies the expense.

You can have a bunch of off-sites with lots of brainstorming, soft drinks, junk food, and scribbling on whiteboards. But even with a strong agenda and a good moderator, too often nothing focused or actionable or tangible results.

Or you can take control of the process. In a very short time-frame, you can build a "Playbook" to guide your marketing decisions and actions—mostly using information you already know. Based on this homework, you can then choose which of five plays is appropriate to your situation, and then apply a set of straightforward guidelines for driving successful action that is practical and proven.

Fine. Sounds good. But, what exactly *is* this Playbook?

First of all, it is *your* Playbook. The Playbook isn't *this* book. This book is just here to help you write and use your own Playbook— the version best suited for your needs. By this we don't mean that your Playbook helps you craft a nicely worded strategy or do a better job managing those consultants or running those off-sites (though it does those things, too). We do mean that your Playbook is the essential guide you will create and keep at your side to help you win, to help you define, establish, and defend your desired position in your market—whatever that may be.

Your Playbook should be the tool you refer back to, to guide your actions and decisions and to motivate those of your team.

What does this Playbook consist of? It's simple. Just three things:

First, your Playbook will identify one of five possible plays that you select as best fitting your situation and goals. (Sure, at this point it's hard to imagine that just five plays could cover all business situations. But as you'll discover for yourself in Part I of this book, five are all you need to have a full range of choices.)

Second, your Playbook will include a carefully thought-out map of your playing field that will allow you to execute your chosen play with confidence. This map will show where you want to get, what you're up against, and what you actually have. You will create this map by reviewing your situation, goals, and challenges in a way that validates the play you have chosen and guides you to the right play for each step in your progress. That's Part II of the book.

Finally, your Playbook will prepare you for the true test of strategy—the reality of running the play in action. It will arm you and your team with a set of simple guidelines to help you successfully run the play you have chosen and to best respond to the live action of the real market. That's Part III.

For each of these three sections of your Playbook, we'll arm you with a corresponding set of basic concepts or rules that you can turn to for making sure that you're actually moving ahead in the most effective way.

The best part: it actually works, and in hours, not weeks.

Here's a quick advance look at what you'll be doing.

Step 1. Your Strategy Options– The Five Marketing Plays

Before you place your bets, before you jump into action, you need to understand your options. You need to choose a strategy with the best chances of success. This basic marketing and competitive strategy is what we mean when we talk about your "play."

One of our favorite examples of an effective play comes from the time when we were still at Microsoft.

The year was 1999, and one of the product groups was gearing up for the launch of Microsoft SQL Server, a terrific new database server product that was a key part of one of Microsoft's most important growth businesses. At the time there was one dominant player in this high-end enterprise database server market: Oracle.

The Microsoft SQL team was all pumped up. They had delivered a great product, the first real contender for the space in a long time. They had also done their homework: they knew everything there was to know about the Oracle product, they had talked to lots of potential customers, and they knew their own product upside down and sideways.

When we first sat down together to map out the launch campaign, their plan was to attack Oracle head on.

And why not? Everybody at Microsoft—and a great many other people, as well—was sick and tired of Larry Ellison's bombast. And we envied Oracle's loud, hard-hitting, and exorbitant PR and advertising claims. So why *not* attack? We had a great new product, it cost a lot less than Oracle's, we knew we were committed to supporting it, and we had the marketing dollars to do it. We were Microsoft, for Pete's sake, we should be able to win.

The problem was, we were making some wrong assumptions. The straightforward, head-on play wasn't appropriate. Even though our product was better in a lot of ways, Oracle still had us beat on a few key dimensions such as the ability to scale up to very big installations and highly complex jobs. Even though most users would rarely if ever need the capability, Oracle always beat its chest over that one issue. To be candid, our competition had us on this one; it was Oracle's true position of strength. And it happened to be the area that a lot of large companies were paranoid about.

Oh, sure, they also cared about price, but not that much. Also, our Microsoft heritage and reputation didn't really help us that much in this market. While everyone trusted that we built great, easy-to-use consumer software, we were far from being perceived as a truly "enterprise-class" provider, at least not for mission-critical applications. Oracle, on the other hand, had enjoyed that reputation for years.

So the smart play ended up not being the direct attack (a.k.a. a Drag Race Play, as you will see soon)—at least not at this stage. Instead, we decided to find the areas where Oracle's biggest strength didn't matter as much. Rather than attack Oracle directly and get compared on the criteria that it had already successfully established, we would have to use something more like a quarterback sneak (which we call a Stealth Play).

The campaign we settled on said in essence, "Go ahead, use Oracle. That's fine in those instances that it's really needed—but on jobs like X, Y, and Z, do you really need to spend so much money and lose so much flexibility?"

Stepping back and choosing the right play made all the difference. With this more humble approach, Microsoft SQL Server was able to gain a true foothold in the market. We reduced the barriers for initial trials and we got people to start using the product and experiencing its benefits. We focused on the targets for whom this made a lot of sense. And although the jury is still out, SQL Server sales have gone from zero to huge and market share from zero to a very significant percentage, in just three years.

Sounds good. But how do you actually pick the right play for *your* Playbook? Every situation is so different.

Don't sweat it too much. It may seem hard to believe, but our experience with hundreds of businesses and their specific challenges has shown over and over that there is always one obvious basic strategy that's right for the situation. Once selected, your play becomes a starting point; it's your path, your line of attack. From it, the rest of your in-market action plan comes to life.

And it gets even simpler. Remember that there are only five plays to pick from. Here they are.

The Five Go-to-Market Plays

Drag Race: In some circumstances, your best bet calls for singling out one competitor and putting the pedal to the metal racing against them to win the category. This can be quite exciting, so it's a really tempting choice. But you better have what it takes to beat them over the finish line.

Platform: Success can be hell. Once you've secured a lead in your category, you have to hold on to it and make the most of it. Standing on your platform at the top of the category, you need to be on the lookout. You must gather allies and defenses. Sounds kind of boring. But it's essential. Success begets envy and you never know from where a new challenger is likely to emerge.

Stealth: Just because you're not strong enough yet to win the battle doesn't mean you can't win the war. In this play, you undermine the status quo in your market by whittling away at the incumbent's weak points. And maybe even by making them look foolish. But remember, you still have to stay out of their way and survive. Big, dumb, slow competitors can still squish you.

Best-of-Both: Go ahead, have your cake and eat it, too. While in many cases the smart decision is to focus, requiring a trade-off at the high end or the low end of the market, in the right circumstances you don't have to. With this play, instead you gain dominance over the whole of a category by collapsing these two ends. If you appeal to the most important needs of each part of the market, you can win them all.

High–Low: Compromise is for weaklings. With this play, you try to close out the competition by splitting the category and owning both halves. It takes a lot of finesse, but when you need to keep a competitor from establishing a Best-of-Both foothold, you need to appeal to the distinct prejudices of both the elites and the common folk, the high end and the cheap. This is the hardest play to manage, but if it's done right, you'll achieve high volumes and high margins at the same time.

In choosing the right play, there are some important questions you will need to ask yourself. Different plays are best suited to different conditions. Different plays require different strengths. Do you have the right ones to pull off your choice? Some plays are riskier than others. How tough are your nerves? Depending on the play, succeeding can take a long time. Do you have the time, patience, and resources? After all that, how big is the goal you're after? Is it achievable? Is it worth it?

Step 2. Mapping the Playing Field

No matter what marketing strategy you're currently following, you have to execute it in the reality of the marketplace. Your play succeeds or fails on the actual playing field. So it's a darn good idea to know everything you can about the terrain.

This is where the second part of your Playbook comes in. Whether you're refining your existing play or moving into a new one, you're making a bet—a bet on finding or recognizing a new gap opening in the marketplace and a bet on your ability to bridge that gap.

You can think of your playing field in the same way. Where should you be placing your bets and investing your time and energy? No one wants to punt from the seventy-yard line against massive headwinds. So before jumping into a market, you had better know what you're up against and what you're aiming for. That's why finding and understanding the gaps in your playing field is so important.

Here are the key gaps to look for, map, and measure on your playing field:

> The overall market—its economics, history, and trends;
> Your customers—their desires, frustrations, and unmet needs;

Your competition—the strengths and vulnerabilities of
the other contenders out there who are vying for the
lead spot with the same customers;

Your capabilities—your strengths and weaknesses; the
gaps YOU will have to fill in your own capabilities
and resources in order to meet your customer needs
and to stake out your position in the market.

Step 3. Turning Your Play into a Killer Campaign

Great marketing campaigns sing. When all of the components hang
together—from your basic sales pitch, to PR and tradeshows, to
collaterals, to ads to Web sites, e-mails, and banners—they complement and enhance one another. Great marketing campaigns take
your play and motivate action in your favor. No matter how well
founded and well chosen your strategy, lousy marketing campaigns
(or even just pretty good ones) lead to defeat or significant loss of
ground.

Whatever the scale, there is no such thing as a marketing campaign that *you* do by yourself or a play *you* run yourself. It takes
all kinds of people. Sometimes these include ad agencies, Web mas-
ters, road warriors, PR mavens, channel partners, and even the
people who answer the phones. You're not just writing *your* Playbook; it's your whole extended team's Playbook. The key is for
everyone to understand what's needed and what they have to
execute.

This is where the final part of your Playbook comes into action.
Here we'll introduce you to a set of simple, powerful techniques, design tools, and guidelines that make it easy to do each of the above,
over and over again, no matter what play you're running or what
kind of audience you're targeting.

So those are the elements of this process: doing your homework to best understand your situation and map it to your play; selecting the correct play; and turning the play into action through a focused, dynamic, effective in-market campaign.

Take-Aways for Getting Your Playbook Started

1. Marketing is not just a barrel of fun. If it is to be effective, it has to be based on sound strategy. And strategy is not some theoretical exercise. It's got to be practical. Doing practical, strategic marketing doesn't have to kill you. You just need to create and follow a simple Playbook to make it happen.

2. Creating your Playbook starts with selecting the correct play— the core strategy that guides all of your actions. The good news is that there are only five plays to choose from.

3. To choose the correct play, you'll need to understand your playing field. This means creating a basic map of the gaps and opportunities of the market, your customers, your competitors, and yourself.

4. The proof of your planning and decisions is in the marketing and sales campaign that takes you to the goal line. To do this you have to rally your squad of players, take the action to the market, and do a better job than the other guy in persuading your targets to choose you.

5. The Playbook is yours. Don't write it and put it on the shelf. It gets better the more you use it. Keep it up to date as the conditions you face change and evolve. Taking your hill and holding it takes constant work. And when you win, the hills just keep coming.

Coming Up

Understanding *The Marketing Playbook* begins with understanding the five plays. That's what we focus on in Part I of the book.

PART I

Choosing the Winning Play–Determining and Executing the Best Strategy for Your Situation

The five basic strategies for establishing and maintaining market leadership:

- What they are
- Which to pick
- How to run them

It's not the size of the dog in the fight, but the size of the fight in the dog.
—ARCHIE GRIFFIN, RUNNING BACK, HEISMAN TROPHY WINNER

2. The Drag Race

Want to wake up the market? Pick a fight.

Not a very subtle solution, is it? But sometimes the direct approach is best. Find the best competitor to beat, and do what it takes to beat them. That's what the Drag Race Play is all about. It's simple, it's easy to understand, and it can really get your blood going.

Besides, people love a good drag race fight between two determined contenders. A noisy, in-your-face battle that at worst will grab the attention of the paying customers.

What Is a Drag Race Play? Simple: Two Cars— The Faster One (with More Gas) Usually Wins

The Drag Race is the simplest of the five plays. It involves singling out and isolating one competitor and beating him in direct comparison (Fig. 2–1). It calls on you to choose the dimensions that count most to the market. And sometimes it means betting the business on this choice.

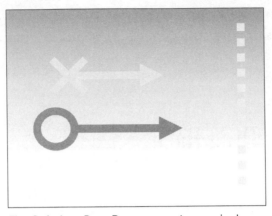

Fig. 2–1. In a Drag Race, you outrun a single competitor.

A Drag Race is one of the most tempting strategies to choose. It's straightforward, it's direct, it appeals to your killer instinct. And it appeals to your ego. *Of course* you're better than the competitor. Everyone needs to know that. And once consumers know, you can count on them to switch to your product or service.

Case in point: Back in the late 1980s, the co-authors of this book were working hard to help establish Microsoft Word and make it known as the very best product in the word processing market. This was already a huge and important market: 90 percent of all PCs had a word processor. It was the best-selling application on PCs. So everyone was in the race. Moreover, if folks didn't switch to a Windows-based word processor, they wouldn't switch to Windows. Period. For Microsoft, winning with Word meant winning the market over to the new Windows world.

The challenge inspired us. But the rest of the market was slow to catch on to the virtues of Word.

On one occasion we went with the product manager of Word, Liz Welch, to demo and promote the product to the CIA. Yep, the Central Intelligence Agency. After numerous security checks, we were led into a large room with no windows, and introduced to the CIA "word processing staff." This was an army of about fifty conservatively dressed, serious ladies, whose sole job it was to type or edit—word process—scores of highly classified documents. All day, every day. Tough crowd. We tried to wow them, but the fact was that people who loved WordPerfect didn't care much about gee-whiz features or cool screens. They just wanted to get their work done. Our audience was polite but bored. We had missed the mark.

So it was back to the drawing board. The mission was to get the WordPerfect crowd interested. We got our next opportunity at the big industry tradeshow Comdex, where our audience was strictly WordPerfect users and experts. Instead of technology demos, we issued a Word vs. WordPerfect challenge. As soon as we said that we knew Microsoft Word could beat WordPerfect, customers woke up again. Their hands shot up. They wanted to know how. Now we had their attention. And that attention rose to real interest when we did a direct Word vs. WordPerfect "shoot-out." We showed them things like autocorrect and automatic table drawing—and snores turned to oohs and ahs.

It worked. Our targets finally paid attention long enough to see our great features and then wanted to try the product. And all because we challenged their incumbent and proved that we could win in a head-to-head comparison. We turned this success into a nationwide campaign, going to twenty cities and demonstrating "shoot-outs" in each one. We won the Drag Race. We became the market leader.

It meant much to win against WordPerfect in the presentation hall of Comdex with a captive audience. Using such direct comparisons with a competitor to focus attention on your superiority is essentially a Drag Race Play writ small.

But doing one pitch doesn't carry the weight of betting your entire business on winning; those are two very different things. In the big world of the marketplace, your competitor doesn't really like being attacked. And they have a lot of opportunity to respond.

So When Does It Make Sense to Run a Drag Race?

It makes sense to run a Drag Race when you can win—if not win the entire market, then at least win enough traction in that market to be worth the gas you will burn in the process.

As such, it makes sense to question and validate your assumptions about that market, which we refer to as a "playing field." What does this playing field look like? Some make great courses for the straight-away of a head-to-head race to the finish. Others are obstacle courses. You can't run a Drag Race if you're not clear about the course.

As you will see in Part II of this book, that effort doesn't have to be too complicated to pay big dividends in your strategy and decisions.

To decide whether the landscape is suitable and to guide your best execution of a Drag Race, you really need to check for the right market conditions, the right customer frame of mind, and an appropriate competitor to race against. And you need to be sure your team has the right resources and determination to do what needs to be done. By the end of this chapter you should be able to determine, every time, whether a Drag Race is the right play for you in any particular circumstances. If it's not, go back to your homework or read on to the next of the five plays.

Here are the conditions you need to satisfy for this Play:

Your market has to be ripe for a drag race.

Two basic situations can call for a Drag Race: when you're in position to be a fast follower, or when you're in position to be a market clearer.

A fast-follower Drag Race happens when there is a big
player who owns too much of the market and you
want to steal share from them.

A market-clearing Drag Race happens when the market
is fragmented with too many choices and you have a
lot to gain by driving these down to just two: you and
one other leader.

In the 1960s, when Lee Iacocca introduced the Mustang as a new
category of American sports car, he shook up the entire U.S. automotive market and drew in a whole new category of buyer. The
Mustang generated amazing public attention and critical kudos,
giving Ford an entirely new level of cachet. Oh, yeah—and the company also raked in huge new revenues as a result.

This, of course, did not go unnoticed by their fiercest rival, GM,
which shortly introduced a muscle car of their own—the Camaro.
This was their fast-follower answer, and while there would always
be some lesser contenders out there (Firebird, Dodge Dart), the real
Drag Race was always between the Mustang and the Camaro. Both
companies worked hard to stay ahead of the other in every comparison, adding horsepower, features, and steel with nearly every
model year. Once entered into this Drag Race, both companies
stuck to their guns and it grew into a full-scale war. From all ap-
pearances, this war is still going on today.

In contrast, the Microsoft Word vs. WordPerfect story is a classic
case of a market-clearing Drag Race. Most people thought that Microsoft Word vs. WordPerfect was the battle royal between the two
preponderant players in the market. It wasn't.

Back in 1990, Word had only around 15 percent market share.
WordPerfect had around 30 percent. But the remaining 55 percent
was in the hands of a wide and fragmented variety of players such
as WordStar, XyWrite, AmiPro, and even the Wang word processor
and the Notepad accessory, each with its own niche.

To depict the playing field of any competitive situation, we use a diagram that we call the Ps and Qs: P for Price, shown on the vertical axis, Q for Quality, shown on the horizontal (Figs. 2–2 through 2–4, and elsewhere throughout the book). Most people we've introduced the Ps and Qs to have been surprised at how useful this method is as a way of mapping all the offerings in the playing field so the situation can be readily understood.

In the word processing marketplace of 1990, prices ranged all over. Several companies were offering mainline products at around $319 for full versions for first-time purchasers of the mainline products; this is depicted in the Ps and Qs map, Fig. 2–2.

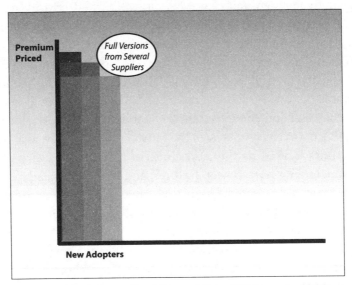

Fig. 2–2. Word processing high end, late 1980s–early 1990s

On the other end were products that came free, included with the PC or operating system as utilities—things as simple as Notepad, which has writing, editing, and printing functions and is still used by lots of tech nerds today for a number of documenting tasks (Fig. 2–3).

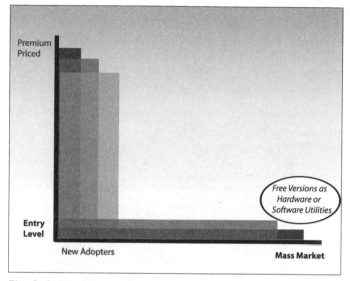

Fig. 2–3. Word processing low end, late 1980s–early 1990s

The Drag Race made all the more sense because the market was so fragmented that Microsoft had everything to gain by competing head to head against WordPerfect. Choosing only to compare itself to one competitor made things a lot simpler.

And the pricing and offerings became tuned to match just that battle. New, "fighting" price points were introduced: $99 for retaining your customers in their upgrades from previous versions and $129 for "competitive upgrades" to get your competitors' users to switch from their current brand (Fig. 2–4). That's where the real action was.

If people paid attention only to this duel, then Microsoft just had to win on criteria that compared to WordPerfect. When these two started their engines and broke away from the starting line, all the other players were left in the dust.

This particular example highlights the value of another important industry/market factor in choosing the Drag Race as your Play: change.

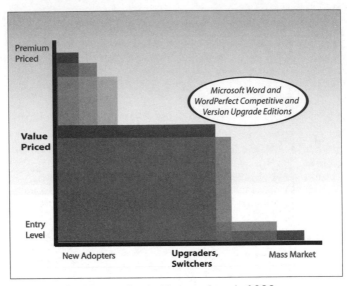

Fig. 2–4. Word processing battleground, early 1990s

In doing your analysis of your industry, you should look for a change that would create a new opening, a new opportunity to win. If the playing field is too crowded *and* the players already well established, you will have an uphill climb entering a new race. Look for some external impact you can make on the structure of the industry, some change, some new way to create customer incentive that makes switching possible or easier than before.

In our case, the change was the entry and adoption of Windows and its impact on the overall word processing market. This change, which was only beginning to take root, still played a huge role in our ability to successfully execute a winning Drag Race against WordPerfect. Originally this battleground was defined as all word processors regardless of operating system or computing platform. This was how WordPerfect defined its own market.

When we entered the Drag Race with them, we redefined the *Windows* word processing market as the only market that really mattered. Windows was the future, all PCs were shipping with it. So why bother thinking about the others. This accelerated the clearing of the market. And it positioned us extremely well given our own advantages and heritage.

Focusing only on the Windows part of the word processing market narrowed the battlefield and shortened the length of the race track. This market segmentation allowed us to define victory more narrowly and put it more within our grasp. It allowed us to claim larger and more exciting evidence of our momentum and growing lead in the race—e.g., as "the fastest-growing Windows word processor" or "the Windows word processor preferred most." It meant that we could show gains and even superior share more quickly. Soon most of the spectators—the people facing the decision of whether to purchase WordPerfect or Word—felt the race was over.

And, again, this hard-won race also had the side benefit of reinforcing the value and importance of Windows itself.

Changing the dynamics of our industry, and the timing of our challenge, made the market ideal for a Drag Race. Before you start your engines and press the gas pedal, make sure that the track you plan to race down is similarly justified.

Your target customers must want to watch a contest.

One of the things that makes a Drag Race so appealing is the roar of the crowd. The spectators whose praise you seek will cheer you on, or gasp at your crashes, or turn their backs when you lose the lead. And they are the ones who pay the price of admission.

You put out all this effort to win customers, to get them to root for you, and, more importantly, to pay you instead of someone else. For this play to work, the customers have to be in the mood for a contest.

In doing your analysis of the target customer, you may be tempted by the large prize of a big potential customer base. Winning that customer base is another story. There has to be some kind of opening in the customers' mindset and in their pocketbooks to stand a chance of making them look favorably in your direction. It could be a regulatory change. It could be changes in their own competition or with their own customers. There's got to be something that motivates them to think differently, more openly.

This customer opening can come in different forms. One is when your customer base generally consists of early adopters, who tend to have a general openness to change, along with an excitement and interest in alternatives and an appetite to try them. This was the case in the examples cited above.

Another, more fertile opportunity comes when customers are dissatisfied with the current incumbent. Picking a fight with a supplier that customers love to complain about is a great way to get some attention.

Take the case of Salesforce.com vs. Siebel Systems. Both companies develop sales force automation and customer relationship management software. In the late 1990s, there had been a vast number of new entrants into this market, each promising huge though rather vague business benefits. For a time all of them competed, offering more, newer, and supposedly better product features—until Siebel Systems, run by a passionate, hard-driving CEO, made the biggest promises and pushed hardest. Siebel took the lead of the pack and eventually established market dominance. Under the pressure of Siebel's huge sales and consulting machine, the other players like e.Piphany, Onyx, and Pivotal gradually receded into their own, ever-shrinking niches.

Game over, congratulations to Siebel. Right? Wrong.

The problem was, all the promises (from Siebel and all the other original players) came with a much bigger real price than originally laid out. The hidden costs of installing, integrating, customizing, and maintaining products as well as training people to use these gargantuan software products were generally proving to be many times higher than the original selling price. And the promised benefits, beyond the initial ones immediately felt, were hard to find and not directly justifiable in term of ROI. Meanwhile the market and the economy collapsed and most IT departments began to suffer the chill of a frozen budget. Several companies couldn't even afford to install the software they had paid so much for. Net/net, a big set of customers was disappointed, frustrated, and getting angry.

The time was right for a race. Customers were motivated to seek alternatives. In came Salesforce.com to exploit these very feelings. They too had a dynamic, aggressive CEO, Marc Benioff, driven by the slogan of "Success. Not software." The company provided a lightning rod to those customers who were tired of the status quo. Salesforce.com took direct aim at Siebel and countered each source of Siebel customer dissatisfaction.

But restless natives are not enough. To get a head start in a Drag Race, you have to make it easy for customers to switch. Salesforce.com was ready. Compared to the time-consuming, labor-intensive project of installing traditional enterprise software, Benioff promised no installation at all. Their offering was a service you used online instead of a product you bought and then had to install and maintain.

He also made the switch worthwhile. With competitors offering feature-glut and complexity, and their packages often ending up as "shelfware," Salesforce.com offered a perhaps less robust but simpler alternative.

Benioff was also in the right place at the right time. Even the most agitated, receptive targets won't move if they don't have the money or if the timing is wrong. Salesforce.com entered the playing field during a big market downturn. They turned this to their advantage and went right after the problem of budget freezes. Compared to the high upfront prices and capital expenditure that IT departments were getting tired of, Saleforce.com sold at a moderate monthly subscription rate.

And they made huge traction, quickly.

There has to be one other car, and it has to be the right one.

Entering into a Drag Race is just the first step. You still have to make sure that you get across the finish line. Finding a player in the market worth targeting is easy. You just have to make sure that the opponent you pick is actually beatable. But watch it—picking on someone can make them mad. So pick wisely.

Remember, a Drag Race really works only when you're racing just one other driver. It doesn't pay to claim that you're better than everyone else. You don't have to be great at everything—you just have to be better than your single opponent. And to start, you should aim at their soft spots, the places where they are most beatable.

Salesforce.com picked on a business model weakness of Siebel's. At the heart of Siebel were highly paid, big-account salespeople affectionately dubbed "elephant hunters." These were the stars who spent all their time winning major multimillion-dollar contracts and getting compensated accordingly. This was really the only way Siebel knew how to sell. For people who make their money this way, it's hard to entertain other models where the winnings have to be deferred over time and gathered over a number of smaller wins.

Salesforce.com made another wise decision by not targeting Siebel's stronghold in the whole market—that would have been too hard to win. They only targeted the part where Siebel was weakest— the midsized-enterprise customer, for whom these issues were most acute. This market also happened to be the most important hope for Siebel's future growth.

Challenging a competitor to a race really only works if you choose an opponent who will take the bait.

At first Siebel pretended to ignore Salesforce.com but then began to see ad after ad, review after review, and article after article indicting the Siebel approach; it just got to be too much. They finally responded. They signed a deal with IBM to serve up their software as a subscription, too. They acquired a start-up company called Upshot, which in one of those amusing twists had been trying to run a Drag Race against Salesforce.com at the middle part of the market.

With Siebel's new alignments in place, the real race began. And everyone who watched the industry wanted to get front-row seats.

The finish line has not yet been reached. The battle continues and the stakes have grown higher for both sides. Regardless of the ultimate outcome, in this case betting on a direct competition worked wonders for Salesforce.com. It helped put them on the map. It helped draw the attention of receptive customers and market observers. It helped drive impressive initial momentum in the market. And it caused their primary competitor to start playing by a new set of rules.

Another example of a less-than-obvious but fun-to-watch Drag Race is that of Visa, the credit-card brand. It all started back in the 1980s. Visa was going strong, but it was unsatisfied. When it asked cardholders who they thought offered the best card, only 40 percent said Visa. That was just not good enough. Time for a little healthy competition. Time to pick on somebody. But who?

MasterCard was the biggest other player, jockeying with Visa for the highest market share position. So the natural target was . . . American Express?

Yes, American Express. Rather than pick on MasterCard and give its biggest competitor any credibility, Visa took direct and aggressive aim at American Express and its upscale image and position. The focus of the campaign became "Visa: It's everywhere you want to be." This campaign has run nearly 20 years and has had amazing results. Highlighting great, exciting places and noting that each place offers something really desirable "but they won't take American Express" generated new attention to the category and became almost a source of entertainment of its own.

Drag Races are popular and this one cemented Visa's image as a premium global provider, which did great things for its position. By picking on the brand it could beat, Visa focused on its own leadership and cemented its lead over its real competitor, MasterCard, with a nearly 35 percent share advantage.

But be careful. Drag Races can also be dangerous. Poking a big competitor in the nose can have unpleasant results.

A lot of new companies feel—by virtue of their high horsepower-to-weight ratio—that they can take on the big, slow-moving, out-of-date incumbents. These low-share troublemakers feel they have everything to gain. But they often count too heavily on their competitor's inability to start their engines until it's too late.

If you have real advantages that you know will be hard to replicate, this logic seems sound. Be careful. It doesn't usually pay to assume that your opponent is stupid or incapable of change. Big companies can be slow, but once they enter the race and turn on their big turbines, they have lots of fuel to burn.

One example of such logic was in what came to be known as "the browser wars." Back in 1994, Netscape came on the scene with Netscape Navigator, the first widely available Internet browser. They gave it away free and generated huge initial momentum. They were growing nicely under the radar screen at first. Then they decided to enter into a Drag Race. With the revolutionary product they had developed and the positive attention they were receiving, it was just too tempting. They claimed that the Internet accessed with their browser was the future of computing and that traditional operating systems like Microsoft Windows would soon be obsolete.

The guys at Netscape took direct aim at Microsoft because they knew they had an edge in the form of a terrific product that people really loved. True believers in the vision they expounded, they were pioneers who believed that the future was theirs. They also believed that Microsoft would be too big and slow-moving to catch them, while they had a development culture and operation that was fast and agile, creating new releases every few months compared to Microsoft's one-and-a-half–to–two-year upgrade cycles. They were one totally focused company, new and nimble compared to Microsoft with its huge divisions and thousands of employees working against long-term plans set in stone.

The Netscape guys guessed that Microsoft's growing bulk would be no match for their speed. They guessed that Microsoft would never be able to turn quickly enough to match them, at least not until it was too late. They guessed wrong. They thought they saw a gap, but didn't fully digest the fact that Microsoft's entire company culture was based on being competitive, on chasing taillights, on being maniacally focused on winning. You can wave a flag in front of a bull, but you'd better make sure you know what to do when he charges. If you don't, you end up like Netscape, going from 90 percent market share and on top of the world, to less than 20 percent market share and bought by another big bull for a small fraction of their once flying-on-top-of-the-world stock price.

So take heed. Before you enter a Drag Race, make sure you look closely at the resources and wherewithal of the other racer, but also make sure you yourself are prepared to do what it takes to stay ahead all the way.

You have to be in the racing frame of mind.

Tune your own engine. Fill your gas tank. And make sure you have the right driver behind the wheel.

This first go-to-market play is definitely the simplest to describe, but it's also the one that requires the most complete commitment.

In most cases, it's all or nothing. Choosing a Drag Race means betting your future on one outcome. Don't even try it if you can't win. Your car has to be faster or you have to have a lot more gas: you need to win before you run out of race track. And your driver has to have reserves of nerve and skill as the race heats up.

When you do your assessment of your own strengths and weaknesses, make sure to stay honest.

First and potentially most important, look closely at your motivations. Are they sound, rational, healthy competitive capitalist reasons? Or are you choosing a Drag Race by default? Or just because you have ego needs? It's one thing to go after someone else's customers because the size of the prize is enticing. It's another to get drawn into an unnecessary, draining contest simply because someone else challenges you to it.

Look at the "space race" of the 1960s and 70s. Make no mistake, we were and are totally excited by the prospects of space travel. But, for all its arguable benefits, the contest between the United States and the Soviet Union for supremacy in manned space travel was certainly motivated in part by a sense of damaged pride. Sure, there was a geopolitical rivalry between these two nations with incredibly high stakes. But billions if not trillions of dollars were spent on a set of risky missions with little economic, military, or (in most cases) even scientific justification. Who won? The U.S. won the Cold War, but it's questionable at best whether the space race was a significant contributing factor.

Yet even when you have sound goals, you still need to have the right resources or mix of strengths to win. You need to be confident of your advantages and of your ability to maintain your lead.

Take the example of Airbus vs. Boeing. In many ways Airbus came out of nowhere and took on the absolute unquestioned leader in its category. At the time, Boeing had the lion's share of the sub-jumbo airliner market. Airbus went right after them in full and direct competition as an upstart challenger blatantly trying to steal share. Aggressive, yes. Risky, yes. But Airbus was confident of some potent advantages. First, they had the European airlines lined up as initial customers. They had some significant cost advantages. They had a great new plane that compared very well with the comparable Boeing entry. And they had a special ace in the hole: they were owned and supported by the national governments of France and Germany. The funding of these gigantic sugar daddies made it possible for Airbus to keep prices extremely low.

Such Drag Races can take a very long time. In Airbus's case, it's been going on for two decades. And they can often turn into trench warfare with each side gaining a little ground and then losing it. You need to make sure you have not only the resources but also the patience, determination, and nerve to keep driving until your opponent is exhausted. Airbus's government backing gave them access to the long-term resources they needed to keep investing, to go all the way, no matter what.

If you're a start-up with great product but little capital, you might be able to manage a Drag Race against others like you, but you enter into a Drag Race with a big player at high risk. Very often such a challenger can get off to a great start, only to find themselves awhile later short on resources, with the leaders of the effort waking up every morning asking the painful question, "Have we won yet?" If you're lucky, the big guy takes the bait, wastes a lot of resources, and eventually cedes part of the market to you. Almost as good (or sometimes even better), they take notice, get tired, and buy you. Worst of all, they ignore you completely, keep on chugging, and just wait it out until you die of starvation.

Also beware of the inverse. Why Drag Race if you're already the winner? Why take the bait when some pipsqueak comes gunning for you? Letting the market compare your twelve-cylinder mag-tired road eater to a little bicycle does not reflect all that well on you.

The Rewards and Risks
of Maximum Acceleration

What are the rewards of running a Drag Race? Big trophy, lots of applause, all the prize money. What are the risks? Total exhaustion, defeat, obscurity.

Rewards

Again, the Drag Race is the easiest of the plays for everyone to understand, and easy to know how to execute. We all relate to such rivalries and we see them every day—better tasting, less filling, 20 percent more whatever, and so on. It's also the easiest play for focusing and motivating your teams: it's clear whom you're supposed to be beating and it's easy to keep score.

Another benefit for marketers is that a Drag Race makes it very easy to generate PR. This benefit is not to be underestimated. Every reporter loves conflict—and that's what a Drag Race is. There's entertainment in a "food fight" among grown-ups; there's drama in a shoot-out. They get covered. Just pick up any business or technology magazine and you will see how often it comes down to a grudge match between two rival providers.

Similarly, Drag Races make it easy to get customers involved. They're great when customers have money and are willing to spend it. The races take place in well-defined territory: they don't require building a new category, just winning one that already exists. If the targets are enterprises, they have clear RFPs and definite dates and processes for buying. If they are consumers, they know what product they're talking about, be it a VCR, a car, or a brand of coffee.

Risks

When you see big guys competing, you don't have to do much research to know that the market for their products is real. The risk is all in the execution of winning that market. Nonetheless, these risks are big and serious.

We've already noted that the level of resources required can be daunting. If you don't have them—product, team, capital, business model—you lose. And losing after an all-out race isn't pretty. Many have found it impossible to recover. Don't start unless you can finish.

The advantages of your offering have to be real and meaningful.

With Microsoft Excel vs. Lotus 1-2-3, for instance, Microsoft had the advantage because it had the best-seller on the Macintosh already. The team thought graphically. Thinking graphically turned programming on its head. It was a major rethinking of applications—a rethinking we turned to our advantage.

Another important risk is profit erosion. After the product war is in full force, price wars generally follow. Look at the pricing of cell phone minutes over the past twenty years: they have collapsed from $2 per minute in 1986 to $0.05 per minute in 2003. Such price battles train consumers to expect to pay less. But for the companies involved, they reduce the size and value of the ultimate prize.

In the arena of software development tools, before Borland and Microsoft began Drag Racing each other for category domination in the early 1990s, a database cost around $599 to $699; today most are $99. Suites of developer tools used to cost $2,000; now they are largely free on the Internet.

Only companies tuned to such price wars really benefit. Companies that have supertight operations and a superior profit model love to draw everyone into price wars, because they know that they can always win on price. Take a look at Dell or Wal-Mart. Once these giants had established their operations and buying advantages, they have always taken the position of low-cost leaders. This makes them very hard to beat.

I'm Up for It–How Do I Run a Drag Race Successfully?

Remember, if you have chosen your market, target, and opponent well, winning in this case is all about execution. The fastest car, the most aggressive driver, and the straightest course make all the difference. It's simple really. Fig. 2–5 shows a summary of how to stoke this kind of internal combustion and how to keep the Drag Race pistons pumping all the way across the finish line.

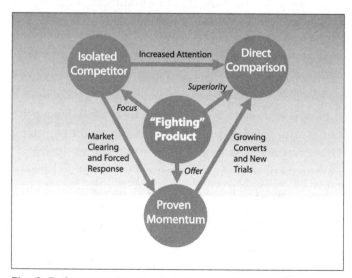

Fig. 2–5. Cross section of a Drag Race engine

Start by placing all your bets on one contender. This is your fighting product. It is at the center of the whole race.

Then, make sure to isolate and point it at just one competitor. Pick a fight with them and ignore everyone else. This creates a very clear focus for you and for the market you want watching the race.

Generate as much heat around this contest as you can. The point of a Drag Race is not to be subtle. It's all about drawing attention to the battle. It can't be boring. If you choose this play wisely, you have little to lose by picking on your opponent. And you have everything to gain from the attention.

That said, you had better be sure to win your shoot-outs. Direct comparison is the name of the game, but if you don't come out on top of this match your engine will sputter and maybe even die. Focus all attention on the areas where you know you have superiority.

Make sure not to waste the opportunities that these contests give you. Whenever you successfully sow doubt, scoop up all the converts you can. Keep the barriers for switching low.

And then make as much hay as you can about their conversion. Once you start to look like the winner, more and more people will start betting on you. And the cycle continues. Making this hay is the job of your marketing. In brief, here's how this play should influence your marketing decisions and efforts.

Marketing Implications

This play is a sales and marketing dream. It's fun for your teams to execute. Set up all the elements so they can just put the pedal to the metal.

Product

Make sure you can claim a clearly better product.

That's a given. You have to be better in some important way. Remember, when taking aim at a competitor, you had better be prepared to stand up to the fire when the other guy starts firing back in your direction.

The dimensions of superiority aren't always obvious. Avis took direct aim at Hertz on the dimension of customer service with its slogan "We try harder." They successfully inverted their position as number two into an advantage. And whatever the source of your product advantage, you have to keep on making it better. One of the biggest motivators in a Drag Race is feature envy, typically represented by long and growing feature lists with all the checks in the good guy's column and all the X marks in the bad guy's.

With the fighting product at the center, you can start the virtuous cycle. Begin with a focus on a single competitor and drive direct comparison to get momentum against them. That ignites even more focus, more comparison, more momentum. Away you go.

Packaging

Package your product to compete—by focusing on one offering only.

Remember, this play is supposed to be simple, so bet on one product, one version of it, one winner SKU or offering. Don't add complexity, options, or alternatives or you'll just end up drag racing yourself. Typically this means putting all your weight behind your fastest model. When the big players in the automotive industry Drag Race against each other, they quote all the stats on their high-end models, even though very few folks will actually buy the top-of-the-line offerings.

Pricing

Price it to win.

Even when you have the best product, you're still going to have to pay attention to price. In a Drag Race you never want to lose deals. You may not always want to be the lowest-cost provider, but you'll find it hard to avoid price competition over the long run. Hyundai has taken this practice and elevated it into a science. For every model, make, and feature of Honda cars, Hyundai matches and offers their version at a lower price. And they let you know about it. They may not have achieved number-one status or even beat Honda in any market, but, boy, this strategy has won them a lot of converts.

Positioning

Position your offering as superior and as the right bet.

Momentum counts in a Drag Race. People bet on winners. So make sure you show positive momentum in any way you can. The more evidence you line up, the better. People can tell that you're in a Drag Race by the size and frequency of the claims: "better than . . . ," "fastest growing," "outselling by . . ."

Sometimes you have to be clever about how you do this. If you're just starting, you clearly can't yet claim victory over the whole market—so focus on the parts where you can. Sometimes this is clear, as when Microsoft Word focused only on users of Windows. Sometimes it's a bit more of a stretch, as in "Choosy mothers choose Jif." Peter Pan may have had more total share, but what mother didn't want to think of herself as choosy?

Promotion

Promote your advantages shamelessly and aggressively with direct comparison.

A Drag Race is a spectator sport. The fans are looking for blood. Give it to them. This play is all about taking direct aim at your opponent. With Word, one of the most effective tactics was the shoot-out. We called it the Word Challenge. The Comdex shoot-out described earlier was our version of a "blind taste test." (Sound familiar?) And WordPerfect users preferred Word. Boy, did we make hay out of that.

As mentioned, the Drag Race is ripe for aggressive PR. Make sure to be in every contest in every trade publication. But make sure you win them. And when you win, make sure to trumpet all these awards.

Drag Races are also the domain of great salespeople. You have handed them a terrific weapon. Make sure they use it. They love to go head to head and win. Give them the leeway they need. Never lose a deal because of scarce resources or lack of flexibility on price.

A Word to the Wise

A Drag Race can be fun and exciting, and it can be very rewarding. What do you do after you've won; or, worst case, what do you do if, after all the effort, your target keeps the lead?

The typical response when someone else challenges you to a Drag Race is to respond in kind. It's natural, it's human nature, but it's not always or even generally the best response. As noted, if the race goes on too long, it can be great for the customer who gets better and better products at better prices, but hell for the players—testing their resources, drawing profits out of the market, and leading to their ultimate exhaustion. Even the winning company may rue the day they started down this path. As we will see in the next chapter, sometimes the best response to this simple, classic strategy is to ignore the bait and avoid direct confrontation in the first place.

Take-Aways for the Drag Race

1. The Drag Race is the simplest go-to-market strategy or play, and the most direct form of competition. It involves singling out one competitor and doing everything it takes to gain superiority over them, for a single product at a time.

2. Drag Races come in two basic forms. One is the fast-follower contest in which a new entrant attempts to grab the lead from the incumbent. The other is the market-clearing challenge, which focuses on head-to-head comparisons with one player taking the spotlight, and eventually the winnings, away from everyone else.

3. Define the contest in terms you can win. Customers need to be receptive to change. Your competitor needs to be vulnerable. If that means focusing on a smaller initial prize or segment of the market, so be it.

4. You need to have what it takes to win. Don't enter a Drag Race unless you're ready to stick it out for the long haul and are willing to bear the risks.

5. Once in the race, make sure to fully exploit every advantage. Drag Races are spectator sports, which is one of the best things about them. Be direct and competitive in every element of your marketing. Trumpet every feature, every award, every victory, every sign of momentum. Never stop pounding on your lead.

Coming Up

If you've waged a Drag Race and won—what next? How do you get the most out of your lead? Winning big makes you a big target yourself. How do you defend your lead over time as conditions change and new challengers enter the market? The basic strategy for accomplishing these goals with the minimum resources and over the longest term is what we explore in the next chapter.

The idea is not to block every shot. The idea is to make your opponent believe that you might block every shot.

—BILL RUSSELL, NBA COACH

3. The Platform Play

It's dangerous at the top. And lonely too. One way to block the shots people will take at you is to make sure you're not the only one who benefits from being up there.

However you got there—by means of a long Drag Race or some other route—once you've established a leadership position of any kind, you want to hold on to it, and even strive to grow beyond it.

Reaping the rewards of being top dog can be inspiring, but the rewards come with a big risk. Success can breed future success; it can also breed contempt. The company in a prominent position offers a tempting target for others to shoot at. The view may be nice, but lots of folks may want to knock you off your perch.

Successful companies that have stayed successful have almost always found ways to intertwine their success more deeply with the success of their whole industry. On achieving a victory, they don't just exit the field to celebrate. They secure the peace. They use their triumph as a jumping-off point from which to reinforce and extend their long-term position. They do not let short-term greed cloud their vision. They focus more on long-term greed—it's a lot healthier and more durable.

How do you do this? By redefining success beyond just your own isolated terms and into broader industry terms. By combining your interests with those of a whole industry, by fostering an industry ecosystem—an interlocking, symbiotic network of players within the industry—that supports and benefits your leadership position. By using your winnings to win new friends—friends who are happy you exist and have a vested interest in keeping it that way.

Companies that achieve this transform their business from just one of many competitors into a shared platform—a platform that a growing number of other companies then use to drive their own successes. Others then invest in this platform and stake their own futures on, and come to have a strong interest in, maintaining and strengthening it. In other words, here's a fortress that you no longer have to defend alone.

This is the Platform Play.

What Makes a Platform a Platform?

Fine—the Platform sounds like a nice place to sit on top of. What does this play actually look like?

A Platform Play is a fortress, a well-defended vantage point from which you can see any enemy coming and fend them off. And, like concrete, it's strongest when it's reinforced, it's strongest when you don't build it alone. This play is the inverse of a Drag Race. Rather than picking on someone head on, you stay above the fray, you involve everyone in your success, and you avoid direct competition or comparison.

Not everyone can pull off this communal play. But when you do, you can achieve something incredibly powerful, in the way that stones added to cement yield much stronger and more durable

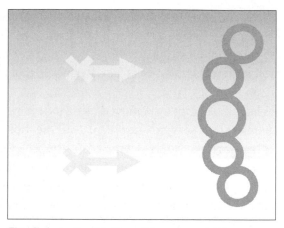

Fig. 3–1. In the Platform Play, you get others to
stand with you, defending against common
competitors.

concrete. As illustrated in Fig. 3–1, you can either face all the on-
coming opposition alone or bond together with an ecosystem of
partners who also want to see you succeed. When you do so, you
gain ever-increasing, ongoing support for your business and extend
your reach and influence at steadily declining costs. And by nesting
your success with that of others, you create ever-increasing barriers
to entry.

The Japanese company NTT DoCoMo, Inc., executed a very
powerful Platform Play to grow itself from a nice, well-positioned
business to a true powerhouse and industry center of gravity.

DoCoMo was formed in 1991 as a subsidiary of NTT, Japan's
regulated telephone monopoly, to handle the modest wireless pag-
ing, car phone, and in-flight businesses. Through the 90s, these
markets grew nicely and evolved into the much larger mobile phone
market, bringing DoCoMo upwards of 10 million subscribers.
They were so successful that in 1997, NTT spun them out.

The IPO brought in more than $18 billion, setting them up in
what seemed like a cozy place. But to DoCoMo's new CEO, Keiji

Tachikawa, it was only the beginning. Not satisfied with the healthy mobile voice calling business he was building, Dr. Tachikawa looked to the future and saw the growth of the Internet and the future of smarter and smarter handsets; he determined that DoCoMo would be there.

Two years later the company launched its i-Mode service, one of the earliest wireless data services anywhere. And the most successful. While other wireless Internet efforts in almost every other country met with only modest success, i-Mode generated an immensely profitable business, achieving over 40 million subscribers and continuing to add hundreds of thousands every month.

Content and application providers were soon knocking down the doors to deliver stuff on i-Mode. Why? Well, maybe the fact that they could make a lot of money doing so had something to do with it.

The smart folks at DoCoMo weren't too greedy (at least not short-term greedy). They only charge these providers 9 percent of their revenues for delivering content or a service to i-Mode subscribers. And they make it easy for them to actually get the money. DoCoMo handles all the billing and collections, providing subscribers with one consolidated bill which then gets reconciled back to the whole ecosystem. Everyone's happy.

The company also makes sure that the rest is easy. They started by using a simple subset of common HTML so that it would be exceptionally simple for anyone to create a site or a service. Most telecommunications companies like to build proprietary technology. With NTT's huge market in Japan, they've built their own radio technology and their own phone technology. Just about everything has been designed uniquely for the Japanese market. But, savvy businesspeople as they are, they kept their own egos in check. They didn't feel that their methods had to become a monolithic standard; instead they made sure that over time more and more alternative standards—GIF, Java, MIDI, http, etc.—were made compatible, too.

Sounds great. But what does it take?

When Does It Make Sense to Run a Platform Play?

If you're in the right place to run a Platform Play, you've probably been pretty darn busy for a while, competing hard in one form or another to gain your present position that has put your product at the top of the pile. It's time then to go back and refresh your view of the playing field to make sure conditions are right for your next move.

You're in position to run a Platform Play if your situation meets these conditions:

Your industry is ready.
Your customers are your allies.
Much of the market sees your competition as their enemy, too.
You're strong, confident, and aware enough to share the wealth.

Your industry is ready.

Most companies do not start out by running a Platform Play. For example, in the early stages of development of a new industry, competition is too no-holds-barred to allow the kind of ecosystem required for a successful Platform. Some shift has to occur to provide an opening.

Take the case of Amazon.com. During the 1990s dot-com boom, it was just one, albeit one of the most prominent, of many dot-coms competing fiercely for our attention and our pocketbooks. Then, as the bubble burst, it became one of a smaller and smaller number fighting to survive.

But Amazon had some important advantages, including a great brand, great technology, and a strong customer foothold with books. The technology had started with the book site, where the company had built advanced searches and recommendations to make it easier for customers to find what they wanted.

The first steps toward turning these advantages into a Platform came in the form of allowing book searches and links on everyone else's Web sites. Originally, the play was just to use this to extend to new Drag Races in other retailing categories, competing on a supply-chain and operations basis with the likes of Wal-Mart and Costco.

But when the dust settled on the dot-com bubble, it became clear that Amazon's key advantages were not in its buying power or scale but rather in its powerful merchandizing and customer intelligence technology. A growing number of brick-and-mortar companies wanted to apply technologies such as these but did not want to face the effort of developing them on their own. This opened the way for a much broader, shared ecosystem.

Amazon is now moving to become even more of a Platform company. A large number of retailers can sell their goods through Amazon's ZShops. A growing number of big players such as Toys 'R' Us, Target, Smith & Hawken, Nordstrom, and the Gap—all of which would have previously been considered competitors—have sites within Amazon. It's a highly symbiotic relationship. These brands get the benefits of Amazon's merchandizing platform—with search, Web presentation, recommendations, and, of course, traffic. Amazon gets a piece of each of their businesses without having to build out new brands, purchasing power, or distribution networks.

Your customers are your allies.

Your customers can become the most dynamic barrier to entry for others. That's the case with ID Analytics, a company that uses advanced analytics to help financial services companies predict and thwart identity theft (where the bad guys steal enough of your personal information to keep getting new credit cards, loans, online purchases, etc.). Although only a start-up, they are actively managing the process of enlisting and binding customers together as allies in a united fight against this growing epidemic.

Their founder, Bruce Hanson, knows how to do his customer homework. As former president of products for HNC (now Fair Isaac), he had seen the power of identifying issues that united customers. HNC brought banking customers together in a form of a consortium that pooled their collective data to give each a better chance of protecting themselves against fraud from stolen credit cards. HNC, as an expert, neutral third party, was able to help all its customers benefit. This shared asset became a key competitive advantage and a strong barrier to entry.

The same common interest appears to be in place with the issue of identity theft, and ID Analytics is in a good position to create a Platform for similar customer alliances and symbiotic value.

One danger lies in the possibility of customers growing restless about supporting a company. They can start to feel trapped or neglected—especially if the company doesn't make sure that the deal continues to be of common benefit. This may be happening with HNC's acquirer, Fair Isaac, which has had a near-exclusive hold on credit scoring for ages. Without continuing to enhance the value of this offering, and ensuring the win–win of all its partners, Fair Isaac/HNC may become more and more vulnerable.

That said, the Platform Play is all about finding the strongest way to defend your turf. So, for it to make sense, you have to have some turf to defend.

Most often this means that you have already won. You're either the most popular player or the perceived leader. In other words, your product or service is in a market-leading position. Most often this implies that you're a large, highly established company, as in the case of DoCoMo. But that doesn't always have to be the case.

One company we work with provides a good example. N'Site Solutions is an outsourced business process solution provider in the absolutely gigantic property and casualty insurance industry. They are still a moderate-sized company in people and revenue terms and as such are in no position to compete with the huge national technology and service players who serve the industry—multibillion-dollar public companies such as IBM, Accenture, and CCC. But all of these folks in fact only target the high end of the market, the biggest insurance carriers. That leaves a big gap in the middle, a gap that N'Site has been happy to fill.

Within this market definition, N'Site has been able to establish a growing leadership position, a position of respect and authority that it can extend but that it needs to defend.

You typically run a Platform Play when the customers are yours to lose. Inertia is in your favor. With the Platform Play, you're taking an active role about not squandering this advantage.

Even though you're the leader, you have to keep listening. Keep in touch with what the most demanding customers are trying. You may be the safe choice, but you can't afford to ignore the issues, however small, that your customers may bring up. Addressing these is the key to staying on top.

Much of the market sees your competition as their enemy, too.

When the customers are yours to lose, the competition has also already lost, at least to a degree. But beyond that, it really helps if the whole ecosystem of the market is set up to challenge your challengers. Platform Plays are best attempted when enough players have a vested interest in you and therefore see anyone who challenges your position as opposing them as well.

In contrast to the Drag Race, in the Platform Play you need to be certain you don't overemphasize the importance of competition or, worse, create it. Just because you're in position to run a Platform Play doesn't mean you're immune to competition. In fact, by virtue of your leadership position, you're a bigger and more tempting target for new entrants.

Sometimes the most important competition is yourself. Instead of making comparisons with other competitors, in a Platform Play you make comparisons to yourself. Each new version of your offering must be an improvement over the previous one. Instead of 25 percent better than another player, you're 25 percent better than your own current version. Once Microsoft Word and Excel had established themselves, all focus moved to Office, where the improvements came from a more combined system. All future comparisons were to previous versions. Mentioning WordPerfect or 1-2-3, ever, would have just served to unnecessarily remind people of their existence.

You're strong, confident, and aware enough to share the wealth.

You may be a Platform company without even knowing it. But having what it takes to run a Platform Play is highly advantageous. It's important to know where you are in the market and make sure to nurture this advantage. N'Site Solutions found itself in exactly this situation. Without focusing on it consciously as a strategy, N'Site developed several key elements of a Platform.

As a neutral solution provider and "broker" in its market segment, N'Site provides large combined benefits to its customers, benefits they would not otherwise realize on their own. By pooling their customers' buying power, the company is able to achieve discounts for them across its supply chain. Managing and monitoring the transaction of its customers with a wide range of partners has allowed N'Site to establish standards of performance for each of them and report and drive down variances from these standards.

Reputation is fundamental. You can't get people to trust you to regulate their ecosystem without it. That was key to both N'Site and ID Analytics in developing their strong customer relationships. The long histories of their founders in their respective industries and their reputations for innovation and integrity made a big difference and allowed them to get started where a lot of other small companies would have stalled.

In the process of building its business, N'Site has developed a number of large and growing networks of suppliers to these customers. These supplier networks find great value in working with N'Site in terms of simplicity, standardization, and increased visibility and reputation than what they could achieve alone. Association with N'Site has become worthwhile. And therefore a virtuous cycle has been created with N'Site supporting, providing value to, and enforcing performance and standards among its partners. In turn, its partners provide N'Site customer leads, reinforcing the value of the network, and erecting greater and greater barriers for others to replace this position.

But it has to stay that way. Patience and attention to detail are key.

The Rewards and Risks of Platforming

What are the rewards of building and supporting a Platform? Lots of supporters. Ongoing leadership. What are the risks? A big target on your back. Constant temptations to traitors—partners, members of your ecosystem who may be lured into opposing you.

Both the rewards and the risks are high in a Platform Play. When well done, though, this play often converts your worst competitors into your best allies. But this can be a very hard play to execute, typically for organizational reasons more than technical or business ones. It's hard to keep any alliance together even under the most urgent need.

Rewards

If executed correctly and under the right conditions of current strength, this play can offer the lowest-cost strategy. It generally avoids costly and risky battles and can co-opt erstwhile competitors by providing them with more attractive alternatives. By distributing risks and rewards across an ecosystem, you help make it more self-sustaining and durable.

Take a look at Marvel, the comic book company. Here's a whole other level of "killer app." Through its incredibly systematic use of licensing, Marvel moved from a focus on comic book Drag Races with the likes of DC Comics, to generating an intricate weave of intellectual and creative properties that support and fuel partner films, toys, books, video games, clothing, and more. All gained huge benefits from applying the imagery and cachet of Spiderman, the X-Men, or some other radioactive superhero, and all provided a share of those benefits back to Marvel in the form of royalties and yet further reinforced brand power. Not to mention the sequels.

Risks

As for risks, in addition to making you the most obvious target, no market ever remains static. Any player growing fat, rich, and successful will stir up the competition and even attract new entrants who look upon your position with envy, desire your profits, probe for your shortcomings, and decide that they might have a chance to unseat you. These challengers can be big or small; they may come after you either as entirely new entrants or as an extension of their existing businesses.

The hard news: most companies are not in position to run a Platform Play. As already mentioned, this one is extremely challenging to execute properly. And if you're not truly strong enough, you could easily find yourself unwittingly in a Drag Race that you may very well lose without much of a fight. If you're strong enough but too complacent, or lack the organizational knowledge, or suffer from organizational inertia, you could easily be blindsided by sneak attacks from your supposed allies or from stealthy newcomers. New entrants could use your very success and weight against you while they still have no critical mass. Their nimbleness and underdog status could be the very thing that helps them gain a foothold.

Remember, success invites resentment and the desire for competition. Take a look at the rise of Linux as an alternative to Windows for a very current example.

I'm Up for It–How Do I Run a Platform Play?

The Platform Play is all about being in the center of an industry ecosystem and benefiting from its network effects. As with Platform end-customers, partners need to be nurtured—even those that have a strong stake in your success. For them to continue to find value in your platform, you have to invest in it, making it more and more attractive.

In some ways this play is like turning your industry into a garden. You have to plant the right seeds, let them grow organically, water and fertilize them (and spray pesticide once in a while), and then harvest the fruits wisely. It becomes an ongoing virtuous cycle. How you can make this cycle work is outlined in Fig. 3–2.

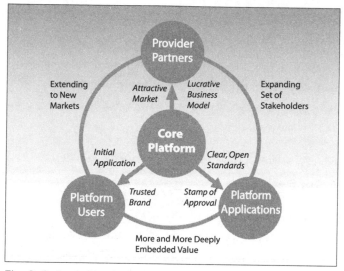

Fig. 3–2. Anatomy of a Platform Play

In short, you start at the center with the value you have in your core Platform, value that can be shared with others in the market. You have to blaze the trail of gathering the first Platform users yourself. To demonstrate the value of the Platform, you use it to build your own initial application.

As you expand to new and attractive markets, you reach out to provider partners; you entice them with a lucrative business model, hoping they will build more and more new applications of their own that will leverage your Platform. Once the first partners are hooked, you need to make it easy for more to join them by providing clear, consistent standards for membership in your Platform "club."

You support this club with smart programs, and turn membership into a valuable stamp of approval. With consistent reinforcement, and because of previous consumer experience, you aim to make this stamp (often in the form of a "certified logo") a trusted brand. It makes choosing additional "Platform-approved" products

or services easier and safer for users than the alternatives. As such it becomes an important buying criterion. This starts the virtuous cycle in motion. Approved "Platform applications" do better than others. More companies want to build them. And with each experience the value of your Platform is broadened and reinforced.
Let's dig into this process in a bit more detail.

Start by investing in and leveraging your core assets.

Rather than putting all your weight behind one "fighter" product as the center of your strategy for comparing with and beating the competition (as in the Drag Race), you use the strongest, most broadly applicable aspect of your technology or business to seed the center of a new ecosystem.

Consider DoCoMo again. They already had a healthy subscriber base and a profitable business. They had great relationships with handset manufacturers. And they had a strong brand from NTT. But they didn't stop there. They used all these to help pull together a new service to these same subscribers offering a deeper, richer, and more personalized experience using not just voice but data.

Innovate to show the way— but make room for others to show more.

Any new technology needs a "killer app" to prove its value. Electricity is powerful stuff, but you can't really tell without a light bulb. In the Platform Play, applications are especially critical in order to validate the importance of the core and to engender trust, not just to customers but also to potential partners.

In the beginning DoCoMo introduced some of its own applications—such as "Doco-Navi," a real-time travel route application—to demonstrate the value and attributes of its service.

But because of its aggressive partnering strategy, DoCoMo did not have to find or build the killer app for its wireless data service, i-Mode. One of the most powerful and popular applications came from a partnership with Bandai, a toy and animation company, that launched an i-Mode cartoon site which included "Miss Kitty" (a mouthless cat with a bow on her ear) and that has generated tens of millions in revenues.

Share the wealth and watch it grow.

Once you've shown the value of your core technology with initial applications, make sure it's applicable to a broader and broader set of markets.

Because DoCoMo has created a huge ongoing ecosystem, the company doesn't have to figure out what the next killer app will be or the one after that, no matter how bizarre. There are tens of thousands of partners to compete amongst themselves for the honor.

i-Mode has grown like wildfire. Not through DoCoMo building and rolling everything out themselves, not by them taking all the winnings or losses all by themselves. No, i-Mode was launched as a means for other companies to benefit. DoCoMo used i-Mode as a new way to make its assets widely available to other parties, who came to benefit from the Platform and in the process supported the Platform.

In DoCoMo's case, these third-party supporters take the form of application and content developers who build new ways to use the core i-Mode service. The applications and services have grown from the few that started out to nearly four thousand official and nearly seventy thousand independent i-Mode content sites.

Take a look at United Way. Their whole mission centers around being a Platform. It is their differentiator. Rather than competing with other charities within a given category, United Way sits at the center of a charitable-giving ecosystem. They raise hundreds of millions of dollars every year with the sole purpose of distributing it out to their over 1,400 community-based United Way organizations. Each of these independent, locally governed bodies is better off because of associating with one central Platform.

Make it easy and lucrative for others to work with you.

Helping others make money always makes you more attractive.

If the central United Way platform takes too much for itself in operations costs, it becomes less attractive to both donors and member charities. Just like with any Platform business, staying on top of this and providing each of the member charities the support they need is an ongoing effort to maintain United Way leadership.

This way Platform players create and support an ongoing win–win cycle, making it easier and more attractive for new stakeholders, making the stakes more and more valuable to all of them, and making it harder and harder for competitors to replicate.

Keep growing the network—give it the support needed to grow.

One of the keys to effectively running a Platform Play is to make sure that being a part of it remains truly attractive. Your Platform is like a currency. It's good to be able to print money, but if you let everyone print it without any oversight, the value of the currency is rapidly debased.

In the DoCoMo example cited earlier, that company separates general content providers from those on its "i-Menu." These premium providers are the true showcase of the service. Their content must be approved by DoCoMo and must meet the company's standards. But these standards are made clear and simple to follow.

All of this creates an ongoing virtuous cycle that benefits all of the stakeholders, reinforcing and strengthening the Platform, while, of course, yielding huge long-term benefits to DoCoMo.

N'Site developed its Platform in response to customer needs. But now the company knows it has to invest in actively managing the networks it created. They are a core part of its value proposition. Investing not just in customers but also in partners makes you much bigger than just your company, it makes you a whole industry together. As such you need to have the right kinds of programs, support, and ongoing benefits to keep this asset healthy.

To stay in this enviable position, you have to extend your reach and make sure that your platform appeals to the whole market, either directly through you or through your partners. The value of the Platform has to continue to increase. The scope of benefit for all its stakeholders has to grow. The virtuous cycle all participate in has to continue.

Marketing Implications

Marketing in this "communal" play is a subtle thing. It is not at all the chest beating of a Drag Race. When you're running a Platform, your own outbound marketing efforts must be limited and very carefully chosen. Marketing in this play is much more about setting things up so that others will do much of the marketing for you and then guiding the process all along the way.

The Platform product:
Be a lover, not a fighter.

Remember that your products and offerings are not out there to win a direct contest with anyone. You're beyond that. Your job is to bring others together under your banner. Whether a technology, service, or other core value, your product needs to be something that others can build on. It is the platform from which additional value gets built.

In a Drag Race, better–faster–cheaper is critical. But in a Platform Play, it's not about being cutting edge. It's about having the right set of products that are safe to bet on. It's about striking a balance between retaining leadership while still appealing to as broad a range of possible user/consumer needs as possible.

When DoCoMo first launched i-Mode, the service was not at all cutting-edge technology. It offered very low data-transfer speeds, making it only suitable for text and simple graphics. But it actually worked, and it didn't require the most advanced, most expensive phones. What's more, DoCoMo didn't overpromise. They set expectations for a "unique mobile experience," simpler and less rich than the Internet on your PC but valuable none the less. So people used it, and they liked it a lot. It was fun, it was affordable.

In N'Site's case, this balance means finding the right set of offerings across market segments. In its stronghold in the insurance midmarket, the company offers a combination of its core technology and services, directly to its insurance-company customers. To the lower-end, small–insurance-company side of the market, it works to offer a much more "in a box" ready-made solution. And to the high end, it focuses on its technology alone, partnering with much bigger players to gain a foothold.

In the same way, to attract both customers and partners, your Platform needs to make sense. It cannot be seen as risky or bleeding edge. It has to be prudent and approachable for each segment of the ecosystem.

Pricing: Maintain affordability and value at all levels.

You need to price all these products—the core platform technology, any demonstration application of it that you build yourself, and the suite of tools and programs you offer to your partner network—to be fair and reasonable. Never let price be something that your stakeholders can complain about. Never appear to be exploiting your position unfairly. But also, avoid discounting or competing with others on price. You need to uphold the perception of superior value.

Intel, for example, has pursued a strategy of flexible market coverage similar to the other cases we've examined. As the volume leader, they made sure to fill the market with product-line variants that cover every shape and size of customer. Typically, some are very-low cost products; these have small margins, but keep competitors from offering products priced to undercut Intel.

Using the Ps and Qs mapping technique introduced in the last chapter provides a map as in Fig. 3–3. They were the current share leader, typically with high volume and a moderate to low price. There weren't really any substantial direct competitors left, the classic situation when you have defined your slice of the market correctly.

But of course they didn't stop there. They also had higher-priced products that captured the revenue and margins at the high end, giving them a Ps and Qs map looking something like Fig. 3–4.

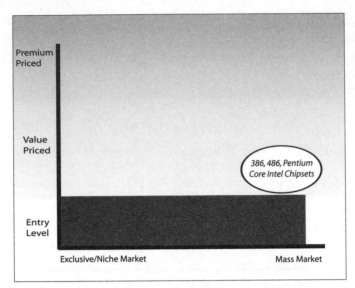

Fig. 3–3. Intel, Drag Race winner, Platform incumbent

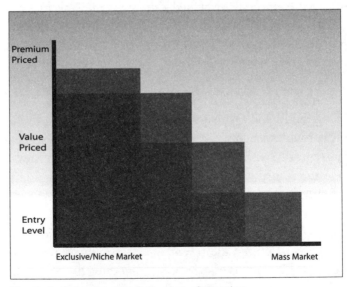

Fig. 3–4. Capturing the full range of margins

Here's their product-line evolution to cover this spread:

1990: Pentium (one size fits all from desktop to server)
1995: Pentium, Pentium Pro (a new server model at ten
     times the price)
2000: Celeron, Pentium III, Xeon (a new, low-price
     model that's half the cost of the flagship desktop)
2003: Celeron, Mobile Pentium, Centrino, Pentium 4,
     Xeon, Itanium

Having such a product and pricing spread allowed them to broaden the scope of their ecosystem. It made them attractive as a platform to a much wider universe of potential device and software partners. And it reduced the room for the other folks to maneuver.

Positioning: Establish yourself as part of an industry.

Everything you do and everything you say should reinforce the value of your ecosystem. But remember to be humble and to stay in the background. Don't compete for attention with partners who are going to mention you anyway as a key asset and source of their legitimacy.

United Way doesn't position themselves as a charity competing with other charities. They call themselves "the United Way Movement."

In examining your own industry, search for openings that could make an ecosystem possible. Aside from your former competitors, are there numerous supporting or related players who could have a stake in your success? Are there a number of other companies that would suffer if your business suffers? Is their success bound up in yours?

This is the most desirable situation for a Platform or fortress. You want the natives of the industry to be friendly to you. When insurgents attack a strong point, they depend on aid and comfort from the locals. But if the natives see no percentage in acting against your interests, they will warn you early on that an enemy is approaching and will harass them or even cut off their supplies in the process.

Remember, it takes discipline to lead an ecosystem. It also takes some tolerance. Because you hold the superior position, you want to avoid direct comparison—you have nothing to gain by it. Don't let yourself be drawn into a Drag Race. Don't let annoying competitors draw you out of the safe place you've created. Don't take their bait. When you run a Platform Play, you need to remain above the fray. You need to reposition anyone who challenges you as someone bucking the system, as a ludicrous upstart with no business rocking the boat. And your allies should carry this message, not you.

Packaging: Guide your partners to package their products with your stamp of approval.

Unlike having a single, drag racing SKU or package, in the Platform Play it is critical that you provide and package the tools that all your partners need to create and support their own offerings using your core.

This is something Microsoft understood almost innately. Master of the Platform Play, they not only built great Platform products (thanks to practical technology leaders such as Brad Silverberg, whose crack teams delivered Windows 3.1, Windows 95, and Internet Explorer), they also supported and fostered a broad community around these products. One of our colleagues, Cameron Myhrvold, formalized and systematized this community into a powerful ecosystem by creating the Developer Relations Group. This organization was charged with evangelizing the value and attractiveness of the Windows and Microsoft platform to the community of independent software vendors and third-party developers. As such it became the central nervous system for all the activities, programs, and offerings and in support of the ecosystem and a key strategic asset to the company.

Package your products to serve and support your ecosystem. Clearly you see this with DoCoMo branding, and with the prominence of "Intel Inside." Logos, membership programs, and partner certification are all key elements of this important effort. But make sure they are open and flexible enough to accept change and to blunt challengers.

Promotion: Leave the driving to them.

Don't work too hard to promote yourself. Let your partners, customers, and other stakeholders do it for you. Most of your promotion should be to these stakeholders. Spend money on co-marketing. Use your promotional efforts to show your network that you're a good partner. Partner conferences are the order of the day. Where the Drag Race was all about feature envy between competitors, the Platform Play is all about attendees, and envy amongst them to be included in your club. Your press releases and media coverage, rather than being about feature wins or switching momentum, should be all about new partners and how existing partners are benefiting.

Finally, Above All: Stay Sharp

Remember, your key advantages are your incumbency and your network of partners. But these can also become weaknesses. You cannot become complacent. Cultivate your ecosystem and allies and make sure that people know that you're continuing to innovate.

Platforms die when innovation ends. New innovations, expanding markets, and the ego temptations of new Drag Races all threaten the delicate equilibrium you have established. It's critical that you continue to reinvent yourself and reinvent the value of your Platform. Loyal customers and partners will wait for some time for you to respond to new issues and needs, but they will not wait forever.

The key to this play is to keep the virtuous cycle going no matter what kind of weather it faces.

Take-Aways for the Platform Play

1. The Platform Play is the strongest, most durable go-to-market strategy. It offers low marketing costs, high barriers to entry, and secure revenue streams. The opposite of a Drag Race, which relies on direct competition, the Platform Play relies on getting others to cooperate. You do this by transcending the battle and convincing others that their success is intertwined with yours, building a whole industry of supportive stakeholders.

2. Platforms are built upon strong foundations. Most commonly they come from companies that have gained a leadership position after a hard-fought battle. Inherently, the Platform Play is about defending and expanding your turf. You have to have some turf to defend for this to make sense. And you have to share it as a common good in some way for the Platform to be viable.

3. Platforms only thrive in specific conditions. The industry has to be able to support a symbiotic ecosystem. Customers have to want security and stability and be willing to accept your mantle of leadership. Your competitors must have mostly left the field or the field needs to be defined in a way that excludes most of them.

Rather than targeting competitors, partners become the focus. They need to be invited to join in your little slice of heaven.

4. Platforms don't sustain themselves. They need care and feeding. You need to be a good steward. You need to be very conscientious and diligent about the ecosystem you have created. It has to remain a win–win for all parties, at the outset and as conditions change.

5. Remember, this is a team sport. Make sure the benefits of being on the team and the risks of opposing it stay high. Being in a leadership position makes you a tempting target. You have to constantly reinvent yourself to head new entrants off at the pass and make competing against you obviously counterproductive.

Coming Up

Becoming your own ecosystem, as in the Platform Play, is an admirable goal. But what if you aren't on that path yet? What if you're still the weaker player? How do you break in? How do you compete with what has become a whole industry or even just the most powerful Drag Racer?

Sometimes the best form of competition is to seem not to compete at all. Whereas the Platform Play is all about staying above the fray, the next play is all about staying below the radar—finding ways to make headway with comparatively few resources, only small advantages, and formidable opposition.

He will win who knows when to fight and when not to fight.

—SUN TZU

4. The Stealth Play

If you can't beat 'em . . . join 'em or at least stay out of their way.

It can get downright discouraging when you find yourself confronting a competitor company that has everything going for them. Whether it's because they're ten times your size, or better positioned, or just the default incumbent, it's still a bummer when they just seem to keep holding on to their lead.

You try so hard, you know you have something really special. Why, oh why can't you win for a change? Well, nobody said business was going to be easy or fair. Don't get too depressed. Don't throw in the towel. When you see another Drag Racer pass you by or find a Platform landing on your head, remember that the loss of a single battle—or even a number of them—doesn't determine the outcome of the campaign. If you have enough fortitude, if you're nimble and truly determined, and if you don't let foolish pride get in your way, you can accept your losses, climb into your tent, and take cover.

The Stealth Play is the one for just such situations. It's a play you turn to out of need rather than strength. It doesn't offer a speedy route to victory, and it's not as dramatic or heroic as the previous plays. When you're not in a position to win one of those, it's the Stealth Play to the rescue, one of the most important to have in your repertoire. You can pull out Stealth and use it as an alternative to slipping into a Drag Race you don't want, or whenever you enter a market where you face tough opponents who have more clout than you. It will help you gain or regain your foothold. Then you can survive, thrive, and even find a way to come back and fight another day.

What Does Survival Look Like?

Survival does sound better than the alternative. But what does this play actually look like?

The Stealth Play is like a quarterback sneak. Rather than running a play where you try to outrace the other team to the goal line, or launch a brutal assault against their defenses, you find a way to slip through while they aren't noticing. Once into their backfield, you find a way to keep their attention diverted. (See Fig. 4–1.)

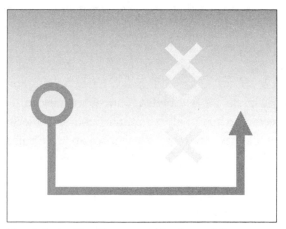

Fig. 4–1. In Stealth, you survive by avoiding direct confrontation.

To switch metaphors for a moment, a cavalry charge may seem heroic, the gallant thing to do. But when facing an opponent too well armed or too securely ensconced behind their walls, it's suicide. There's not a lot of profit in self-destruction. The smarter course is to find other, safer ways to undermine their advantages, ways that won't draw too much attention to you.

So when you're not yet able to win a direct confrontation, you avoid it. If your opponent controls the central position, find another place to make inroads. If they are more popular than you, hitch your wagon to them. But you will always be on the lookout for their blind spots, for opportunities to fill the gaps they leave or to address the needs and desires they overlook. And whatever you do, you won't draw attention to your actions or allow them to feel threatened until you're good and ready for them.

This is the essence of the Stealth Play.

The story of Enterprise Rent-A-Car offers a very telling example of a company that found itself confronted by massive opponents. Rather than duke it out with the heavyweights, the company removed itself to more protected terrain. There it could safely watch the top dogs beat each other to a pulp while it built a stronger and stronger business—only to reemerge as a head-to-head competitor and arguably the biggest in its class.

Enterprise was started back in 1957 by fighter pilot Jack Taylor as a small, local car-leasing company. Early on the company did very well because of local knowledge and good service. It eventually grew to become a national car rental business, offering, among other things, daily rentals to people whose cars were being repaired. It continued to grow nicely until, in the 1970s, it found itself embroiled in the airport car rental market, where a fierce battle raged between the big players like Avis and Hertz, with millions spent on national advertising and promotion.

The company took a step back and asked itself some tough questions. Were they ready to go "head to head to head" with the two biggest players in this market? Did they even want to? Was struggling to compete for the spot of third car in a very expensive version of what we label the Drag Race worth the trouble? Was something like "We try even harder" consistent with their strengths and their modus operandi? The answer in every case was no.

Enterprise looked back to its roots in local, hometown markets and decided to remove itself from the cutthroat playing field "at the edge of America's runways." Instead, it found plenty of remaining gaps in its own backyard. It continuously expanded its footprint in hometown locations that the big airport travelers neglected to address because they were too busy slugging out rates and location fees at airports.

Enterprise decided not to bother competing for your travel-related business. It left that bloody field completely to the "big boys." It focused on being your nearby source when you need a temporary replacement. It enhanced its offering to include a "We'll pick you up" service, making its differentiation complete.

Under the cover of highly localized small rental agencies, Enterprise was able to build a very powerful alternative business model. And because they listened and were low to the ground, they found and filled one of the most boring gaps in the business. Boring, but one of the biggest.

Other than business travel, one of the major reasons for renting a car is as a temporary replacement after an accident. And who, in the end, is paying the bill? Insurance companies—making them huge potential customers.

The other major differentiation Enterprise came up with was based on the issue of, Who wants to have to find their way to the airport to pick up their rental after their car just got totaled? Hertz and Avis would like you to. Instead, with Enterprise's multiple in-city locations and its "We'll pick you up" service, the choice for the carless car owner was obvious. On top of this natural grassroots advantage, Enterprise also made sure that it built its business to target the insurers—who rent tons of cars every year and whose checks don't bounce.

The result? Enterprise now owns the vast majority of the insurance temporary replacement market. And they captured this share right under Hertz's and Avis's noses without ever having to Drag Race either one of them directly.

Lo and behold, after biding their time and sticking to their knitting for so long, Enterprise reemerged in the mid-1990s as a huge player, with over five hundred thousand vehicles, and over five thousand locations. Now they were ready to start opening rental offices at airports again. Is another Drag Race about to begin? Wonder who's in the best position this time around.

When Should You Go Stealth?

What does the playing field need to look like if you're going to hide out in it?

Frankly, if you're not in a strong enough position to drive to immediate victory, this strategy makes the most sense. But getting it right requires a very, very precise understanding of each element of the playing field. The vigilant, close-to-the-ground guerilla fighter who studies the territory and curries favor with the natives survives. The sloppy and overconfident gets executed.

Astute and ongoing gap analysis (which we'll address in detail in Chapter Eight) is probably more important to the success of this play than to any other because the market gaps are smaller and your own competency gaps are bigger. Nimbleness and flexibility are the keys to this play, but it's pretty hard to be nimble if you're winding your way through an obstacle course blindfolded—which explains why gap analysis is so important.

Your Competition—Knowing them really well

Your competition is the king of the jungle that you don't want to find loping across the landscape, eager to gobble you up.

If you were facing competitors weaker than you, you would not resort to jungle-warfare tactics. The general situation analysis is simple. You're outgunned, but the incumbent's dominance isn't absolute—otherwise you wouldn't still be alive. So you need to find a place where they aren't and stay there until you can win.

Even a big lion has weaknesses. The reason you choose this play is the very size or position of your competition. It is their Achilles' heel. But you need to understand your competition's biggest strengths so you can stay out of their way. Look keenly for the chinks in their armor or for their most weakly guarded territory.

There are three basic competitive situations that lend themselves to a Stealth strategy, and each implies a slightly different mode of operation.

A losing Drag Race. The first situation, as embodied in the Enterprise example above, is a Drag Race in which the strength and advantages of the top player(s) are too great or their lead on this particular racetrack is too long. Finding some other place to play, off the progressively beaten path, is the prudent thing to do.

An impregnable Platform. This second competitive situation is one in which the dominant player still has lots of allies—allies it rewards. A Stealth Play offers the best way to reap some rewards while filling in gaps in the Platform. If you can't beat 'em, join 'em. At least until you're strong enough to go it alone.

*A **declining but still huge incumbent**.* This last situation is one where playing by Stealth is more an opportunity than a last resort. Because of some of this competitor's flaws, there are inroads to be made, but because of their continued power, their wrath is still to be avoided. This was certainly true of IBM decades ago as Microsoft was moving into the computing category.

In each of these cases, the incumbent is big. They "own" the market and there's not enough room for you to join the leader or leaders (Fig. 4–2).

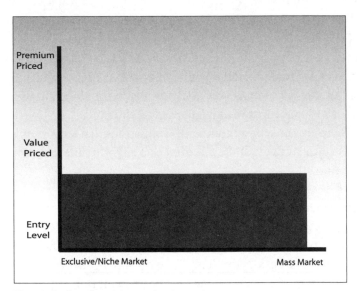

Fig. 4–2. Dominant incumbent

Your job is to keep finding places where you can add (or steal) a bit of value (Fig. 4–3).

You pick off one bit at a time, until you've added enough to be in a position to challenge the leader once again (Fig. 4–4).

And where do you find these places to add a little extra value? With customers, of course.

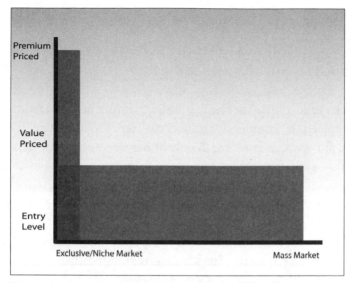

Fig. 4–3. The Stealth player picks off a premium-price niche.

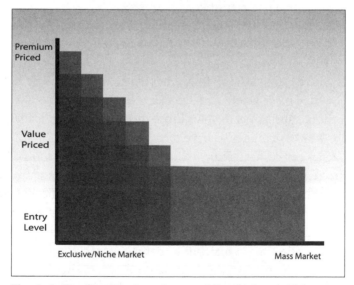

Fig. 4–4. The Stealth player keeps adding niches until in a position to challenge.

Your Customers—Finding people who will provide you aid and comfort

Key to this strategy is finding and exploiting customer situations that match the competitive situations. Here too it's critical that you look for gaps in how the big kahunas are addressing customer needs—gaps that are interesting and important enough to these customers to be worth filling but small or unexpected enough to avoid the attention, desire, or paranoia of your still-secret nemesis.

Just as there are three basic competitive situations leading to three variations on the Stealth Play, there are three kinds of customer gaps to be looked for and exploited:

> *Niches* that are overlooked,
> *Add-ons* that supplement existing offerings, and
> Alternatives that *feed off* the failings of others.

If you're losing a Drag Race, then *find a niche,* a clearly defined and isolated place where you can gain a lead. One where customers have more specific needs than those met by the broad leader. And where they have money to have those needs met.

Niches can come in many varieties. Suitable niches should be attractive enough to build a business in but remote enough to avoid undue attention. They can be vertical-industry–specific, like property and casualty insurance; functionally specific, like the corporate treasury department; or, quite often, locally or regionally specific. Supply may become global, but all demand is still local.

Location doesn't get much more local or more remote than the home base of Extend America: Bismarck, North Dakota. That's where the company found its niche. Not only did they find a niche, they went after it in a smart, stealth way. Rather than try to compete for the top metro markets in the brutal and increasingly costly wireless wars of the national wireless telephone carriers, Extend America's founders decided to focus on underpenetrated markets. They chose the more sparsely populated, rural, "square states" of North and South Dakota, Wyoming, Nebraska, and Montana, where the distances between population centers had previously made building out a wireless network and attracting a critical mass of subscribers too costly. But those same distances made the need for mobile communications and the pain felt by their absence all the more acute. Extend America is filling a real need, one that the "majors" currently just can't be bothered with.

They have also been smart enough to ally themselves with another platform—in this case, Nextel. Rather than pay the price for all spectrum licenses themselves, they allied themselves with this premium yet still nimble carrier. They got to benefit from the strength of the Nextel brand and product offerings as well.

If you're facing a strong platform, then *add on to it.* Target customers who want the value of the platform to be extended. Focus on areas that are seen as complementary, additive, and nonthreatening to your newly found host.

Peter Norton of Norton Utilities (now owned by Symantec) built a multibillion-dollar software business out of ongoing utilities that filled in security and other, often temporary, holes in the never-ending versions of Microsoft Windows. Visio built a very nice software supplement to Microsoft Office before it was acquired by the "host" for $1.3 billion.

In a different industry, the so-called feeder airlines like Mesa Air Group have built solid businesses almost entirely by extending the reach of other major carriers. While the big carriers stay focused on their "hubs," they don't get "spokes" out to many remote cities. But there are real customers in those cities. What are they supposed to do, drive?

That's where the feeder airlines come in. Mesa makes its business by extending the reach of the hub airlines through to these spokes. And by connecting its "spoke customers" seamlessly with the hub carriers, the customers get all the benefits of traveling through a major carrier. They book their spoke-and-hub travel as one. Traveling from, say, Durango to Phoenix to Boston, they get charged a lower combined Durango-to-Boston fare, and their frequent-flyer miles count directly on their major airlines. And they don't even know they are on a Mesa Air Group flight. But Mesa gets their money just the same.

Customers also have complex, evolving needs—needs that even the most sophisticated Platform company can't always supply completely. Add-ons that fill such gaps, while extending from and leveraging the core supplier, also come in different shapes and sizes. These can be utilities, supplements, or extensions of the platform.

Finally, if facing a weakening or sleeping giant, then *feed off it.* Identify areas or categories where their grip on customers is loosening, where evolving demands are passing them by, where dissatisfaction is creeping in, but where your gains don't itch so much that they scratch you out.

As customer tastes, requirements, and expectations change, sometimes the biggest players don't always change with them, at least not fast enough. One thing is constant with consumers: change. Old strengths don't always hold. Established brands don't always extend easily to new areas. This dynamic can present significant opportunities to shave off some of the big guy's business. Look on the margins. That's where the change begins. And the margins can get bigger and bigger, until they're not really marginal any more.

Take the big daddy of the fast food business, McDonald's. For the longest time, it truly saw itself in the hamburger business. And in this business it had taken on challenger after challenger, and hadn't just survived, it had thrived—so much so that it had to stop counting how many billions it had served. The number wouldn't fit under the golden-arches sign anymore. But with a growing national awareness of new food tastes and choices, a new slate of quick service restaurants (QSR is the acronym that everyone in the industry uses) quietly entered into the market.

Rather than drag racing on burgers, as Burger King and Wendy's were doing (or staying totally local, like Dick's or Kid Valley Burgers near us here in Seattle), these upstart, focused, menu-specific QSRs began to appeal to evolving tastes. It doesn't seem obvious, but a lot of dollars that used to be spent on fries and burgers are now being spent on things like tacos, wraps, and hot, high-priced brown water. It wasn't obvious to McDonald's either, but companies like Taco Bell, World Wraps, and even Starbucks have been taking "not so obvious" changes in consumer tastes directly to the bank.

A similar thing happened in the movie-rental business. Blockbuster built a very big business offering a consistent, wide selection of videos in what seemed like every midsized shopping center. The owner of that nice little video shop around the corner from you began to tremble that, any month now, Blockbuster would open in the neighborhood, featuring more titles and more copies of each.

But then along came the Internet; with it, consumer expectations changed forever. With the near infinite choices of merchandise available from the likes of Amazon and eBay, more and more customers came to expect the same in just about every category. They also came to appreciate not having to drive to a store every time they wanted to pick up an item, or worse, when they had to rush to return it before midnight or face the late fees.

In 1999, Netflix launched its Internet rental business of videotapes to take full advantage of these changes, offering thousands more titles (all viewable and searchable, with no late fees) than the largest video store could hold. The video you want can be waiting in your mailbox a few days from now. Netflix filled a gap that just wasn't there before. And Blockbuster's many brightly lit locations can't compete at all in this new game.

Movie addiction and the desire to never, ever stop staring at your screen proved ridiculously powerful; while other companies were folding left and right, Netflix came through very well, thank you. With no existing business to cannibalize, no retail employees to threaten, and no storefront rents hanging over its head, dot-com start-up Netflix has been able to sheer off a growing number of couch potato video enthusiasts as subscribers, generate hundreds of millions of dollars in revenue, and eventually go public with over $1 billion in market cap. Not bad. Not bad at all.

Such customer gaps, whether regional, vertical, supplemental, or alternative, not only present an opportunity to smaller or weaker players, but also are a warning to the largest and strongest. If you're a small guy, don't stop looking for ways to fill in such gaps. And if you're a big guy, don't lose touch with your customer base or with your potential target customers. Don't forget what business you're really in. Or you might turn around one day to find that you've lost much of it.

Your Company—Finding the grizzled, living-off-the-land survivalist inside

Survival is a lot more about being resourceful than about having lots of resources. Running an underground Stealth strategy is often the soundest path for new companies entering a market or for existing companies trying to find a good grip on their tough climb.

But this play requires a unique combination of skills for you to be successful. You have to have sufficient knowledge of the market terrain to find your way to the goal line. You also need the competitive humility and good sense to know when to avoid sure defeat, the nimbleness and flexibility to keep avoiding it, and the grim determination and patience to keep at it for the long-term game despite the short-term hardships.

The niche you choose to focus on, of course, had better be one where you have a snowball's chance of developing a real advantage. At Extend America, as noted, they did this by focusing regionally, on rural states, starting with North Dakota. It probably didn't hurt that their founder is the former governor of the state. When we started Ignition Partners, we knew the woods were already full of venture capital firms, many that had been around for decades. We knew we had to have a focus—a niche for investing our capital and for differentiating ourselves. Surprise, surprise, we didn't choose biotech or energy science. Why? Because we didn't know the first thing about those areas. Instead, we chose software and telecom because—please excuse the shameless self-promotion—as a firm we had over 150 years of combined experience in these areas.

The essence of Stealth is avoiding direct confrontation. That means putting your ego or your injured pride to the side in favor of more important concerns, such as not getting your butt kicked. Humility becomes a key asset.

Take the case of Entellium, a start-up in the CRM/SFA (customer relationship management/sales-force automation) categories, using the same kind of subscription model of selling this software that Salesforce.com has been using to Drag Race against Siebel Systems. But they are targeting an important gap that neither is focused on. Because Entellium is humble enough (some may say smart enough) to let others put their own brand on the Entellium product, they have been able to open up whole new channels of distribution that the prouder players miss out on or alienate. Private labeling may be a humble strategy, but used right, it can be powerful.

The same is true if you're going to add on to an existing platform. You have to recognize that there is no shame in submitting to another player's requirements if the benefits are large enough.

Look again at Mesa. Although they maintain complete owner-ship of their airline, they fully embrace the notion of integration with their bigger brothers. They blend their flights right into the other airlines' reservation systems. You never even know that you booked a Mesa flight. In fact, they take it further: you never even know that you flew on a Mesa jet. They paint their feeder planes the same colors and brands as the hub airlines they feed. Their attendants wear the same uniforms. Talk about swallowing your brand pride. Talk about stealth. Talk about a very profitable airline in the midst of scores of potential bankruptcies among their huge competitors.

When you run this kind of play, you can't rest on your laurels. You don't have any. You have to be quick. You have to stay ahead. To maintain your value and hold your territory on the playing field, you have to keep finding new gaps and new ways to fill them, fast.

Symantec has done just that. More often than every month, they send me a new virus signature (or updated definition of viruses against which to be shielded) to protect my computer—orders of magnitude in greater frequency than most versions of traditional software get upgraded. And they don't stop at that. As the environments and modes of computing have changed, Symantec has continuously pumped out new utilities to fill one kind of hole or another that these new environments expose, from Internet firewalls and virtual private networks, to intrusion detection systems and overall security management.

By delivering this value over and over again, they have built one of the most trusted brands in computing—all with the logo of whatever is the most current version of Microsoft Windows on their box. Humility, real value, and quickness can pay off big time.

Nonetheless, without persistence and patience these payoffs can all be undone. The Stealth Play is generally a means to an end. But it's human nature to be impatient. It's also human nature to want to toot your own horn. The more successful you are at running this play, the more tempting it will become to come out of hiding, the more galling it will become to sit quietly while some larger, more entrenched player continues to claim superiority. But don't be hasty. Don't make the mistake of showing your hand too quickly. Don't poke an opposing lineman in the eye.

Take a lesson from what happened to Netscape. As described earlier, they had everything going for them after discovering that terrific new gap to fill with their Internet browser. They were nimble as all get-out, creating new versions of the product almost every week, running circles around everyone else in the software industry. They were the darlings of Wall Street. They were delivering huge value and ongoing utility both to users and to a whole new class of developers—Web site creators. And they were getting all kinds of kudos in the process. They seemed to have it all.

But they couldn't resist. They just couldn't stay stealthy. They felt the need to drag race. Maybe it was inevitable that Microsoft would come after them. Maybe it was inevitable that Microsoft would see them as a threat and put their best developers on the task of matching them. Maybe. But telling the world openly that you intend to make the world's largest and richest software company irrelevant, that you're going to supercede the need for their most important and profitable product line took "maybe" right out of the question.

Netscape left Microsoft no choice but to respond. They underestimated the nimbleness and, strange to say, humility of their huge competitor, and they paid the price.

Your Industry—Making sure the market is dynamic enough

Stealth is a great play for many who want to gain a foothold, but it's not a play for everyone. And not for every situation.

In order for you to be able to find the right kind of gaps and keep finding them, the industry you're playing in has to be dynamic and shifting. It has to be growing as a whole or changing in some way. Whether a new industry or old, there has to be room for a smaller player to gain traction. Without such change and opportunity, rather than sitting back and focusing on the low-hanging fruit, the big guys would be desperate to fill every little gap.

In each of the examples above something was changing in the industry that made alternatives, add-ons, and supplements not only possible but well received.

In the case of Extend America, the tight financial markets made it even harder for the big wireless carriers to stretch into new locations. And new rural-focused legislation made its own potential financing situation more favorable.

For Mesa, airline deregulation opened up a whole new range of opportunities and added a great deal of urgency to the major airlines to partner quickly.

The recent availability of high-performance, lower-cost offshore labor has been a huge asset to Entellium. Access to such a resource has allowed this small company to be much more nimble in updating and delivering their sales-force automation software, and to deliver it at a much lower price.

Underlying changes in technology standards and infrastructure—distribution, form factors, power sources, etc.—have opened up opportunity to other companies. Of course, the Internet itself, as we have seen, has been a huge factor in making many markets dynamic enough for new entrants to find their own stealthy openings—at least initially.

Netflix included. But the simple switch to DVD from VHS also played a huge role in the rise of Netflix. Without the smaller size and portability of the DVD form factor, their shipping and warehousing operations and costs would have been prohibitive.

Whatever the cause of change, doing your industry homework is critical, to understand the terrain incredibly well. This play is all about being low enough to the ground that you can find gaps others haven't—and being smart, fast, and persistent enough to keep finding them.

The Rewards and Risks of Being Stealthy

The trade-offs are pretty simple—lower cost and survival versus discovery and death.

Remember, in the Stealth Play, you're always at risk just because of your limited resources and weaker position. If you were more powerful, more established, or more advantaged, you would not choose to run a Stealth Play.

Be that as it may, once you're in it, you're in it to succeed. So you might as well take maximum advantage of the benefits such a strategy offers.

Rewards

Most importantly, this strategy is safer than the alternatives. Keeping a lower profile and nibbling away at the edges is much less likely to awaken the bear. If the competitor is running a Platform Play, as was the case with Symantec and Mesa, they often literally invite you to service their customers. And they make it easy for you to do so. You get to ride their coattails on things like their reseller and co-marketing programs, you get to go to their industry conferences, and, if you're supersmart, the CEO of your biggest long-term potential competitor even puts you into his/her keynote address.

Also, remember, this can be the right play when you have limited resources: it just doesn't cost as much as other plays. You only choose this play when you don't have the money but do have the time and the skills. Going under the radar implies an "economy of force" approach. Using this strategy, you can build a growing business with much less because even to execute it well (which is the only way you'll try it—right?) requires an amazingly small team and budget.

In the cases above, you get to surf in the wake of other huge brands without spending all that much green on marketing. But the savings go beyond marketing. Look at Netflix and its start-up costs compared to those of building out a huge network of retail outlets. Look at Extend America: they were able to avoid the incredibly expensive wireless spectrum auctions because of their partnership with Nextel.

Following a Stealth strategy has another implication that is either a reward or risk depending on your situation and goals. This play is one of the best ways to prepare your company for acquisition. If the business gets big enough to be interesting to one of your partners, among the fastest way for them to take advantage of it is to buy you out. If you do it right, you can even structure your arrangements with the big guys to set this option upfront. It all depends on your aspirations.

For this to make economic sense, you have to be certain that you're attractive enough to warrant a good price and compatible and unthreatening enough not to draw your competitor back into a Drag Race you're not ready for. Which highlights the biggest risk—being discovered too soon.

Risks

The big guys you're trying to avoid may be slow, but you can't count on them being stupid. Smart players will know that everyone in their ecosystem is trying to take their marbles away, or at least tempted to try. So you should count on them being conscious about which gaps they choose to let you fill and which they don't. In software, the giants like to incorporate your key benefits in their next release, leaving you as a low-margin utility player with a nearly empty basket.

This happened consistently with folks such as Norton/Symantec in the early days. When they did a disk defragmenter or other utility that users started to depend on, the operating system vendor would incorporate one of their own relatively soon thereafter.

Another risk comes in choosing which gap you're going to focus on. First and foremost, the gap has to exist. It has to be real enough to give you a footing. But it also has to be remote enough to keep you off your competitor's immediate war plans. Choose wrong in one direction and you find yourself on a desert island. Choose wrong in the other direction and you find yourself back in the cage with your old friend King Kong.

Geographic and vertical industry segments are pretty easy to validate as niches. Customers identify themselves in these categories. Huge numbers of businesses are built around these dimensions. But other segments make less sense and may get you nowhere. Microsoft put huge energies into trying to make traction in the "MORG" (medium-sized organizations) segment. It seemed to make sense on paper. Medium-sized companies represented a gap in the sales metrics compared to large enterprises and small business. Gates and company spent years and years—and millions and millions of dollars—trying, only to discover that it wasn't a segment at all because in this business no one really considered themselves a MORG. Either they were small businesses happy to stay that way, or they aspired to be big.

Microsoft could afford to make this mistake. If you're running Stealth, you can't.

Because, yes, finally, resources are a risk. Sure, this is a less resource-intensive play than others, but you still have to have the resources to stick it out. You have to have the time to establish your foothold. You have to have time to establish your initial value. And you have to have time to keep adding to that value. Time means money, and money can be more scarce when you're chasing small gaps one at a time. You have to have the wherewithal to take advantage of this play, go the distance, and emerge all the stronger. And things can get pretty gloomy in the interim.

This is a common problem when you're a start-up or a new business unit. Your betters (either the exec management and/or your investors) can often be too impatient and cut off your sources before you've really had sufficient time to win.

I'm Up for It—How Do I Run a Stealth Play?

Once you start, maintaining your momentum and surviving long enough to thrive, grow, and live to fight another day takes a lot of discipline. You will have to use all of your skills. You will have to be resourceful and you will have to keep at it. And you will have to keep the long view in mind.

The more you can see this as a process or a system, the better—a system whereby you find numerous gaps and build numerous businesses in each of them, and ultimately bind them together into something bigger.

This system should work something like the representation in Fig. 4–5.

Getting this Stealth Play "cloaking device" up and running follows roughly these basic steps. First, you start by identifying a key gap that the incumbent does not address. Your addressing this gap with a nonthreatening, complementary utility gets the process started. This gap is likely targeting a specific niche market that is underserved by the core competition's more generic offerings. Fill-

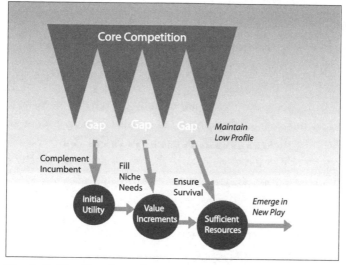

Fig. 4–5. Stealth schematic

ing more and more of the needs for the customers in this niche increases your value over time. If throughout this process you keep a low profile and continue to add value economically, your survival is assured. And if you play your cards right, you get strong enough to emerge from Stealth into a new play.

Let's go through this process in a bit more detail.

If you're giving up on another play, choose a more achievable initial gap.

Remember that you will often be coming to a Stealth Play because you've been trying a Drag Race or a Platform Play, and it didn't work out. Find an underserved need in a vertical or other niche. You have to be honest and brave enough in terms of your limitations. Then choose a more achievable gap, and move on.

Provide an offering that is supplemental but that will actually fill the gap.

You have to make sure you can actually do what it takes to make some real business in this protected territory. Don't pick a gap or opportunity that you aren't naturally suited to. You will just die more quickly if you do. Make sure that the folks in this niche value what you have done sufficiently to reward you for it.

Fill the gap, then keep finding other gaps to fill.

Once you've filled that first gap, make sure you can stay there. You have to keep one step ahead. Guerillas cannot afford to rest. At any time, you may fall into the sights of your competition; your nice little hideout can be raided or your tidy little foothold can get gobbled up. Keep investing in new areas of added value. Find new ways to secure and fill the next gaps of your targets. That's the way to grow.

Stay one step ahead.

Even if you have exposed a chink in your competitor's armor or found a safe place to hide from them, you might nonetheless get crushed or just die of starvation. Survival is still up to you. You have to have an unwavering will to survive. Beyond that, you have to have the cunning and endurance to stay undetected. Keep a low profile. Stay on the lookout. Stay nimble. Stay one step ahead.

Keep building new protections.

Don't be in a rush to show yourself. Make sure you're firmly established in your niches, whatever they are. Bide your time, establish yourself, stockpile resources, and keep building new protections. Beware of calling undue attention to yourself until you're ready to step out of the Stealth mode. Make sure you're getting the maximum yield out of each of the gaps you fill. And as your resources grow, invest in the things that will make it harder and harder for your customers to leave you, regardless of what the big guys eventually decide to do.

Marketing Implications

All the core marketing elements have to come together to make this play work.

Product

You do have to have a product or service solid enough to keep you in the game.

In most cases your offering has to be highly compatible with the big fella who dominates the industry, so this can take quite a bit of engineering or operations work. Also, if you're trying to grab a particular segment of the market, then you'd better have some hard features that will be tough for others to replicate. This is how Sun hid for years in the graphical workstation market even as Intel enabled the manufacture of more and more powerful PCs. Remember, you may be forced to keep updating your product to keep it relevant. And more small products make a better gamble than one big bet.

Packaging

Even with robust products that might otherwise threaten a big player, packaging can really help you maintain a Stealth profile.

In most of the cases described above, some form of subservience of the brand played a role—whether by private labeling, ingredient branding, compliance with the big player's logo, brand, and style, or even complete anonymity. This important tactic can become a key benefit. Remember, Mesa didn't even have to design its own uniforms.

Pricing

The price level really depends on the gap you're focused on.

If it's a utility or add-on, it needs to be priced to simply top up the core platform you're supposedly supplementing. But in many cases the pricing can be pretty high, given the specificity of what you're targeting. It will have to be high enough to compensate for the low unit quantities you can achieve in a specific niche.

Positioning

Stay stealthy.

Note that across all of the Stealth Plays described, across all of the gaps filled, the wily insurgents never tried to fully replace the incumbents, especially when the vestiges of a platform still serve to benefit them. At least not as far as these real-life cases have progressed to date. I still get both happy meals and lattés, run both Windows and virus protection, and subscribe to Netflix and run out to the video store when a new release seems too good to wait for. The watchwords are *low profile, complementary, isolated,* and *specialized.*

Promotion

Your actual marketing activities have to follow your stealthy positioning.

Rather than doing your own broad PR, advertising, or tradeshows, join in those of others. Tag along. Ride their coattails. Or hide out and stick to your knitting by addressing customers directly in a one-to-one sales approach. Whatever you do, don't become a tall poppy—you will risk getting mowed down.

Finally, Decide Carefully When to Emerge and in What Form

Normally with this play there are three basic options once you're ready:

> If you become strong enough, you can go back to a Drag Race on the bigger track.
>
> If your combined offering is robust enough, you can replace, supercede, or pave over the existing Platform.
>
> If you're well positioned enough among all the other smaller offerings cropping up, you can drive up the middle to collapse them all into a new or consolidated category.

Remember, this play is really a means to an end. Few really want to hide out in the hinterlands forever. Think ahead on what play you're going to run once you're strong enough to move beyond a Stealth strategy, when you're positioned well enough to be more than an add-on, complement, or niche alternative.

Take-Aways for the Stealth Play

1. The Stealth Play is the lowest-level, most durable go-to-market strategy. It is all about avoiding direct confrontation. And as such it offers small, less dominant players a relatively safe opportunity to find entry, maintain a foothold, and grow at low costs. This is not a play you would normally seek out; more often it's forced on you by competitive conditions.

2. Stealth businesses can come in different forms. They can be niche businesses that don't threaten the big guys. They can be add-ons that supplement or enhance an existing Platform. Or they can be opportunistic alternatives that feed off the weaknesses of large, complacent, or weakening behemoths. In all cases, stay lean and leverage as much as you can of the big players' resources—in awareness, marketing, partnerships, and so on.

3. To run a Stealth Play, there must be customer niches or gaps that you can identify. The overall industry structure has to be dynamic enough for you to stay on the move. And your own abilities have to be up to the task. You have to be resourceful and able to do more with less. And you have to be humble and patient to avoid premature exposure and execution.

4. Stealth players must be guerilla fighters. You need to stay mobile, one step ahead of the big players at all times. Once you have a

foothold, you cannot sit back. Keep finding other gaps to fill. Each time you conquer a niche, you have to secure it and find the next one. You never know where your next meal is coming from. Stay sharp.

5. Remember that this play is just a means to an end. Once you've gained a foothold in the market, you will quickly shift to a Drag Race or another of the plays—doing your homework all over again and determining which of the other four is appropriate. By the same token, you may find yourself returning to this play when you expand to other markets with new products and offerings.

Coming Up

If enough time has elapsed since the formation of a category, or if the technologies or businesses have evolved enough from their niche beginnings, you may be able to combine all the formerly distinctive groups by providing a solution that satisfies them all. Such opportunities can be of truly historic proportions. The play that we call "Best-of-Both" is all about how to blow right past the current choices and create and capture just such an opportunity.

That's next.

When you come to a fork in the road, take it.

—YOGI BERRA, BASEBALL PLAYER AND MANAGER

5. The Best-of-Both Play

We face choices every day. Choice is a good thing. Choice is downright American. Choice is power. But what about when neither choice seems best?

Which would you prefer: the high-risk or the low-return investment? Would you like the safe but really slow model or the fast but really dangerous one? How about the ugly one that works, or the stylish but impractical one? The simple but low-power version or the cutting-edge version that's harder to use? So maybe you don't want to have to choose after all. Maybe you want to have it both ways.

Then you understand the mindset of a Best-of-Both Play.

What Makes a Best-of-Both Play?

In most circumstances you're forced—in one way or another, as a consumer or as a company—to pick sides. But in the right circumstances, you don't have to. If you appeal to the most important needs of each part of the market, you can win them all. The Best-of-

Both Play means finding a category with these kinds of trade-offs, where the approach is that you don't choose between one or the other extremes, but focus on the best of both and then collapse them into one.

With this play you draw attention to the unfairness of current choices, highlight the pain caused by the current trade-offs, and offer real relief—a better, more complete alternative, the third or middle way (Fig. 5–1). The Best-of-Both Play means running right up that middle way, blowing past the current alternatives, to a new customer finish line—and watching the category collapse in your wake, right into your waiting hands.

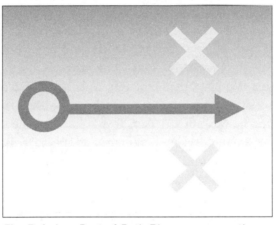

Fig. 5–1. In a Best-of-Both Play, you run up the middle between opposing alternatives.

Making this play work can result in truly historic outcomes, creating whole new business categories in the process. There are tons of categories that we now take for granted that used to be considered impossible combinations, until some brave, resourceful soul jumped into the breach and showed us the way.

An Example: Japanese Luxury Cars

Before 1989, the phrase *Japanese luxury car* was an oxymoron. The real choices were simple and extreme. On the one hand, you could buy a very, very expensive luxury car from Europe—hand-crafted to near perfection, with no detail overlooked, the result of a century of tradition. Or, on the other hand, you could buy an inexpensive, mass-produced, reliable, and fuel-efficient little car from Japan.

There was nothing wrong with either choice, but a vast gulf separated them. Everyone knew that never the twain would meet. That all changed thanks to Eiji Toyada, the chairman of Toyota, who saw the market differently.

Mr. Toyada was pleased to look at his business in 1983 and see that Toyota was selling Corollas, Tercels, and other nice, reliable, small cars like hot cakes. But he also looked across that vast gulf between Toyota, Honda, other Japanese cars, and Mercedes, BMW, and a host of other European luxury cars. He saw their tremendous margins. And he was not satisfied. Toyota had become too strong, too excellent an engineering company, and too successful a business for him not to capture at least some of that high-end market.

So he called a top-level, top-secret meeting to plan how to create the first Japanese superluxury car, one with all the panache, performance, and fit and polish of the best that the Europeans were offering, combined with the reliability and value people had come to expect from Japan.

This was no easy task. They had to get it right. With the entry of Honda's Acura line in 1986 and Nissan's Infiniti shortly thereafter, the heat was on—and the ground was laid.

In 1989, the Lexus LS400 and ES250 hit the streets to much fanfare and admiration—supported by highly stylized branding, superb advertising, personalized service, and incredibly high-touch, low-pressure sales. By 1990, Lexus was raking in awards—including JD Powers Best Car Line and Motoring Press selection as best imported car of the year. The awards kept rolling in and so did the sales. Within three years, in 1992, Lexus outpaced BMW and Mercedes-Benz to become the sales leader, number one among all luxury imports.

What seemed like the impossible has become commonplace: the combined ideas of "Japanese" and "luxury" are now firmly established and totally natural in the car market. These days, as you may have noticed, all the players in this relatively new, highly attractive segment face off against each other continually in competition to establish or defend their dominance—using variations on the play we've labeled the Drag Race.

So it goes. That is the way of competition. The play that made so much sense originally and got you where you are makes a lot less sense once you're established there.

Of course, Lexus didn't get this extraordinary position overnight. And the original conditions had to be right for their run up the middle.

Just what were those conditions and how can you tell if you're facing similar ones in your market?

Indicated Conditions: When Do You Run Up the Middle?

For one thing, there has to be a middle to run up through. Or at least, there has to be the possibility of creating one.

The middle represents a huge opportunity, but conditions have to be right for the play to have a chance of succeeding. To grab this juiciest of apples, it must be hanging low enough to reach, ripe enough to be worth eating, but well enough hidden that nobody has spotted it before. Where these conditions differ from the Stealth Play is that the gap has got to be big.

Where do you find this middle? Look to your playing field.

Finding that gap in the middle calls for a simple gap analysis (see Part II for detailed tips on how to perform this in depth). The gap *is* the middle. Pretty simple really: The current situation involves the trade-off between two extremes. In the future, a combination of the best of these extremes could be made available. Something has to change to bring these two ends together, and you're just the folks to do it.

The playing field has to possess such a middle in all dimensions of the market landscape for you to be able to execute this Best-of-Both Play. Start by looking at the industry. Conditions need to be ripe at the highest level first.

Your industry has to be ripe and ready for change.

Unlike the Stealth Play (where you bet on being able to continue finding small or moderate-sized gaps that you can fill peaceably), the Best-of-Both Play is all about finding and filling the one big gap that will really shake up the industry. But in order for you to be able to pull it off, a lot of things need to have already happened.

This play is all about change—change that may seem revolutionary, combining two ends of a trade-off that previously seemed impossible to combine. But in terms of the industry it affects, this play is actually evolutionary. As you'll see, it has to be. Otherwise, such a combination would be impossible.

In order to combine two ends of an industry, look for situations where both ends have existed long enough for their contrast to be real and noticeable. Both ends of the trade-off have to be established and mature enough to be worth the effort to collapse them.

Take Lexus, for example. If the British and Germans hadn't developed the luxury category first, it would not have held much interest. Meanwhile, by the time that Eiji Toyada and his compatriots started dreaming of entering the luxury market, they had already put in decades of hard work to create and improve their position on the other end—moving the Japanese car beyond being just a cheap little import, to establish it as a reliable, economical, desirable alternative. Without the strong low-cost car on one end of the market, he wouldn't have dared enter the true luxury segment on the other.

Once these extremes and the trade-offs between the far points of the industry have been clarified, you face the job of figuring out how to fill the side of the trade-off that you don't already have a position in. You have to project the market into the future, beyond its current limitations. Companies that run the Best-of-Both Play are inspired by the chance to reinvigorate their market, and to reap the benefits.

Of course, it helps if there is some dynamic in the overall industry that's helping propel change—some fundamental shift that enables new things to happen in already established territory. Find that thread of forward momentum and underlying change. Grab on to it earlier and more firmly than anyone else and use it to pull yourself right up through the middle.

In his launching of the Lexus, Toyada-san followed a pattern in an industry that has seen variations of the Best-of-Both Play over and over again to segment and subsegment its markets, allowing manufacturers the opportunity to sell more and more targeted vehicles both as replacements and as more specialized second or third family cars. The minivan, and then the whole progression of sports utility vehicles, from the originals to all their variants—the luxury SUV (Lexus, Mercedes, even Porsche), the compact SUV (the Toyota RAV4, Honda CR-V, Chevy Tracker), the hybrid wagon-SUV (the Subaru Outback, Volvo XC90, Audi Allroad Crossover)—are all examples of Best-of-Both market segmentation and further subsegmentation.

All are attempts to refine previous categories, increase penetration, and drive up margins by better targeting.

But these innovations didn't happen just because the manufacturers felt like doing some targeting, but because they were able to find the right combination of underlying conditions. Usually, long-term trends had to come together to favor all these variations. Otherwise we would all still be choosing between Model Ts in black or in black. The Best-of-Both Play is all about being the first to recognize and exploit the trend. The whole point of this play is to break the mold. We've seen a few variations, but the vast majority of such change tends to focus on change in process technology, change in regulatory environment, or some radical technology improvement.

Building model variation after model variation would seem to imply the opposite of the economies of scale generally needed to pay off all the long-term investment in R&D and capital equipment for manufacturing. But since the 1970s, manufacturing technology and methodology have gotten a lot more sophisticated. With massively improved supply chains, just-in-time production lines, standardized drive trains, and interchangeable parts, the "economic order quantity"—the minimum required number of a category's units sold to pay back the investment—has gotten smaller and smaller. This in turn has made variations of the same core components more and more feasible and desirable.

In the case of the original SUV, another external dynamic enabled and accelerated the desire to collapse the truck and wagon categories. In 1975, Congress passed the Energy Policy and Conservation Act. A response to the high gasoline prices and fuel shortages of the early 1970s, the act set strict fuel efficiency requirements for automakers. Failure to meet these standards would result in fines based on the total number of vehicles produced by an automaker in a given model year. This was a very big deal and was destined to put a serious damper on the U.S. auto industry compared to its import rivals.

Luckily (or unfortunately, depending on whether you own an SUV or carry an environmentalist badge), this legislation had separate standards for automobiles and light trucks. Since light trucks were at the time used primarily on farms and ranches, they were held to a less stringent standard. The manufacturers saw this and recognized the possibility of a new category. Surprise, surprise, it was a new class of "light truck" that acted a lot like a very big, very powerful station wagon for soccer moms but was subject to these lower fuel-efficiency standards. Thus in the early 1980s, the SUV was born. And now no suburban block is without its fleet of Suburbans, Lexus RXs, Range Rovers, or, God forbid, HumVees. To some, that's progress.

Such technical, economic, and regulatory trends have allowed Best-of-Both categories to emerge in numerous other industries.

Another heartening example came just recently in the unpretentious category of snack food. Since time immemorial, two things that just plain did not go together were sinful, delicious, satisfying, can't-stop-eating-'em junk foods and nutritious, wholesome, good-for-you, healthy diet foods. Nowhere was the insidious power and enticement of this temptation more clear than with the lowly potato chip. *Potato chips* and *fat-free* were clearly contradictions in terms; they could not belong together. God wanted it this way. Then, as he so often does, Man, with his science, entered the picture.

In 1968, Procter & Gamble researchers synthesized a fat substitute called sucrose polyester, originally intended as a substance for increasing the intake of fat by premature babies, a noble goal. But as it turned out, the substance, which was a big molecule of fat, actually made it possible to replace fat in foods with this fat substitute that the body would not digest. So, for about ten years, P&G thought about making the substance, which they later dubbed Olestra, as a cholesterol-removing drug. This was another noble goal, but they still couldn't get it quite right.

Finally, after years of additional work by P&G, the FDA approved Olestra for use in "savory snacks" such as potato chips. Frito Lay began to market its Wow chips and P&G its Fat Free Pringles as one of the most inspiring Best-of-Both stories in history: "*No Fat/Low Fat And Fewer Calories But All The Great Taste Of Original Potato Chips/Tortilla Chips.*" Come on. Who could resist temptation any longer? This seemed like a miracle. Why fight it?

Most Best-of-Both combinations do involve some compromise—you combine a truck and a station wagon and you lose some truckness and some wagonness, but for many consumers what you gain is truly worth it. In this case, you combine tempting and delicious with low-calorie and fat-free and you get . . . well, how to put this delicately . . . you get *leakage . . . from you know where*. The FDA warning label clearly states, "This product contains Olestra. Olestra may cause abdominal cramping and loose stools." Sorry, those fat-free chips just do not seem worth it. For most people, if being able to eat diet/junk food means they might have to wear a diaper, they'd rather go back to being either fat and satisfied, or thin and hungry.

Here's one last example of a key industry trend that enabled a true Best-of-Both Play. One that is a little less odious: the continuous scrunching of the laptop computer.

Back in 1982, Rod Canion, Jim Harris, and Bill Murto invested $1,000 each to found Compaq Computer Corporation (later acquired by Hewlett-Packard—then well known for its calculators). They were inspired by what they saw at two opposite ends of the spectrum—a continued trade-off between size and power. On the one hand, the extremely popular IBM-PC had legitimized a whole new category of computing, one that was much smaller and more personal than a mainframe that had to be guarded by professionals in white coats. But on the other, if you wanted something portable, the only real alternative was a calculator. These guys knew—they were all ex-pats from Texas Instruments (another calculator company).

The outcome of their inspiration was the Compaq Portable, the first 100 percent compatible IBM computer clone. More than that, it was something new, a run-up-the-middle between power and portability. The Compaq Portable, which looked something like a Singer sewing machine with its little screen and attachable keyboard, was actually transportable (though we snidely referred to it as a "luggable"). It was the first computer that you could travel with as carry-on luggage.

Compaq made $111 million in its first year, $329 million in its second, and $503 million in its third, each industry records. Running up the middle between portability and power paid off—so much so that it became a massive industry habit. In 1989, IBM announced the IBM 5155 Portable Personal Computer, a clone of the clone. Then Compaq followed up in 1990 with the first real laptop PC, the SLT/286, which weighed only fourteen pounds and brought the promise that you might actually be able to use it aboard a plane in flight. After that the Best-of-Both combinations kept coming—the notebook PC, the subnotebook, and the mini-PC—all further runs up an ever narrowing but ever more attractive middle.

What made this possible? Of course, the ingenuity and vision of the people who created each new generation of products. The success of each previous generation also played a role in setting a new level of expectations and reestablishing the opportunity for success. But behind it all was one of the most important and robust industry/ technology trends in business history—the unabated doubling of the number of transistors that could be placed on a chip, first pointed out by Intel's Gordon Moore and familiar to us all today as Moore's Law.

The ever-increasing power of microprocessors from generation to generation played a key role in driving the same trend of ever-decreasing economic order quantity (which, again, is the minimum amount you can manufacture and still make economic sense). This allowed PC manufacturers to continue experimenting and to continue releasing more and more targeted subcategories or variations, driving up the same middle between power and portability.

How do you find this middle ground? How do you tell if it's real? One good place to look is at your industry's customers. They are the ones who will tell you, and they are the ones who will pay you if you get it right. So what kind of customer situation is best suited to pulling off this Best-of-Both Play?

Your customers must be willing to come from all sides.

The Best-of-Both Play is not about small gaps. It's all about finding the big gap and finding a way to close it. Unlike previous plays, the Best-of-Both aims at the broadest and yet most reliably profitable customer set possible. It sets its sights on the jackpot—regular, value-conscious customers. Unlike the Stealth Play, it's not at all about targeting a niche, but rather about appealing to the combination of previously separate niches. Unlike the Drag Race, where early adopters are the key target to win over with your extreme power or functionality advantage, the Best-of-Both Play is all about inviting everyone to the party. Such extremes should become less meaningful if this play is executed successfully, making it possible for customers to take the advice of Yogi Berra, quoted at the beginning of this chapter: "When you come to a fork in the road, take it."

People naturally fall into or put themselves into groups. It's human nature. It's also human nature to compare yourself to the group you aren't in. The Best-of-Both Play is egalitarian. It invites everyone from every group, even groups that have thought of themselves as forever distinct. In fact, in collapsing two previous extremes of a category, this play can offer a new way for people—on both sides of a target—to think about themselves. It lets people feel entitled to what was previously denied them. Successful Best-of-Both Plays have faced down undaunted some of the biggest and longest-standing gaps in human history.

Take, for example, the gender gap. The gender gap has historically translated into an extreme marketing gap. Any way to fill this one? Women and men have been working diligently since time immemorial to be as distinct from each other as possible while at the same time finding ways to be more attractive to each other. Tough problem. And in almost no domain more so than in . . . well, odor. Smell, that is. Men and women both want to smell good (however that is defined in their culture). But they generally smell different from one another. There just isn't any middle ground on this one. Or is there?

Of course there is, if you're one of those open-minded, free-thinking, ever-creative packaged-goods companies. Like Irish Spring. At the height of the women's movement, out comes a soap that's "manly," as proven by the hearty Irish fisherman in the TV ad, cutting into a bar with his trusty fisherman's knife, showing that the bar has green cleaning stuff all the way through. And the stuff works—as attested to by the lovely raven-haired lass who's looking forward to his landward homecoming with some olfactory trepidation after his unwashed months at sea. But, she's so happy that he uses the stuff, it's so effective that she exclaims it's "Manly, yes, but I like it too." Finally, there's a soap that you can share with your woman without threatening your manhood or her womanhood.

Lingering on the lovely topic of smells a bit longer, note that another amazing up-the-middle product took the inverse approach with massive success around the same time: the underarm deodorant product marketed as Secret. You really can have it both ways. As the slogan incites, you can be empowered and still retain your femininity because it's "Strong enough for a man. But made for a woman."

The Best-of-Both Play tackles the generation gap, too. It's been a fact of life that when you're young, you wish you seemed older and then when you're old, you really wish you were younger. And it's also been a fact of life that you can't do anything about it.

Nonetheless several companies and products have been incredibly effective in driving demand by appealing to the desire to collapse this gap. We can attest to this phenomenon from deeply personal experience. Look at cars (sorry to go there again but we're guys and we like cars, so bear with us).

When you're really young, all you care about is getting your hands on the keys. Then you're psyched just to have a reliable car to get you to college or to your part-time job. But pretty soon, if you're ambitious and lucky enough, you feel you deserve a better choice. When your co-authors were in that early-twenties age bracket, we both looked at the choices and saw an extreme trade-off between a Honda Civic as the terrific fresh-out-of-college car on the one hand, and the big Mercedes Sedan as the impressive, substantial, "I've arrived and I want you to know it" established professional's car. Then along came the BMW 320i, first launched in 1975 right after a major oil embargo, and just as people were first beginning to figure out that the brand-new word *yuppie* meant Young Urban Professional. This classy BMW, with the size and pep of a small Japanese car and the sleek finish and cachet of a German automobile (a German compact car—sort of the inverse of the Lexus), appealed to that newly formed and massively growing middle—so much so that it became an icon of the group.

But the world keeps turning, doesn't it? Turn around twice and you're older, you have a bunch of kids whom you have to take to soccer practice, ballet lessons, and the dentist, and you don't like the next set of trade-offs you see. Recently entering that age and finding ourselves in that situation, we were not very heartened to consider the prospects of being trapped in a minivan on the one hand or looking obvious and ridiculous in a red convertible sports car on the other (no insult intended to the illustrious and clearly more courageous owners of either vehicle type). What to do?

Here comes another Best-of-Both Play to the rescue—the Volvo 850 series. Consider the 850 T5-R. Yes, dear, it's a station wagon. Yes, dear, it's incredibly safe—it's a Volvo, isn't it? The first car to have side impact airbags, it's built like a tank to protect the kids. And it has a 250-horsepower turbocharged engine that catapults you from zero to sixty in something like one nanosecond. This was a cake-and-eat-it-too offer if there ever was one. It was the midlife crisis car that your spouse actually let you get away with.

Each of these Best-of-Both alternatives is more exciting and interesting because it's a contrast—a contrast to the existing choices. But just as it's human nature to want some of what the other group has, to want the best of the alternatives, it's also human nature to shun complexity.

So if you're thinking of choosing the Best-of-Both Play, you had better make sure that the alternatives or trade-offs you're combining are not numerous. In fact, there should only be two—otherwise how are you going to be the third?

Competition: For this play, you need it

The Best-of-Both Play is defined by its competition. This play is your answer to another competitor or really to competitors, plural. It's the breath of fresh air you will bring to an otherwise stale space. But unlike the Drag Race, where you pick one segment of the market and overrun it, in Best-of-Both you seek out a competitive space with two competitive alternatives, and devise a solution that combines the best of those alternatives.

Jonathan Roberts, who helped pioneer several play strategies while at Microsoft, was a master at using the Best-of-Both Play to shake up a category. One example: In the mid-1990s, Jonathan was head of marketing for Windows NT and the company's server offerings, marketed under the product name BackOffice. By that point Microsoft had built its reputation as the pretty nearly undisputed leader in desktop software. Yet that was not just a blessing but also a curse. The reputation for excellence on the desktop did not translate everywhere, especially when it came to the enterprise customer and the more mission-critical back-office functions.

A straight Drag Race for the server didn't make sense. If a server fails, people get fired. No one would easily believe that the same people who made the PC game Flight Simulator could also build a true enterprise product.

The gulf was too vast between productivity functions handled by desktop computing and the functions such as accounting and payroll handled by mainframes or minicomputers. Jonathan and his team turned this gulf to their advantage. Laying the ground-

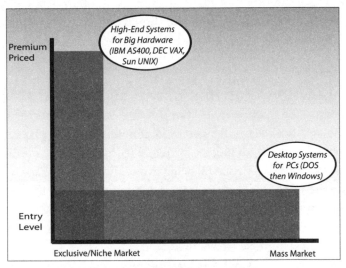

Fig. 5–2. A bifurcated systems software market

work for a Best-of-Both Play, they looked at the market and saw it as divided into two limited parts (Fig. 5–2).

On the one hand were the high-end software solutions that ran on big hardware systems such as IBM AS400s, DEC VAXs, or even heavy-duty Sun Microsystems UNIX-based server boxes. For a long time this was really the only way to do the large, transaction-oriented functions that were everyday work at every large enterprise. No one thought about the problem any other way. But these solutions were incredibly expensive, hard to upgrade, and very costly to expand, forcing you to spend way ahead of needed capacity with each new addition—like buying an entire additional house each time you have another child.

On the other hand were PC-based desktop systems. These had changed the rules of the game. The cost of adding each new PC including the software was actually pretty minimal. This made the economics of adding capacity much more attractive. The problem was that back then the only kinds of things you could really do with a PC were spreadsheets, word processing, and maybe a little simple bill paying. The possibility of connecting and adding up the power of many PCs over time was intriguing but still relegated to things such as file sharing and printing. If you were a big enterprise, these economics were clearly attractive, but they remained tantalizingly out of reach given your requirements for stability, security, and other essentials.

Then Microsoft Windows NT arrived on the scene. This more powerful, reliable, and scalable operating system for servers made it possible to begin bridging the gap. Jonathan and his team saw that they could position NT as a solution for using little desktop computers to perform big tasks, driving up the middle of what had been two distinctive, separate markets (Fig. 5–3).

Deploying a Best-of-Both strategy, the team milked this development for everything it was worth. They proclaimed that you could now have it both ways—this time going from the bottom up. Now you could capture the benefits of PC economics without giving up on security, stability, reliability, and the rest. You could grow your computing infrastructure one low-cost machine at a time instead of spending a huge amount for extra capacity you wouldn't need for months or maybe even years. Now there was a middle path.

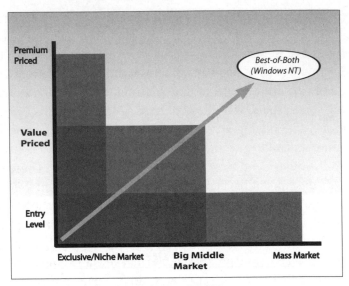

Fig. 5–3. Driving up the middle with NT

And many people took it. Playing this card allowed Microsoft to establish a foothold in the category. From there, each core technology advance brought more and more areas of applications and functionality into the sights as Best-of-Both targets. And the story continues today.

Best-of-Both allows you to play your competitors off against one another; when you drive up the middle, their markets begin to collapse.

Driving Your Capabilities Toward the Upper Right-Hand Corner

Jonathan Roberts referred to this play as the "Two-by-Two Matrix," based on a layout that was his choice for mapping it (Fig. 5–4). Each of the cases we examined above can easily be placed in such a ma-

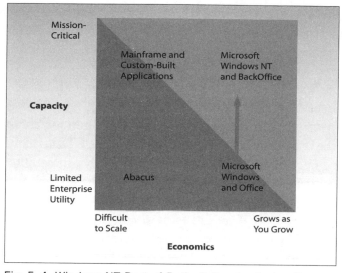

Fig. 5–4. Windows NT Best-of-Both: Collapsing trade-offs between cost and capacity

trix, with one market segment on the left and the trade-off market segment on the right.

And the so-called "magic quadrant" (as the Gartner Group termed it)—the one on the upper right—was at first vacant (see Fig. 5–4): an impossible solution waiting for some eagle-eyed innovator to fill with a Best-of-Both amalgam, like BackOffice and NT in this case.

In your own industry, that entrepreneur had better be you. To run this play, you will have to have some new but lasting product, technology, or other advantage that allows you to collapse both ends and run up the middle.

You can get there in two basic ways. The first is as a new version or upgrade of your own previous offerings. In this case you move beyond whatever play first established you and use it as a launch pad to capture a much bigger territory. You highlight your own product for the trade-offs it represents in one dimension (what easier product to criticize and to know you have beaten than your own?). You then demonstrate how you have transcended those limitations in your new product and capture the most important elements of the opposing dimension.

This was the case with the Microsoft NT and BackOffice play where the trade-offs were between capacity and cost. The Best-of-Both Play here first collapsed these trade-offs from the bottom up with the version improvement over Windows itself. Then it collapsed them from the top down in contrast to the big mainframe and minicomputer systems (and blew right past the limited-purpose, low-cost systems like Abacus).

This same kind of version-to-version Best-of-Both Play is also represented by Volvo, which was really competing with themselves when they picked on their previous image of their vehicles as slow and stodgy cars, retained the best elements of those products, and then grabbed the pizzazz and punch from hot sports cars (Fig. 5–5).

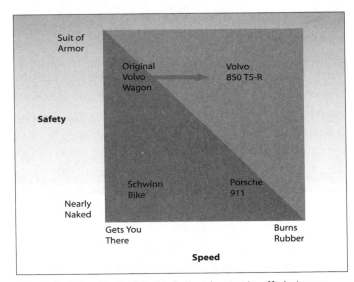

Fig. 5–5. Volvo Best-of-Both: Collapsing trade-offs between safety and speed

The other way to get to the top right corner—that is, the other approach to running this play—is the approach for a company that is a new entrant.

Here, too, you had better be sure you have some real advantage that keeps you up there.

That was the tactic of online jeweler Blue Nile. Men of every age face a challenge when the time comes to pick out an engagement ring. You don't want to screw it up either by turning your intended off with a subpar rock or by spending so much that you forfeit your future children's college education. And given the complexity and stress, few men recognize when they're making one of these missteps until too late. Blue Nile founder and CEO Mark Vadon recognized this dilemma from his friends' experiences and from his own. He decided that there had to be a better way, and in 1999 he found it. The Internet was the impetus and a key tool for collapsing two opposing alternatives. With it he launched Blue Nile and blew up the economics of the category (Fig. 5–6).

Targeting men who are on the hunt for an engagement ring but intimidated by the process, Blue Nile brought together several innovations to break new ground in how people buy diamonds.

The company sells their products from a central distribution center and so avoids the expense of stocking and protecting multiple retail outlets with expensive jewels; with this arrangement, Blue Nile can often sell for less than the local jewelry store. At the same time, because of their national direct-customer reach, they've been able to sign up scores of distributors around the country to offer jewels that wouldn't otherwise be available online without a huge investment in inventory. Since diamonds have long-established standardized ratings of color, cut, clarity, and carat weight, engagement rings can be an ideal e-commerce purchase despite the high average dollar value of the orders. Thanks to those standardized ratings, the buyer knows what he's getting before he makes his purchase.

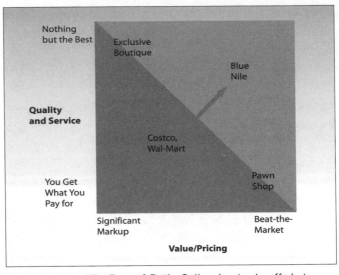

Fig. 5–6. Blue Nile Best-of-Both: Collapsing trade-offs between quality and pricing

Finally, beyond this integration of quality and value, Blue Nile is relentless in their pursuit of functionality and service to enhance and simplify the decision and purchase process. With such features as a very robust but easy-to-use diamond search engine, in-depth diamond and jewelry education, and even on-the-phone hand holding, Blue Nile has been able to offer a true Best-of-Both alternative, successfully using the Internet and savvy buying to shake up a very stodgy category. And they have been taking this practice right to the bank, becoming one of the few Internet-only companies not just to survive but to achieve profitability at significant scale.

Things such as this can be truly historic opportunities—but only if you're ready for them. You really do need to have something special in your product/offering to pull off this play.

The Rewards and Risks of Trying to Drive Up the Middle

Best-of-Both will never be an easy play to manage successfully. It makes sense to look at the odds before laying down your cards.

Rewards

As all of these cases have shown, the ultimate rewards of this play are huge. You're going for the whole enchilada. If you can make it happen, the Best-of-Both Play provides you defensible category leadership in one fell swoop, and leadership of an even bigger, more inclusive market than you started out with.

And while this is a tall order to carry out, there are some advantages to this play in terms of execution. By its very nature, Best-of-Both implies a competitive response that is more fragmented into at least two "worse thans." Often you discover two opposing market segments so dedicated to fighting each other that they've become confused and unable to focus on the long-term threat to both their positions. For you, that spells opportunity.

Another opportunity is the message. This play offers a naturally appealing marketing message. Tough decisions and hard trade-offs give people headache and heartburn. The Best-of-Both Play is the Alka Seltzer® for such confusion. If you really do have a Best-of-Both offering, every wide-awake buyer will want your combined best-of-both-worlds solution.

But that's a big IF. Without truly powerful, truly integrated, truly differentiated Best-of-Both advantage . . . well, that's where the risks come in.

Risks

When you're playing for these kinds of stakes, you had better make sure that you feel very, very good about the cards in your hand.

The first and foremost risk is being too cocky. A Best-of-Both Play doesn't work unless you truly can offer the best of both. Make sure, very sure, you have something powerful, something different, and something that actually brings both extremes together before you try this play. And that has no fatal flaws—remember Olestra. Don't go there.

As in a Drag Race, you have to have the patience and resources to drive that point home to the market. But unlike the Drag Race, this play requires differentiation—differentiation not just against one competitor but against two. Shaking people out of their old assumptions takes time and persistence.

Many companies that have a Best-of-Both offering recognize the need to be patient, biding their time until they're sure that they have the resources to successfully trumpet their advantages to a very broad universe of people. Until then, they're smart to keep a Stealth profile.

Beware of drawing profits out of the market. When you attack the high end for its exclusivity and its elevated prices, you had better have a way to still make good money at prices that are significantly lower. And your margin for error is less because you're also promising a big improvement over other rock-bottom–priced alternatives. Threading this needle can be really tricky.

Success at this play, like success in many other things, can attract copycats who like what you have achieved and think they can outdo you in "Best-of-Bothness." Also beware the new fast-follower Drag Race challengers.

I'm Up for It–How Do I Run a Best-of-Both Play?

This is a great play. You should try to execute this one whenever you can. Making it happen means that you will have to look ahead, keep your eyes on both sides of the road, and drive like blazes. It's a play you can even execute against yourself to stay fresh and keep your position moving forward in the category.

The Best-of-Both Play can pay long-term dividends, but it requires combining some pretty volatile elements. Fig. 5–7 represents the play in action—bringing together the extreme low end and the extreme high end, and fusing them as if in a forge. In the process, you'll take the best qualities from both extremes, while at the same time getting rid of all the worst qualities. Whatever the catalyst—new technology, economics, or other trends—if Best-of-Both players are successful in pulling off this new combination, they're on the

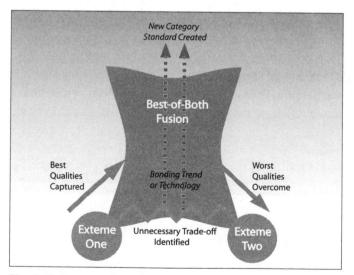

Fig. 5–7. Cross section of the Best-of-Both Play

way to producing a whole new frame of reference and standard for the category, even to the extent of creating a new, merged category. To run a Best-of-Both Play, you'll follow these steps:

> Identify a key trend that promises to shake up your category.
> Target the current most annoying trade-offs and drive them to extremes.
> Capture the best of each end while discarding the worst.
> Once you have a real Best-of-Both offering, trumpet it to high heaven.
> Target one end first and then drive right up the middle.

Identify a key trend that promises to shake up your category.

Find one key trend that's very hard to deny—whether based on Moore's Law, ongoing economies of scale, declining economic order quantity, or some other business or technological phenomenon. This has to be a trend that helps you see into the future. And it needs to be something strong enough that you'll be able to convince first yourself and then others that a Best-of-Both synthesis is actually possible. Once you latch on to this trend, keep a firm hold.

Target the current most annoying trade-offs and drive them to extremes.

Do your situation analysis to highlight the key gaps that you will fill, remembering that you want to focus on two opposite poles or alternative courses currently available in the marketplace. Based on this, you'll lay plans to play directly off the customer dissatisfaction caused by being forced to choose between these poles.

Capture the best of each end while discarding the worst.

Having identified a trend or technology that you can leverage and/ or augment to overcome the current gaps in the market, do what it takes to use it correctly. You need to deliver a true product advantage. Don't try to get started until you have it.

Once you have a real Best-of-Both offering, trumpet it to high heaven.

You're aiming to hit the customer jackpot. If you really do have a synthesized offering that makes possible what people normally thought of as an impossible combination, don't be shy. Tell everyone. The big middle is your target. If you've created a party for everyone, you had better make sure they know they're invited. Be sure to educate people on your two-by-two matrix, either directly or thematically in your communications, to underscore how you compare to both previous alternatives.

Target one end first and then drive right up the middle.

Usually it's easiest to convince one target segment at a time. Depending on how you look at it, you may want to start by targeting the folks who are willing to pay for the high end. Once you convince them that they aren't going to lose anything important, you'll usually find it a lot easier to convince everyone else.

Another choice: start by targeting the folks who find themselves forced to buy at the low end. To them, you're simply lowering the price or removing some of the other barriers to moving up. But whatever you do, don't wait too long to appeal as broadly as possible: a key risk here is not being ambitious enough about establishing your position. Once you've shown the third way, competitors may want to jump in—so you had better stake your claim and be ready to defend it powerfully.

Doing such targeting and making it stick will depend a lot on how well you establish your new position with effective marketing.

Marketing Implications

Positioning

The beauty of this play is in the way you position your offering: you claim the high ground right off the bat. In some ways this isn't quite as simple as a Drag Race, where you pick a fight with one other player, beat them on every dimension, and keep adding other dimensions you can beat them on. But in other ways you'll find Best-of-Both even simpler. Yes, you do pick on two alternatives rather than just one. But these alternatives represent the only criteria upon which your customers should base their judgments. Instead of a long list of features with lots more checks on your column (Fig. 5–8), you have only two items. And, of course, you're the only one who can check them both.

You're positioned as the savior, the harbinger of the future. You offer something better than what has been out there and you appeal

Drag Race Play

	Competitor	You
Criterion 1	√	√
Criterion 2	√	√
Criterion 3	√	√
Criterion 4	x	√
Criterion 5	x	√
Criterion n	x	√

Best-of-Both Play

	Option One	Opposing Option	You
Criterion 1	√	x	√
Criterion 2	x	√	√

Fig. 5–8. Winning by comparisons: Drag Race vs. Best-of-Both

to the human sense of justice. "Why be forced to choose—the trade-offs shortchange you. We're offering you another way. Your way."

Packaging

Much as with the fighter product of the Drag Race, you cannot complicate your offering with all kinds of variations and versions; you have to keep this really simple. Best-of-Both also means less than both, in the sense that you're providing a single offering instead of separate high-end and low-end alternatives—so you should put all your weight behind one winner SKU or one line. Make this single offering the tool that drives you up the middle.

Pricing

Price is a key weapon. If you aren't priced competitively with the high-end offering, you may well be presenting a false solution. You don't have to take the combination of both extremes all the way. This play is the "best" of both, not absolutely everything of both. Your offer needs to represent very good value for the money, so pricing should naturally be value based, not deep discount. As mentioned, beware of the slippery slope of price erosion, but at the same time don't let price be a barrier to moving up to your middle path. Don't lose deals because of it.

Promotion

Finally, this is a play that really can benefit from broad appeals. You're going after the big middle ground of customers; you have to make sure to reach them. Targeting the early adopters in tradeshows does not really buy you much. They don't want to be in the middle anyway. Word of mouth, share of mind—those are your approaches. PR as well as Web, in-store, and even print and broadcast advertising can be strong weapons. Depending on your market, getting analyst support can be a key promotional asset as well. If industry analysts endorse the trend you're riding as inevitable, that will speed the move of customers to your corner.

Finally, Keep On Doing It

Once you've launched your Best-of-Both Play and you're running it successfully, don't forget that you can't sit back and relax. You have to keep on working it. In fact, whether you've just come off being totally successful in executing a Best-of-Both Play or you're coming off another of the plays, you always need to be on the lookout for other opportunities. That's a terrific way to reinvent yourself and to keep yourself on top of your game.

Some of the best companies in the world run plays against themselves over and over again, never allowing themselves to rest on their laurels.

It gets better: the Best-of-Both Play can truly project you to the next stage of your development. Coming off one play (even a play against yourself), you can use the position you've gained in your category to build a new platform and offer some halo of your synthesizing power to a broader and broader array of partners.

This whole play is about thinking ahead and seeing into the future. But at the same time you're planning for your next harvest, recall the point we've made before: you also need to anticipate others' response to your success.

One obvious next move is for the competitors you ran past on each extreme to attempt a Drag Race against you. This can be dangerous if they've learned enough from you—but if you play your cards right, and keep on innovating, they could easily end up in a double Drag Race and cancel each other out.

Take-Aways for the Best-of-Both Play

1. The Best-of-Both Play is one of the most ambitious strategies, aiming to capture the heart of a category in one fell swoop. In a Best-of-Both, rather than picking on one player, you borrow from two, blowing right past them both. It's all about seeing future trends and using them to play two competitors at different ends of the market against each other by offering a new synthesis and driving up the middle of a market. It can be one of the most rewarding plays.

2. Best-of-Both Plays come in two basic forms. You can use it as a new entrant to the market by finding a fresh path that allows you to run directly past previous alternatives. You can also use it as an established player on one dimension of the category; by creating a true upgrade of your offering, you become able to transcend both your own past offerings and the current offerings of others.

3. The Best-of-Both Play has nothing stealthy about it. Competition is what defines your play. This is not about niche targeting, it's about the whole market. But it's not for the faint of heart. It requires a big bet so it should only be played by those with a true advantage. It should only be played by those with the right trends on their side.

4. Best-of-Both Players are loud. You need to have a simple message with a compelling offer. You need to shout it from the rooftops. And because everyone won't be convinced overnight, you have to keep on shouting and keep proving that you're right—that your way, the middle way, is both possible and preferable.

5. Finally, consider this play as a fact of life, a force of nature. Collapsing previous categories together as a way of synthesizing new value has been a source of innovation and change for a long time. Embrace change in yourself to bring change to the category. If you don't, others will.

Coming Up

The Best-of-Both Play asks customers the question, "Why choose?" by offering a solution that gives the best of both the worlds offered by your competition. The final play, a counter to Best-of-Both, asks the question, "Why compromise?" By holding onto both the high and the low ends, you can offer each side an alternative to the beige middle ground.

That's coming up next.

Don't compromise yourself. You're all you've got.

—JANIS JOPLIN

6. The High-Low Play

All things to all people often means nothing to no one. Why not try giving different things to different people instead?

> *"It slices, it dices, it grills steaks, it fries shrimp, and it's only $9.99!!!"*
> *"It's totally modern and totally classic!!!"*
> *"It's the highest quality and the lowest price!!!"*
> *"It's the most elite, and anyone can get in!!!"*

Do promises such as these sound familiar? Do they sound good enough to make you think about buying? On occasion, maybe pitches like these really do make you pause for a moment and consider. But the more important question is, Do you really believe them? Probably you find yourself feeling a wee bit skeptical the moment you hear them. And then you recall the old saying about things that seem too good to be true.

Sometimes the promise of the best of both worlds can end up meaning just a mediocre muddle. Sometimes both worlds were better off all by themselves.

The High–Low Play is the play for just such situations.

The Nature of the High-Low Play

As you saw in the Best-of-Both Play, driving through to capture the middle can be very tempting. It's bold. It's big. The High–Low Play is the inverse of Best-of-Both. Instead of collapsing a category, this play splits it or keeps it divided, working both ends to oppose the middle. Rather than combining elements of both the high and the low end of a market into a new, all-inclusive middle ground offering, this play aims to deny that such a middle ground exists or that it's actually worthwhile or even legitimate.

By attacking a large middle-ground offering from both the high and the low ends of the market simultaneously (Fig. 6–1), this play places its bets on the enduring, deep-seated value of choice and raises a battle cry against compromise. The goal is to attack at the top with the most premium, expensive offering and attack on the bottom with the lowest-price, entry-level offering.

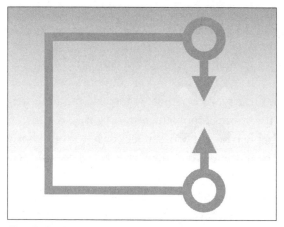

Fig. 6–1. The High–Low Play: Attacking the market from the top and bottom simultaneously

The High–Low Play is number five on our list for a reason: we saved the toughest for last. Squeezing your competitor between two offerings—putting them in a "pincer"—sounds cool, but executing it is anything but easy. Rarely run, High–Low is the specialty play of this book.

In general, simpler plans are better, but this one is not simple. Instead of just putting all your weight and messaging behind one offering, this play calls on you to split your forces and put your weight behind two very different offerings. It's challenging and tricky, which is why you could call this the extra-credit or the "consult your physician before engaging in strenuous exercise" approach.

Nonetheless, the High–Low Play is an important strategy to have in your repertoire. However difficult it may be, there are two special circumstances when it can come in terrifically handy. This play pulls your fat from the fire, and it can help you keep what you have while grabbing a bit more of the other end of your market. If the promises of a Best-of-Both offering are too weak to really stick in the current state of your market, this split play offers a unique opportunity to profit from both ends.

When the other guy has a viable Best-of-Both offering and you don't yet, then this play can help you stave off defeat until you're ready to compete. It can buy you time—time to hold off the collapse of your category. Time to solidify your own future offering. And time to let marketing and branding work their magic while the product side of the house catches up.

Here's an example of just such a situation. Microsoft and IBM had been partners through the 1980s, with IBM building the lion's share of PCs and Microsoft building their operating system software—first DOS and later Windows. Then, in 1992, this partnership ended when IBM and Microsoft each began to offer competing operating systems.

With a new version of its operating system, designated OS/2 3.0, IBM hoped to drive right up the middle of the market. This version promised the Best-of-Both: it had Windows-like ease of use, compatibility with Windows and DOS applications on most current PCs, *and* the stability, reliability, and speed of a higher-end operating system (which, with IBM's history in mainframes and minicomputers, the company was well positioned to market). This was the holy grail for IBM and they were betting huge resources on this play, not just for existing markets but also to help them lock up the coming new generation of PC hardware models.

This presented Microsoft with a problem. The then-current version of Windows ran both Windows and DOS applications and was floating on a wave of popularity. On the other hand, it crashed and didn't run well on newer, faster, more powerful machines.

The company had reason for hope, but it lay in the future with a new-generation operating system code-named NT (for New Technology). This future product promised to be a true quantum leap that would fully outrun OS/2. It was blazingly fast and crash-proof and yet it was totally Windows with all the familiar look and feel and ease of use.

The problem: NT would require users to buy new, more powerful, faster hardware—hardware that had only begun appearing in the market. NT, though powerful and way cool, was compatible with less than 1 percent of all of PC-based computers at the time OS/2 3.0 showed up.

Under other circumstances, Microsoft could easily have waited for the market to catch up with the great new operating system, NT. But suddenly there was no time to wait. OS/2 would eat Microsoft's lunch if the company didn't find some more immediate alternative. What to do? Well, first things first. The coach needed a new game plan for his team. Dave Cutler, head of development for Project NT, thought about it, poked around in the software code, and saw a way to drop some items scheduled for the full version of NT that would allow fielding an interim version, a version that would be compatible with some less powerful machines.

This new project, subsequently launched as Windows NT 3.51, took a little more than twelve months to finish and ship—an incredible achievement for such a complex piece of software. And in the interim, another part of Dave's team was able to create software that ran very well with the majority of fast PCs then on the market.

That landed an opportunity in the laps of the marketing folks, a perfect setup to run a High–Low Play. Now they had enough to pull it off. They had the current Windows version for the low-power majority of the market, and they had the bigger, more powerful NT product for the elite users—and for the future. Each product alone competing with OS/2 would lose—Windows because of stability, NT because of compatibility and speed. But together, with the right marketing, the NT product team was able to pull the rug out from under OS/2.

With a clear call for no compromises, Microsoft designed a double–shoot-out with OS/2. This typically began with a simultaneous demonstration of Windows and OS/2, running side by side on a common, low-power machine. In thirty seconds, Windows was up and running and waiting for instructions; after five minutes, OS/2 had a user still twiddling his thumbs with impatience. Who would want such a slow machine?

Next came a demonstration of Windows NT on a four-way multiprocessor box that had more computing power than a medium-sized country. And NT was put through its paces running all kinds of cutting-edge applications no one had seen before on a PC—applications that OS/2 couldn't even get to. Wow—match *that*, OS/2. The close: Why settle? Your needs are specific. Get the right tool for the right task.

The upshot: game, set, match, Microsoft. It was tough going, but with such a well-executed pincer, OS/2 fizzled and Microsoft maintained its lead in both ends of the PC operating system market—meanwhile buying itself enough time to complete the full version of NT.

Ideally, Microsoft would not have chosen this High–Low Play. As a play for special circumstances, it demands a powerful combination of resources and talent to pull off. What are those circumstances exactly? Under what conditions will someone want or need to resort to this complex play?

When Should You Go to the Trouble of Splitting Yourself in Two?

Normally, the shortest distance between two points is a straight line. So naturally if you want to win, you run straight up the middle, right?

Not if there's a giant hole in the middle of the field, or a thirty-foot–tall barbed wire electric fence blocking your way. Then the only thing to do is to run along the edges, stay sharp, and hope you don't fall in or touch the wire. Oh, great—sounds like a barrel of laughs.

So how do you know when this is the right thing to do? How do you see the obstacles before you run right into them? And how do you determine that splitting yourself in half and running on both sides makes more sense than building a bridge or just plain turning around?

The conditions for this final play are special. You're not going to look solely for one element or feature within your playing field terrain. *All* the dimensions have to come together to indicate whether conditions are right for attempting a High–Low effort.

Given the often reactive or defensive nature of this play, it makes sense to start by looking at the competition.

The Competition—Deny them their middle ground.

Rather than finding an untapped middle market that you can capture with a Best-of-Both offering, this play is about doing just the opposite. When you run a High–Low, you're operating in direct contrast to a Best-of-Both. Instead of being the play of the future, it's the play of denial. Success hinges on successfully denying the legitimacy of a competitor's claim that he has combined or collapsed the category—and on denying the middle ground to someone else.

As we saw with Windows and OS/2, the High–Low Play is often called for when someone else is trying to occupy that middle ground and take away your hold on the top or the bottom of the market. Sometimes you just can't afford to let that happen. You can't let them get that foothold.

So you squeeze them from both ends. You make the ground they're trying to stand on smaller and smaller, and less and less stable. That's pretty easy to visualize. In the OS/2 story, IBM entered the market with its own Best-of-Both Play, trying to beat Windows at its very own best-of-both-worlds game on the combination of power and ease of use (Fig. 6–2).

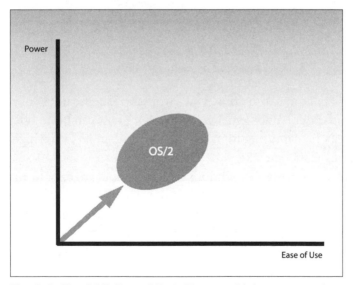

Fig. 6–2. The OS/2 Best-of-Both Play, combining power and ease of use

But, undaunted, Microsoft said, "No way!" and proceeded to squeeze OS/2 from both ends of the market (Fig. 6–3). By attacking the legitimacy of IBM's offering on both the high and low ends, Microsoft was able to make it harder for IBM to gain a foothold.

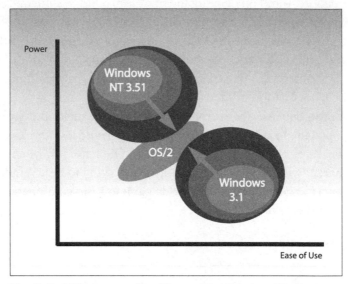

Fig. 6–3. OS/2 squeezed by Microsoft's High–Low Play

In addition to providing you a workable defense until your own Best-of-Both reinforcements arrive, High–Low can be an offensive strategy for capturing more of the market than just your high-end offering alone can take.

The competitive conditions for High–Low are easy to map to the Ps and Qs. Take a look at Sheraton. Their brand has long stood for consistently high-quality, high-service, large luxury resorts and hotels around the world. That gives them a strong position in the market, a great place to be, appealing to affluent, frequent travelers, and commanding premium rates and higher margins.

At the same time, here comes Marriott, moving smack dab in the middle of the market—also with big, clean, reliable hotels and resorts all around the world. Not as luxurious or as full-service as most Sheratons, but offering lower rates and more discounts that were good enough to attract more and more travelers.

Marriott, with its more middle-of-the-road brand and its middle-of-the-road pricing (Fig. 6–4) came to occupy a great position in the market, above discount motel chains yet below the more exclusive names. This put a greater squeeze on the market for high-end travelers who might be looking for a deal than on the low-end market (people who would have to save up for a splurge at such a classy joint). In other words, Marriott had landed right where Sheraton had its key advantage.

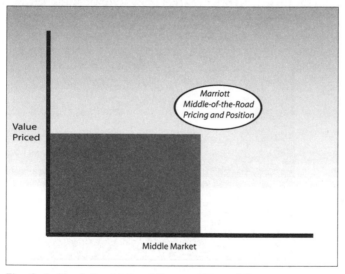

Fig. 6–4. Marriott middle-of-the-road Ps and Qs

What to do? Not pack up and go home. But also not compete directly with Marriott by trying to compare the premium Sheraton brand with the Marriott midmarket position. What's left?

Rather than offer one thing that you claim combines the Best-of-Both, offer both—one of each. That's what Sheraton did with their

Four Points® offering: "All you need in a full service hotel, for a sensible price." They focused on promoting strong price performance with highly competitive deals, such as "Weekend packages from $89 including in-room movie, breakfast in bed for two, late 4 P.M. checkout." What a contrast from the top-of-the-line resorts that cost hundreds a night.

This High–Low combination allowed the Sheraton brand to straddle the market and win on both ends. By having an entry-level offering for cost-conscious travelers who are still attracted to the Sheraton brand, while maintaining their high-end, luxury business, Sheraton is able to keep its brand cachet and high-margin flagships, while cashing in on the bigger, broader market of everyday travelers (Fig. 6–5).

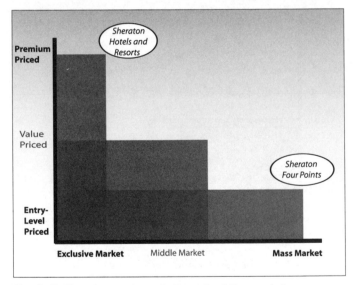

Fig. 6–5. Sheraton captures both ends of the market.

An example of a High–Low Play with competitive dynamics is the SUV market. As we saw in the previous chapter, the SUV category itself is a Best-of-Both Play combining cars and pickup trucks. As the category grew, a whole additional Best-of-Both Play emerged to combine luxury cars and SUVs, with Best-of-Both Play veteran Lexus once again in the vanguard.

These plays where categories are merging can be hugely beneficial, but not to everyone—especially if you don't have a strong Best-of-Both offering yet. For example, what if you're DaimlerChrysler facing the new Lexus luxury SUV? What's your answer? Sure, you're hard at work on improving your own offering in the middle, but in the meantime you need to deny the validity of this new category. As for your true luxury line, you push the high-end Mercedes SLR "supercar." And you start running ads pushing Jeep as the *real thing*—pointing out all the tough, rugged things a real SUV should be able to do.

Real is a word that typifies a High–Low push. Deny the merging of the category. Highlight the sacrifices and compromises inherent in a Best-of-Both offering. Rather than Best-of-Both, insist that it's the least of both. This competitive push says, "Make no compromises," or "Accept no substitutes."

Now, this may be the best thing you can do under the circumstances, as an interim strategy, but you can't pull it off by sheer will alone. You can't keep people out of the middle if they really, really want to go there. You need customers to support you on both ends.

Customers—This play works if they like it right where they are.

From the customer perspective, too, the conditions are the inverse of the Best-of-Both Play. Rather than an underserved gap between high-end enthusiasts and low-end price shoppers, the gap is the opposite. Either customers at the high end of the market are dissatisfied with the low quality of existing offerings and willing to pay more, or customers at the low end feel that they are forced to pay too much for extras that don't matter enough to them. Or both.

The High–Low Play offers you an opportunity to profit from sources of both frustration and desire at once. But there have to be enough customers at both ends.

Most often this bipolar line extension works best starting with strength on the high end and moving downward. That's what winemaker Robert Mondavi did. They started making superior California wine in 1966 as a premium alternative to French imports. They worked diligently for decades helping to establish the legitimacy of California as a source for truly world-class wines that even the snobbiest oenophile (a wine connoisseur's word for wine connoisseur) would prize.

But over this period, more and more domestic wineries cropped up, expanding the market and the supply for very high-quality wines from California, Oregon, and Washington. In all of this Mondavi maintained its high standards and its premium brand. But as awareness of the wine culture grew, they also took note of the rapidly increasing, everyday consumption of wine by average Americans as an alternative to beer at meals. How could they get a piece of this?

By introducing Woodbridge Wines. This winery, owned by Mondavi (and promoted on their Web site), filled this need on the lower end with "quality wine for people to enjoy with every meal." Now, with both of these efforts, Mondavi could straddle the market for California wines—and take it to the bank on both ends, whether you only want a 2001 Woodbridge Cabernet Sauvignon for just eight bucks or you're willing to spring for a very special $150 Robert Mondavi "To-Kalon Vineyard" 1999 Cabernet Sauvignon.

The market was one where the buying criteria were very well set and where moving customers to some compromise between price performance and quality would just be hard to imagine—except the market had moved and evolved to the point where there were now enough customers on opposite ends of the buying spectrum to make it worth addressing them both.

Robert Mondavi could pull this off, extending the quality of their brand and the value it represents, down to the broader market. (But it would be pretty hard to go in the opposite direction. Could you imagine a $150 Premium Boone's Farm Strawberry Wine? Who would buy it? Or a luxury offering from Motel 6? Who would stay there?)

For Robert Mondavi, this was a sound play in part because of who they were. It is therefore of critical importance to do an assessment of your own assets and capabilities before determining whether or not you should run this play.

Your Capabilities—What you can't do is as important as what you can.

In doing an assessment of your capabilities for this play, first start with what you don't have.

A key consideration: you don't have a compelling Best-of-Both offering. If you did, you'd use that position either to enter the new market or to Drag Race the competitor currently claiming Best-of-Both. Remember the stories of Microsoft and DaimlerChrysler: the High–Low Play functioned as a holding action until the product guys could hurry up and provide the needed offering.

The other thing you don't have is a Platform—at least not one that works well enough for this market. If you did, your allies would never let some upstart come in and challenge your space.

That said, you have enough strength—and enough at stake—not to give up your territory without a fight. If you were too weak in product, brand, or customer relationship, you would just exit the field and go hide in some niche with a Stealth Play. The High–Low Play is usually not one for start-ups, either. If you're a start-up, you don't likely have enough resources to win two different and contrasting market positions at once and then defend them both.

No. If you're running this play, you have to have something good enough and powerful enough to fight for and fight with. If you're going to straddle the market, you have to have a position of strength to start with—some real assets that you can parlay into advantage at the other end.

One of those assets is your brand. Sheraton did it with their brand—extending its value to a more market-entry offering but protecting it with a clear variation and contrast. The brand has to be elastic enough to allow pulling this off. As mentioned earlier, it's usually easier to do this from top down rather than the other way around.

The brand can take different forms. It doesn't have to be a logo backed by tons of advertising. It can simply be your reputation, backed by your track record and accomplishments. The famous designer and architect Michael Graves has built an amazing name for himself among the design cognoscenti, creating stunning and unique household objects since 1960. In particular he established a lasting impression (and a tidy, ongoing business) with his fashionably whimsical housewares for Alessi, the high-end Italian line.

So, of course, he had the high end of the market pretty well covered. But what about the rest of the market? What about regular folks who want nicely designed stuff, too? Well, a few years ago Michael Graves added the lower end, creating a High–Low Play. He signed a deal with Target Stores to create accessible but fun designs for their housewares lines. So now people at one end of the market can buy a Michael Graves Bird Teakettle from Alessi for $124, and people at the other can buy a Michael Graves Ferris Wheel Kettle from Target for $13.99. And everyone is happy. Especially Michael Graves.

How did he do it? He had an extensible brand and reputation that was strong enough but elastic enough to stretch across both ends without breaking.

Which leads to another thing that you really have to have: excellent marketing. It's one thing to promise people all the things they want in one complete package; that's a promise that people will at least listen to. It's another thing to remind them that they really do have to make trade-offs, that they really can't have it all, not without paying a price one way or another. Even if the customers are there in sufficient quantity on both ends of the market, it's no easy task sending out two very different but entirely convincing messages from the same source, i.e., convincing people that they really should buy both a luxury car and an SUV. And doing it all without confusing the heck out of everybody. You have to keep your targets straight. This takes finesse, terrific timing, and very coordinated messages.

At a minimum, you have to inject doubt that some new Best-of-Both will be worth the risk of compromising on either the quality or price people have become used to. Forcing them to pause in their consideration may give you some breathing room to develop just such an offering yourself. If you don't have a well-tuned marketing machine, think twice before going for this tricky play.

Finally, not only are the marketing folks the heroes of this play, but the product folks are, too. They're the ones who hurry up to design and manufacture that luxury SUV or superpowerful, supereasy PC operating system before the rug has been pulled out from under you. Or the ones who keep pushing the edge of the quality envelope of your high-end offering while figuring out how to extend some of the same values to the bottom of the market without ruining your margins. That is no small trick.

Industry—Move and change, but not too fast.

Finally, industry conditions need to make sense for this play to work, too. Other plays rely on basic changes in technology or economics to drive a new opening in the market, whether opening up a niche, supporting an ecosystem, or enabling new combinations not before possible.

In a High–Low Play, overall change is still fine so long as it's in your favor and not happening too fast. If innovations are making it possible to reduce costs or add functionality—great, leverage them. But these changes can't be so dramatic that they change the buying criteria you have been relying on. Such innovations also can't be coming so fast that they pass you by while you're trying to defend your position on the high and/or low ends of your market.

Timing, therefore, is one of the most important aspects of making this play work.

The Rewards and Risks of Trying to Split a Category or Keep Its Ends Apart

The High–Low Play is all about underscoring the importance and value of the trade-offs that exist in the market, and being there whichever side customers decide to go for. Whether you're doing it to hold on to your positions or to reach down to grab a new one, it's critical that you be aware of the trade-offs you face before deciding on this course.

Rewards

The rewards of the High–Low Play may not be quite as monumental or dramatic as those of some of the other plays where you race someone across the finish line or lay claim to the big fat middle, but this one does offer you an opportunity for something more than mere survival. If you run it right, you truly get to reap double rewards— kind of a Best-of-Both in the low and high worlds simultaneously.

As mentioned, one of the biggest rewards of this play is the time you gain. Time to stave off the collapse of your category. Time to hurry up and build your own future offering. Time to do the marketing and branding you need to keep customers on your side while the product guys come up with the next big thing.

In addition, as we saw in several of the cases above, a well-executed High–Low Play can pay handsome dividends in terms of retained or even fattened margins with your high-end product, and extended reach and volume with your low-end product or offering.

Risks

While hopefully running this play can buy you some valuable time, time is also the biggest risk. You have to have enough of it. Running out of it means disaster.

As we saw with the Microsoft example, the marketing folks all hustled and pushed their messages of "no compromise" as hard as they could, and all the while they were begging the product guys to send in the reinforcements. If you're going to attack a Best-of-Both challenger, you need to do it fast before the competitor has a chance to get people questioning their own normal sense of trade-offs—reinforcing the rationale and supporting the reasons behind having both a high- and a low-end offering before people start wondering why they can't just plain have it all. You're going to have to make it stick long enough either to reinforce your bifurcated offering sufficiently, or to introduce your own more competitive Best-of-Both offering.

Another key risk is that you will be all too successful in half of your strategy—the lower half. You need to make both high and low offerings worthwhile in their own rights. Otherwise they will both lose.

And if you're too successful at making your entry-level offering compelling and high value, you may risk cannibalization: once people start seeing that you can deliver a high-quality product at a low price, maybe some of your exclusive, enthusiastic customers will start wondering about why they are still paying a premium. And then, instead of reaping double rewards for all of your extreme efforts at supporting this play, you get to sit back and watch your margins collapse.

It's all a delicate balance. Misjudge your customer set, mistime your messaging, or misalign your offerings and you could end up with a whole lot of nothing while the other guy walks away with the treasure.

I'm Ready to Give It a Try—How Do I Execute This Tricky High-Low Play?

Because this is such a complex play, you will reserve it for special circumstances—where either your core position is at stake or a unique opportunity is presented. Don't think you can pull it off without an all-out effort—it's like walking a tightrope. But if you have to do it, make sure you keep your balance and throw your opponents off theirs. Do it right, and you can put the squeeze on them and on the market, and benefit both ways. This really does take a great deal of finesse applied to each unique situation.

First, by preserving a price advantage for one option and by reinforcing the importance of the highest standards in choosing the other option, you make it possible to and have to maintain both entry-level and premium offerings as viable positions. Then, by highlighting the painful compromises inherent in choosing something halfway in between, you sow fear, uncertainty, and doubt in any Best-of-Both alternative, converting it from something interesting to something too good to be true (Fig. 6–6).

Here are the steps.

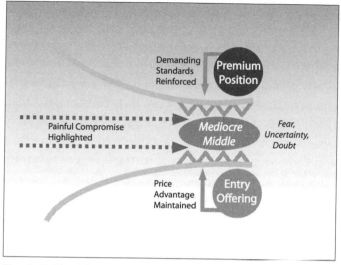

Fig. 6–6. The High–Low squeeze

Identify opportunities to extend your position up or down.

If you have a strong position established, especially in the high end of the market, with a great brand, reputation, and/or capabilities, then make sure you fully understand each of those assets and how flexible they would be in other parts of the market. Either as part of your two-pronged defense or as an effort to expand your reach, select the elements of your advantage on one end of the market best suited to drive further advantage on the other end.

Go high first.

Remember, this play is about denying the legitimacy of a Best-of-Both Play and about maintaining the unique power and appeal of very different offerings. You start by going high first: it's often easier to start out by relying on your premium attributes, differentiating, and highlighting the pain your customers will feel if they trade them off for a more holistic alternative.

Then you move on to the other end of the market. With these customers, make sure to underscore how unnecessary the costs are of adding mediocre new features versus simply sticking with the trusted basic value and price advantages of your low-end offering. You can ensure that an appeal to the least common denominator doesn't make sense if you successfully position it as the lowest value, targeted at groups who really have little to nothing in common.

Cut the mediocre off at the pass and win margins, volume, and time.

If you're aggressive and agile, especially in your messaging and marketing efforts, you can prevent your customers and targets from being tempted into some alternative. Doing so buys you several things. It allows you to keep the margins you like on the high end. It allows you to gain greater sales volumes on the low end. But most important is the time it buys you.

If competitive, economic, and technological trends inevitably favor a combination across the extremes of your category, make sure to work on building an appropriate combination. And use the time you gained by holding the high and low grounds to build a combination that will win against any Drag Race contender. If the market remains split, make sure that you use the time you have to shore up and extend your leadership on both ends.

Anticipate a threat from the middle.

To avoid being caught off guard by a Best-of-Both Play, make sure you keep your eyes and ears to the playing field, watching for any new entrants or openings in the middle of the market. Be prepared. Start building up your defenses on both ends of the market in advance.

Protect and maintain your image as you provide an entry-level alternative.

Avoid the risk of ruining your image on either end as you straddle the market. If you have a premium brand, make sure to modify it appropriately as you go broad. Add a suffix or a specific version name or other element that makes it distinct. Otherwise you will undermine your ability to command strong margins at the top. Also, as you offer an entry-level product or service to a broader universe of customers, make sure that you have the resources in people and money to support this business in the long run.

In large part this is a battle best left to the veteran marketing heroes who don't shrink from this challenge but embrace it in each aspect of their efforts.

Marketing Implications

Although High–Low can be characterized as "for professionals only" or only for your special situations/special team, there are still some basic marketing pointers you need to note. All of these follow the basic premise of inverting the Best-of-Both Play.

Positioning

The key to this play is its positioning, but that is also its biggest challenge. Remember that where the Best-of-Both Play asks, "Why choose?" the High–Low Play asks, "Why compromise?" The whole strategy is predicated on the notion that people should not have to settle; it denies the validity or viability of a Best-of-Both story in the first place. Different people have different needs, and they should have a product or service that fits their needs. If a customer is really picky, why should he settle for a mediocre, watered-down version of something just to save a few dollars. If, on the other hand, a customer is truly cost conscious, why should she have to pay more for attributes and supposed enhancements she considers superfluous?

Remember that the fundamental principle calls on you to position yourself as the answer to both of these audiences, to somehow convince them that, drawing from the same source of value and legitimacy, you can serve them both. Often, you can even provide a migration path between the two extremes (from entry level to premium, of course—not the other way around).

Another important positioning element is authenticity and tradition. As we saw with Jeep and Microsoft, you have to leverage your heritage and appeal to people's desire for the real thing, not offer some mediocre compromise.

Packaging

The product or service offerings themselves need to be packaged and presented in a way that supports the two-pronged strategy. That means instead of one "fighter SKU," you have two. In most instances you put the weight behind the most powerful or full-featured offering so as to best wow people and best reinforce the prestige of your brand. Then you offer your less robust offering as an entry point or beginning alternative. Sometimes it's possible to do the opposite, drawing people in with a low-barrier, low-price no-brainer and then tempting them with a clear migration or up-sell path.

Pricing

The pricing for this play is two-pronged. One high-priced product should allow you to hold onto greater margin, and one-low priced product should allow you to generate more sales volume. Make sure it actually works that way; if margins suffer, you ought to be looking at an alternate strategy, such as trying to Drag Race for the middle of the market instead.

Promotion

This is primarily a play to counter a play so, if you choose it, your efforts need to cut off Best-of-Both–type promotions at the pass. But unlike Best-of-Both, you need to focus on early adopters or connoisseurs. Meet them at tradeshows and events—wow them with the unrivaled power or perfection of your high-end offering. Where Best-of-Both goes broad with its "Why choose?" appeal, undercut them with lower price and stronger value.

This is also a play where experts can be on your side. They tend to look down on compromises. And across it all, especially with your PR effort, you can sow doubt as to whether a new middle-of-the-road offering is really worth it. This is a play where "the FUD factor"—fear, uncertainty, and doubt—can work a lot more in your favor than the other guy's. Such messages can cut off a Best-of-Both offering before it has a chance to take hold. Or these messages can provide a smokescreen for you, convincing people to wait until you come in with the really good stuff.

Finally, Be Careful Out There

Given this play's complexity and the difficulty of pulling it off, you're a natural target when you run it. The high end is attractive to poach and the low end is tempting to challenge. If you're not using this play to respond to somebody else's Best-of-Both, remember that you need to anticipate someone coming after you with a Best-of-Both challenge. But as well as being on the lookout for one big threat, be fully prepared for two different players to call you out to a Drag Race—one on each end of the market. If you've been successful in maintaining the split in the market and the attractiveness of each end, it should be natural for someone to be tempted to make a grab for the prize in each one.

With this kind of precarious play, you can never afford to let up. Of all the plays, this is the one in which looking toward your next move is most urgent. That's why we kept it for last. When you run a High–Low, you should not only be highly practiced enough at your playing field strategy and tactics to feel confident about doing this play, you need to know all the other plays well enough to move directly to them when the time is right.

Take-Aways for the High-Low Play

1. The High–Low Play is one of the most difficult strategies to pull off, requiring a bifurcation of your efforts on opposite ends of

the market. It is about splitting a category or keeping it split on both of these ends. As such it is more complex and requires both more resources and more finesse than other plays. That's why it's number five. Nonetheless it can be an important strategy for your survival or for grabbing a bigger share of a bigger pie—so keep it in your bag of tricks for just those special circumstances.

2. You'll run a High–Low Play in one of two circumstances: either to prevent a new Best-of-Both player from entering the market and undermining your previous position; or to maintain a high-end, high-margin premium business for the early adopters or elites of your market. In the meantime, you also need to be leveraging your strengths to present a price-competitive entry-level offering to a bigger market. Generally, neither version works well for start-ups; you need some kind of position to start from.

3. The High–Low Play is the inverse of the Best-of-Both Play. Rather than pushing everyone into the middle, this play denies the viability or legitimacy of a middle at all. Whereas Best-of-Both is all about simplicity and getting it all, High–Low is all about keeping things pure.

4. High–Low Players are stubborn. They say, "No compromises. Down with mediocrity, up with choice." So what if it makes life more complicated? You deserve the right thing for you. One of the key tools in the High–Low Player's bag is FUD. Sowing fear, uncertainty, and doubt as well as underscoring the risks of going with a middle ground are key ways to buy time.

5. Finally, you will find this play precarious to pull off but even more precarious to maintain. In choosing this play, it is critical

to keep your eyes on what's next, both in terms of other players trying to knock you off your balance and in terms of the right next play for you to evolve into.

Coming Up

Understanding the right play for your current circumstances isn't enough. The playing field is always changing and evolving. The very fact that you chose a particular play to start with will have an impact on the conditions you face in the long run. This movement from play to play and the response of one play to another is the topic of the next chapter.

I skate to where the puck is going to be, not to where it has been.

—WAYNE GRETZKY, HOCKEY SUPERSTAR

7. Shifting Gears—Moving from Play to Play

Knowing your current play is not enough. You have to know your next move and those of your opponents.

You now know all of the five plays and have a repertoire of core strategy options at your disposal. The five are varied enough to choose from but few enough to remember. Just go figure out what you really have and what the other guy is doing, get set for the play, and go, go, go.

If only it were that simple.

For one thing, there are those pesky competitors. They're watching you. They're reacting to you. They have their own plans.

As with all other strategies in business, your Playbook strategy cannot be static.

Your play interacts with those of your competition. Your actions in executing one play will affect your ability to execute another. As you move forward, you need to keep in mind the reasons you chose your current play in the first place. And you have to be mindful of signs that you need to make a change.

Leaving One Play to Start Another

When conditions are right, or when a competitor has made a countermove that changes the game, it makes sense to move to another play. In fact, it's imperative. Sticking with a strategy that's no longer working or has run its course is an invitation to disaster.

Migrating from play to play brings an additional level of strategy. Even as you go about choosing your first play and focus on executing it, you should be keeping an eye out for what might be next. You will have to map your own route, of course, but you don't have to start from scratch.

There's a natural flow or evolution from one stage of your business to the next, from one stage of the market to the next, and from one play to the next; see Fig. 7–1.

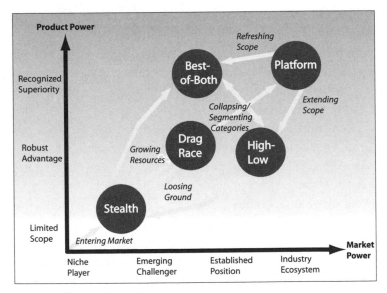

Fig. 7–1. The cycle of plays

When you're first starting out, whether as a start-up or as a new line of business, it generally makes the most sense to go with the Stealth Play initially. There are cases when you may begin by declaring a Drag Race or attempting a Best-of-Both right out of the gate, but more often as a new entrant, you have the least legitimacy and the most tenuous position. So you start by finding a niche that you can win before you try to prove yourself more broadly—and before you provoke direct confrontation.

In this mode you often sit under and benefit from a more dominant incumbent provider who is possibly running a Platform Play. As you gain strength, either by adding new niches or by extending the scope of your product or offering, you can enter the fray of more direct competition for market preeminence, even against the very platform you previously partnered with and paid tribute to.

Most often this move leads to a Drag Race. Once you become confident of your advantage, you can use that advantage to grab the hearts and minds of leading customers and take a straight and clear path to a more established position. But be careful: this is the most common and most tempting play—don't be drawn in unless you're sure you have adequate resources to stick it out until you win.

Drag Races can be costly. They can drain a lot of the profit out of a market if you compete on price. One way to get some of this profit back is to segment the market using a High–Low Play. By adding a premium edition or version for the top of the market, you can offer a high-value up-sell. Or, by retaining an entry level offering, you can continue to invite in the mass of the market. But watch out— don't try to split the market unnaturally or create choices that people don't want to make.

If the market is more mature and you have a truly breakthrough product, you can go for the whole enchilada with the Best-of-Both Play. With clearly established categories and a broad product advantage, you can drive up the middle and capture a wider leadership position. This play allows you to appeal to the desire for value and simplicity, and collapse the high and the low ends into one big net. But you had better make sure the middle ground is big enough and that you've really addressed the majority of needs and desires.

Ultimately if you're successful in any of these battles, you will need to defend your position. The Platform Play is the most enduring strategy. By sharing your success with others and making it beneficial for them to support you, you create an ecosystem of allies—and huge barriers to potential challengers. But beware, the top is the real estate everyone else wants to acquire, too. So make sure your allies remain pleased and won't be drawn out by the taunts of the challengers. Don't let your ego or your appetite lead you into unnecessary and fruitless conflicts.

This cycle of evolution doesn't go in just one direction. You can and should return to other plays to stay ahead of your game. As they say, sometimes the best defense is a good offense. Even the strongest platform is in need of creative destruction from time to time to stay fresh. One of the best ways to do that is to play Best-of-Both against both yourself and an emerging alternative. Using your old offering as the base and the challenger as the catalyst, you can create a stronger compound in an upgraded platform. When you're in the process of rendering your existing offering obsolete, this can be a great way to leapfrog the competition by including yourself in the Best-of-Both comparison.

If you're winning a Drag Race, you can reach down into niches to leverage your lead and extend your momentum. Or you can fall back into the Stealth Play as you enter new markets. Or reposition your Drag Race or part of your High–Low product.

Whatever the case, it pays to be nimble. And it pays to be successful at the play you're running before moving on.

Making Sure Your Play Is Successful

Once you've chosen a play, you have to actually run it on the real playing field. You have already learned many of the essential marketing elements implied by each play, as summarized in Fig. 7–2.

	Positioning	Packaging	Price	Promotion
Drag Race	"Better than..."	One fighter SKU	Don't lose deals	Feature wars, Winning reviews
Platform	"An industry..."	Embedded core, Partner tools	Make partners money	Partner events, Momentum
Stealth	"Extends platform to..."	Smaller, more specific options	High as niche will bear	Low profile, Ride as partner
Best-of-Both	"Why choose?"	One fighter SKU	Value-based pricing	Own trend, Broad appeal
High–Low	"Why compromise?"	Entry product, Premium edition	Lowest and highest	In-store, Up-sell/down-sell

Fig. 7–2. Basic marketing implications of each play

Getting these right in advance will go far to set you up for driving your strategy to success in the marketplace. These elements constitute the final preparations of your go-to-market plan. With the right battlefield intelligence, the right resources, and the most logical mode for deploying them, you should be ready for whatever your industry, customers, and competitors have in store for you.

But the true test of your plans and of your generalship only comes in the heat of the campaign on the playing field. There you will need more than just great plans. You will need craft and skill. You will need terrific execution.

Coming Up

Now that you understand the plays, it's time to take a much deeper look at some of the tools and analysis techniques you'll use to map your playing field—an essential part of the homework in your decisions about choosing a play or deepening your efforts of your current play.

Part II takes your playing-field intelligence to the next level.

The Terrain of Your Play–Mapping the Gaps and Opportunities in Your Market Playing Field

Understanding the situation, key factors, and market dynamics essential to your line of attack:

- What the factors are
- What you need to know about them
- How to gather and analyze the information

You can observe a lot just by watching.

—YOGI BERRA, BASEBALL PLAYER AND MANAGER

8. Mapping Overall Industry Gaps

What separates industry has-beens from industry heroes? And what does this have to do with your Playbook?

One very important common element distinguishes companies that will become has-beens from those that will be their industry's heroes. Something big.

They pay attention. In many cases if not most, the biggest element that separates the players we remember from the players that came and disappeared is that the winners held a profound understanding of the dynamics of their industry. They found a hole, a gap in the market. The bigger the gap they filled, the bigger the company's success and legacy. They found this by, guess what . . . looking.

Picking the right play for any particular situation begins with discovering the gaps that represent the best opportunities in your overall industry. Doing homework on your industry will help you discern between a pothole, a challenging but manageable leap, and an insurmountable grand canyon. That homework can spell the difference between being lauded as a champion, being forgotten as an also-ran, or being scraped off the pavement as roadkill.

An example: We all drive cars, but whom do you think of as the biggest heroes of the enormous automotive industry? Car history buffs might name people like Nicolas Joseph Cugnot, Siegfried Marcus, and Nikolaus August Otto.

But for the majority of Americans the name of Henry Ford is the one that comes to mind.

What Does Your Business Have in Common with the Model T?

Cugnot built the first automobile in 1769; it was steam powered and was a milestone even though it only managed 2½ mph. In 1864, Marcus, figuring that gasoline might work better than steam, stuck a gas-powered engine on a cart and managed to drive a whole five hundred feet. Three years later, Otto invented the four-stroke internal combustion engine.

All three were supersmart, pioneering guys who made tremendous contributions to our lives. Without them or others like them, we'd probably still be measuring horsepower in one-horse and two-horse units. So why don't we remember them? Why is it so much more likely (unless you're an auto industry historian) that you think of Henry Ford as the father of the modern automotive industry?

What makes the difference is that when Cugnot and Marcus and Otto were developing their important innovations, the other elements of the automotive industry just weren't there yet.

In contrast, Henry Ford found his industry gap, and it had nothing to do with engines or suspension or braking or any other automobile technology.

Whether you're setting your sights on shaking up your industry like Henry Ford, or your aspirations are more humble—say, just trying to make a lot of money—doing research on your industry and doing it right lays the groundwork for everything that follows. This research, which we call "doing your homework," helps in three ways.

> It helps you discover, define, or refine the vision that inspires you and the mission that motivates you;
> It helps you reach conclusions that define the boundaries and constraints for choosing your strategy and your operating philosophy;
> Finally, it can help define your investment priorities.

Fine. These sound like valuable goals. But what are the things you need to look at that will help you achieve them?

First, look at the developments that came before you and define the state of your industry today and the state of the other industries that support it. Ford saw scores of previous innovations that helped support the safe development and use of autos: improvements in roads, in tires, in engines, in steel.

Next, look for the openings in the dynamics of the industry. What should be happening that isn't yet? Ford saw that cars—despite all the innovations to date—were still the domain of elites or aficionados, not regular people.

Then, isolate the key economic and other levers in the industry that are required to exploit that opening. Ford recognized that reliability and cost were the key barriers and the key opportunities to reaching the mass market with automobiles.

Finally, focus all your energies, priorities, and decisions on moving those levers. Ford became maniacally focused on cost and reliability and on everything needed to improve them. He made bets on scale and focused on standardization at the sacrifice of consumer choice. He focused on innovations like the conveyer belt, interchangeable parts, and mass marketing. And he delivered the Model T—the first mass-produced, low-cost/low-price car.

Sounds like a tall order. Don't worry. Doing your own industry homework and drawing pointed observations that will inform your vision, mission, and strategy will not require you to take night school classes in economics or hire Paul Volcker or Alan Greenspan. All you need are the few simple tools and methods outlined below.

The ABCs of Industry Opportunity

The most straightforward way of identifying the right industry challenges and opportunities or to verify those you're pursuing is to do a simple gap analysis. It will lay the groundwork for almost all the other strategic and tactical work you do. We've referred to gap analysis in describing the best conditions for each play; now it's time to take a closer look at this valuable tool.

In the hundreds of companies and literally thousands of different situations we encounter, we follow a very simple three-part formula for doing a gap analysis.

We call this formula the ABCs (Fig. 8–1). *A* represents the current situation, *B* represents the desired future, and *C* represents the gap you have to cross to get to that future. How you'll use this becomes clear quickly with an illustration; in this case it's from our familiar playing field, Microsoft.

This first step of the gap analysis is the *A*, or starting point—your current situation. In Microsoft's case in the early 1990s, the industry situation in question was what would come after the IBM PC. Back then, PCs were cheap but had significant limitations. They couldn't run big programs and they weren't easy to use.

This was frustrating for people in the computer industry—especially when you considered the promise of the new Intel 386 chip that offered more memory, more performance, more multitasking, more programs running simultaneously, more everything. A better future was tantalizingly possible, but not yet there.

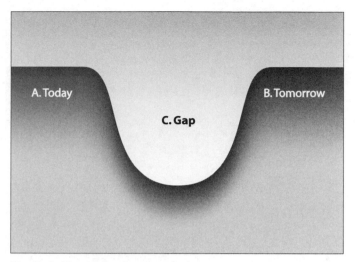

Fig. 8–1. The ABCs of gap analysis

That's the next step: to define a desirable destination—a goal describing the position you want to reach. For this, we use the terminology devised by presentation expert Jerry Weissman, calling your desired destination "Point B." It's the answer to "There's gotta be a better way," an inspiring but still believable alternative for how the industry could operate.

By examining all the existing factors in the computer industry, Microsoft was able to pinpoint a spot on the map that no other company had yet chosen or been able to claim as their own: an inexpensive personal computer that would be as easy to use as a Mac. This point B was one where PCs would be so easy and accessible that in the future there would be "A Computer on Every Desktop and in Every Home." (See Fig. 8–2.)

The third step of your overall industry gap analysis is determining the C—the challenge that, if met, will allow you to bridge the gap you have identified (Fig. 8–3). You have to understand the size and nature of the gap, and commit to crossing it.

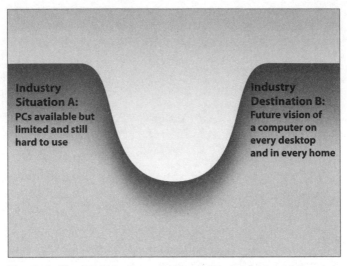

Fig. 8–2. The PC industry and Microsoft's points A and B

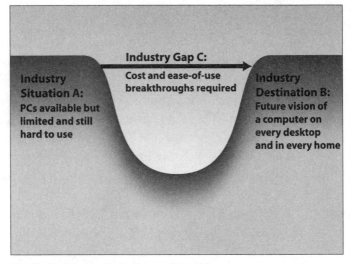

Fig. 8–3. Microsoft challenge: The PC gap

Microsoft found exactly that bridge, which was composed of two primary elements: cost and ease of use. Integrating these factors became the motivation and focus for an entire industry. By focusing separately on key enabling software and allowing for lots of different hardware alternatives, the structure of the industry changed. Software became separated from hardware and really easy, really powerful computers that cost a fraction of the price of a Macintosh became available from lots of different manufacturers. Harnessing the innovations available, aligning the elements required, and driving improvements in these two elements of combined power and ease of use became the source of Microsoft's truly historic growth.

In Bill Gates's case, similar to Henry Ford's, his view of the industry gap focused his vision and his company's mission (Fig. 8–4). The fundamental insight that cost and ease of use were hindering the growth of the PC industry proved the essential secret for suc-

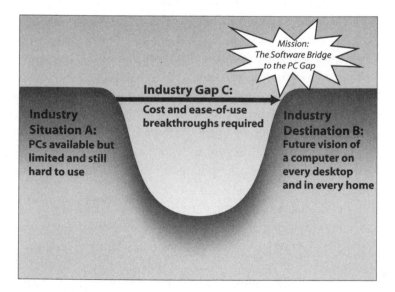

Fig. 8–4. A software mission to fill the gap

cess. Understanding of the key working parts of the industry and how they could be influenced allowed Microsoft to play the critical role in breaking this logjam.

The gaps that you most need to fill become your own mission. Thus at Microsoft, the company's leaders knew the company could not accomplish the vision of "A Computer on Every Desktop and in Every Home" all by itself. Microsoft understood that it was a software company and had to focus its mission on making the software that best aided this movement.

Finding New Places and New Ways to Fill the Same Old Industry Gaps

Looking at all the economic and structural factors, what is the current way of doing things in your industry? What are the biggest gaps and challenges in your industry? Are trends moving in the right direction to narrow these gaps? What role do you want to play in closing them? Visionary, fast follower, late bloomer? How do your vision and view of the current or evolving dynamics of your industry affect your operating principles? Your key bets?

Not every industry gap analysis has to be earth shattering. Not every analysis will point to the creation of a whole new industry. But taking a fresh look at your industry on a recurring basis can reveal new and still very enticing gaps and challenges not yet surmounted.

One company that found a great mission by taking a fresh look at an industry gap that had supposedly been filled many times over was Extend America, which (as noted in Chapter Four) provides wireless telecommunications carrier services to rural markets. Ignition Partners, the venture capital firm where we work, had been studying the wireless telecommunications industry since its inception, searching for the most promising gaps and for the right ingredients to fill it profitably.

Our investment in Extend America was the direct result of some specific insights and observations of recently opened gaps in the economics and politics of the telecommunications industry.

Several of Ignition's team members, no strangers to this industry, had been pioneers in helping discover and cross many of the previous gaps and, in doing so, had helped to shape the telecom industry of today.

But with some 20 million handsets sold and 150 million wireless subscribers in the United States, the gap between telephony and mobility seemed pretty well closed. After the amazing structural insights of Craig McCaw and Steve Hooper helping to launch the first truly national wireless service, it seemed that all the key industry gaps had already been analyzed, the key levers pulled, and the opportunities completely covered.

Add to this the 1990s decade-long overinvestment and overleverage in telecom infrastructure and the subsequent complete collapse in telecom market valuations, and the horizon for new investment in the industry seemed pretty disheartening.

But this did not dissuade the founders of Extend America, a great mix of industry veterans, politically savvy businesspeople, and business-savvy former government officials. This team did their own gap analysis of the telecom industry and of the political and economic landscapes in the country. And from their simple set of ABCs, they discovered opportunities and points of leverage that had not yet been addressed.

A: They looked at the current state of the telecommunications services and related equipment industries. They saw that wireless was now widely available in most places. They saw that despite continued grumbling about rate plans, such wireless service was pretty darn affordable. They also saw that there were a number of big players all competing, struggling to maintain profitability, and actually shrinking in number as they got gobbled up by others. Not necessarily the most promising territory for a new entrant.

B: They set their sights on some possibilities and needs that should have been obvious but were confoundingly unsolved. They saw that despite all the big national players, several geographies remained almost entirely unserved by wireless telephony. They saw very large but not densely populated areas like the Dakotas, Wyoming, and Montana, where the demand was acute but the supply—or coverage—was as yet nonexistent. They saw this and felt it deeply . . . because they were from those places.

C: So, they assessed what needed to change. By integrating the elements, they determined what needed to be done to fill that gap. And they discovered the key levers to make it happen. They recognized that these geographies had remained untouched by the major carriers because of scale economics, finances, and regulations. The low-density populations made it harder to justify the upfront costs of infrastructure (setting up cell towers to guarantee decent coverage, creating all the billing systems, etc.). Their huge debt burdens and a sudden scarcity of capital made this even worse.

The recognition of this gap drove their vision. Maybe it wasn't as grand as starting the entire wireless industry, but profitably delivering service to people who couldn't get it before was and is still pretty darn exciting.

The focus on low-cost infrastructure, low-cost capital, and solid service motivated their mission. With that mission, the founders were able to assemble the key pieces that made launching such a service possible.

Their basic focus on infrastructure, capital, and service costs has helped guide all their major strategic and tactical decisions. It has also helped define their play in the market. And while the jury is still out on this company, we are very excited by their vision, their mission, and their progress. It's a great example of how taking a fresh look at what may seem to be a static industry can yield great results. Doing your homework can really pay off.

A Gap at Thirty Thousand Feet

The ABC process can be applied in every industry, not just technology. It was used by a "little up-start, three-jet airline" that "got off the ground to become one of America's largest and best-loved commercial airlines in history."

Sound familiar? That's Southwest Airlines. Even though at last count the company is the fourth largest airline, the same observations and insights that drove its foundations thirty years ago still drive its vision, mission, and operating philosophy today.

Southwest is a great example of a company that, despite all conventional wisdom to the contrary, figured out that the excitement in their industry was not yet over.

Even back in 1971, when Rollin Kin and Herb Kelleher founded the company, it was easy to see what a mess the current state of the airline business was. But the two men were able to see beyond this sorry state and analyze the gaps, which they proceeded to fill cleverly and uniquely.

Their *A* assessment of the situation was simple. Air travel had become much more available. Everyone seemed to be flying more than ever before. Everywhere Kin and Kelleher looked, they saw lots of airports, lots of airplanes, and lots of flights. Nonetheless there were already huge problems with on-time departures and arrivals. And, boy, was flying expensive.

But looking at all these airplanes and airports, the two men were puzzled by how limited air travel remained. Flights were only available for long trips, and the industry positioned flying as a big deal, with their facilities centered around huge carrier hubs. Why was that? When air travel was theoretically so fast and there were so many airports, why couldn't airplanes be used for more basic kinds of travel—shorter trips than the Los Angeles–to–Detroit or New York–to–Miami hops that the industry was focused on?

Their point B became obvious—people could be flying to places where until now they had been driving.

What key factors or levers made up the gap (C) between air and car travel? Simple: time and total cost. Hopping on a plane to go to someplace three hours away would continue to be something that big-shot businesspeople would do—in the company aircraft. It was still just too expensive for Mr. Average Citizen to fly from Dallas to Houston. And once you considered check-in time, likely delays, and waiting for your baggage, the door-to-door time by car might actually be faster. (There used to be an East Coast flight instructor whose favorite expression was "If you have time to spare, go by air.") The Southwest founders figured that if they could address these two issues, maybe they could close that gap.

The gap and the goal it suggested became Southwest's vision and Southwest's mission. Relentless attention to the industry levers that could cut costs and keep flying fast became Southwest's strategic advantage and the core of its go-to-market play.

They saw this untapped need and decided to become "the Company Plane" of regular people. They designed their strategy and decisions around becoming the "only short-haul, low-fare, high-frequency, point-to-point carrier in America." Getting you on and off fast has guided their innovation investments through the years: ticketless travel, self-ticketing machines, Web check-in, etc. Keeping the costs low guided their business model and service operations: no meals, one-class service, no major hubs with their burdensome hub fees.

As a result, they took what looked to be a stagnant industry and shook it up. They found the gaps and filled them profitably. And as a result of very astute ongoing assessment of the dynamics of the industry, they have continually tailored their vision, mission, and philosophy to keep doing this over and over again.

Take-Aways for Mapping Overall Industry Gaps

1. Understanding your industry is a big deal. Doing the right homework to get a sharp-eyed perspective on your industry can mean the difference between shaking up your industry and getting shaken out.

2. The analysis doesn't have to be painful. It just takes getting a fresh handle on your industry, integrating the elements you discover, and drawing very pointed conclusions using a simple gap analysis.

3. Look for industry gaps repeatedly and frequently. Keep your eyes focused on the right gap. Doing so helps you make sure you don't fall in. And it keeps your vision fresh. Every industry keeps moving; you need to keep moving with it.

4. Figuring out the ABCs of your industry will tell you where your industry needs to go or is capable of going. Your assessment of the possible point B yields (or refreshes and refines) the vision of the future you want to support and promulgate. Your assessment of the gap and obstacles together with your commitment to overcoming them yields (or refreshes and refines) the mission that motivates you and guides your operating principles.

5. This same simple method of ABCs will help guide all the homework you do on the other key elements of your business terrain—your customers, competition, and your own competencies.

Coming Up

Now that you understand the lay of the land from ten thousand feet, it's time to drop altitude a bit and get closer to the everyday pulse of your business. The same situation and gap analyses are critical to understanding the people who make you money: your customers. That's the topic of Chapter Nine.

The purpose of business is to create and keep a customer.

—PETER DRUCKER

9. Your Customer Playing Field

It's amazing what you learn when you actually talk to the people who are supposed to buy your stuff.

Sounds obvious. What's the point of deeply understanding your industry, its dynamics, its gaps, and its opportunities unless you can use that knowledge to sell something to somebody?

Moving from the macro-level analysis of your industry to the micro-level analysis of your target customers within that industry is the second element of choosing the right play. Doing your homework diligently can mean the difference between an academic exercise and a sustainable business.

The same simple ABC gap analysis process you applied to your industry as a whole can also tell you some hot and valuable stuff about your customer landscape—such as exactly whom to sell to, what problems to work on solving for them, how best to turn your solutions into a product or offer, or how best to adapt and adjust your existing product or offer to provide the solution to a customer need. And in general, how to have the best chance of actually selling it to them.

You have to know who your customers are. "What?" you say. "Of course, we know." Are you sure? You might be surprised how often smart, experienced businesspeople have incomplete information or hang on to false assumptions about the people they want to sell to.

So how can you be sure you really know what you think you know? Are you ready for this? You actually go out and personally meet with customers. Scary. They might do something awful, such as talk to you.

And just watch what happens: you'll learn things you couldn't find out any other way.

We saw this simple tactic work for Intelligent Results, a company with founders who knew in depth the dynamics and the gaps of their technology and industry. They also had powerful and proprietary technology that promised to close those gaps. Their timing seemed spot-on, too. A shoo-in for success, right? Guess again. They had more homework to do to get the play and its execution right.

The ABCs of Customer Demand–Turning Compelling Vision into Solutions You Can Sell

Intelligent Results (IR) is a software company in a specialized area called customer relationship analytics (CRA); it's a start-up founded by world-class analytical scientists and engineers—people who were quite used to doing complex, thorough analysis. And, surprisingly enough, they were also practical.

In terms of product, they had already done a lot of their homework when they first came to see us at Ignition. They had done their industry ABCs. They understood the benefits and limitations of current statistical modeling methods of analysis, methods that had provided lots of insight but that the IR folks recognized made use of only a limited portion of corporate data. They also knew that there should be a better, more complete way that would also take advantage of data types that current analysis methods couldn't handle. And they had a key insight on the technology that would take analytics from point A of the current situation (where analysis was based only on limited information) to a much better, more complete point B.

As shown in Fig. 9–1, this understanding of the industry gap had yielded the Intelligent Results vision. It was this: Companies ought to be able to use more than just the numbers at their disposal to do business analysis. They ought to be able to use *all* their sources of data—structured and unstructured, numbers and words—to gain the most complete intelligence and most accurate analysis. IR even had a true technology breakthrough, all their own, that could make this possible. Making it easy to integrate and usefully apply the combination of structured transaction data and unstructured textual data became the Intelligent Results mission.

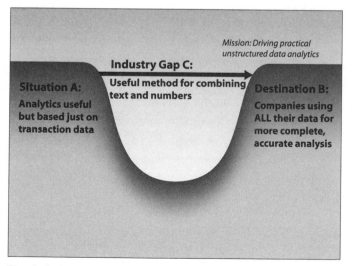

Fig. 9–1. Intelligent Results' industry ABCs

We found all of this very exciting. IR was gaining the attention of the industry cognoscenti, in particular sophisticated analysts (people like them), who were intrigued by their product.

But, despite their thorough and accurate industry assessment, they were barely making traction in actually selling the stuff.

Highly motivated to get to the bottom of the problem and start making better traction, they went out and talked to all their current customers and prospects. They came back, compared notes, and realized that their understanding of the situation, the possibilities, and the gaps was incomplete.

So they took their gap analysis to the level of potential paying customers and found the real sweet spot, the point of market entry, and the most compelling story, offering, and sale. Here's what they did:

1. They dug into their target customers' priorities—their critical needs.

   The founders' former boss, Jeff Bezos, CEO of Amazon, had given them the advice that "the key to success is intense understanding of the customer." And in this they found their answer. Intelligent Results' own clients' most relevant and critical need was to better understand their customers and to predict their future behaviors. Nowhere was this more true than with the banking customers.

   They dug deeper into the needs of the banking customers and discovered that with the market and economic downturns, the priorities of consumer banks and other lending institutions had shifted. These companies were progressively less focused on acquiring new customers versus predicting and mitigating potential losses from existing customers. While the banks had been using statistical analysis for decades to help predict default, there was a new sense of urgency to find new tools to bear on the problem. And they were willing to spend real money to do so.

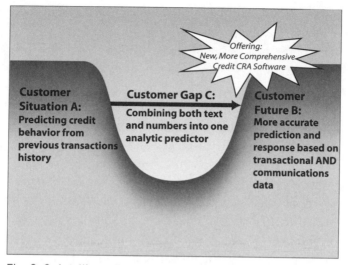

Fig. 9–2. Intelligent Results' customer ABCs

This observation identified Intelligent Results' best initial customer target and yielded a now truly concrete offering (Fig. 9–2). They courted risk and credit officers in consumer financial institutions, offering new customer relationship analytic (CRA) software that would allow lenders to utilize much more information about their customers, from all the various sources, so they could more accurately predict and address potential defaults. And they began to find plenty of people willing to write a check for it.

To be sure you know what your customers want, you have to get answers to these questions:

What are the priorities of your customers?
Are they urgent?
Are they willing to pay for a solution?
Do you understand their critical needs?
Are you prepared to address those needs?

2. The company chose the specific customers they wanted to target initially, and evaluated their obstacles and issues.

One of the great things about the banking target was their level of sophistication. The banks' own analysts and credit people had intuitively understood that there ought to be predictive value in the unstructured text they possessed from customer communications. But they had been frustrated in their efforts to make it useful.

So, even with all their urgency and with the no-brainer ROI promise of reducing losses, the company's target customers' constraints were limiting their options. They had existing processes and software that helped them manage collections. It was important that they be able to efficiently tap into this new source of data and make it usable quickly, without requiring a big change in behavior or a daunting infrastructure investment.

Understanding these constraints helped Intelligent Results refine their offering even more. To avoid barriers to customer adoption, they made sure their solutions integrated with the common banking software and did not interfere with existing systems. This made its unique value more immediate and useful by reducing the barriers of customer adoption.

For trying to reach your own customers, what are the issues and purchase constraints? Do you know how to overcome them?

3. They looked at other products and systems that their customers and prospects had already bought.

They respected those decisions and they made sure to interoperate with those products easily.

4. They looked at how these customers went about buying.

Intelligent Results discovered that their clients' shift in priorities had also caused a shift in their purchase dynamics. The relative power of the credit or risk officer had increased inside the bank. But so had his or her accountability. The company recognized that selling to these folks would have to include real proof of the solutions' effectiveness using live data. This added some time to the process, but eventually it significantly greased the way to making the sale.

How do your customers buy? What steps do they need to take before making decisions? What are their relative roles in the purchase process?

Who Are *Your* Customers?
A Hint: Follow the Money

We worked with a company that found out their assumptions were wrong about their target, so they then re-aimed and hit the bull's-eye.

Avogadro was a start-up that had developed technology for mobile phone users which greatly improved their ability to do wireless instant messaging. Thomas Reardon and the other founders of the company were experts in creating end-user products: they had come from another industry that sold and distributed directly to consumers. All their materials, their story, and their product were carefully crafted for their prospective end users.

But, despite that, these geniuses (honestly) had totally missed the mark. In pitch after pitch their audience would say something like, "Well, that's very impressive. Sounds wonderful. How does it make money?"

In this scenario, brilliant people don't take long to sense that something is wrong.

Soon they realized that many of their assumptions about their customers and markets were off because they were attempting to translate past experience to this new market, and the market of mobile wireless was very different from what they were familiar with.

The end users they were appealing to weren't the real buyers for the product. Unless the user's telecom carrier (AT&T, Verizon, etc.) was set up to allow use of the technology, the customer couldn't take advantage of the Avogadro offering.

So those big players were the real customer. Only through them could Avogadro reach the end users; without them, Avogadro could not get paid. But the AT&Ts wanted to know what all this neato end-user technology had in it for them. Avogadro's positioning, pricing, and pitch were interesting but not sufficient to motivate the real customers, the telecom carriers.

Avogadro went back to the drawing board. They studied the telecom carriers and adjusted their offering with the right kind of focus.

The next time Avogadro pitched their instant messaging option, the telecom companies understood and listened. In time, Avogadro was purchased at a handsome profit by a publicly traded company that also had these telecom carriers as its primary customers.

Who uses your product or service? Do they pay you directly? If they don't, who does? Who pays you the most money? (Or if you are moving into new territory, who would?) Does your offering appeal to their needs?

Don't just stop with the obvious suspects. In many cases more than one part of the value chain pays you money. Make sure you have a great offering for all of them.

Another Hint: Follow *All* the Money

In the 1980s, American Express spent all of its time focused on its cardmember customers. The AmEx card was a premium brand. It was prestigious. And its cardmembers were its crown jewels, precious people willing to pay a premium for the upscale privilege. The company made a science out of mining their base of customers to sell them more and to offer incentives that would spur increased purchasing with the card.

The company knew that it faced competition for its cardmembers in the battle for what it called "share of wallet." So the company focused on adding benefits for the cardholders, maintaining a premium image and so on. Despite the onslaught of new cards, many of them with no annual fee, American Express fared quite well.

Meanwhile, amid all this attention to the cardmembers, the company had never bothered paying much attention to the merchants who accepted the card—the stores, hotels, restaurants, and so on. They had neglected to see these merchants as true customers. Perhaps that's easy to understand: the company *got* money every month from the cardholders, but had to *send* money to the merchants. American Express paid the price for the oversight.

The merchants finally got sick of paying high rates for accepting the American Express card when Visa and MasterCard were offering much lower rates and were beginning to issue premium cards. Soon many service establishments started taking their AmEx stickers off their windows. Worse, it didn't seem to make a difference: the same people were still shopping there, eating there, staying there. Cardholders cared more about the establishment than about what card they were using to pay their tab.

This really hurt. It didn't just hurt the revenue streams flowing into American Express from the merchants, but it also threatened cardmembers' annual fees. If your favorite restaurants and stores no longer accept the American Express card, why keep it?

Since then, American Express has done a bang-up job being creative in attending to both sides of the business. But, boy, was that a hard-won lesson.

In your own company, what's the relationship between all your sources of revenue? Do you treat each one like a customer? Are they each happy?

A WORD OF CAUTION: Even if someone else decides, pays for, and delivers the product or service, don't lose the hearts and minds of the people who actually use it. Listen to them, too. If your users stop using you, no matter how well you support your channel or intermediaries, your channels and partners will end up losing interest, too. It's always easy to hear what you want to hear. Don't.

When analyzing your customers' playing fields, you have to be willing to remove the filters (e.g., a quota-driven sales force, a fee-generating market research firm, deal-negotiating channel partners, or your own only-want-to-hear-good-news ears) that may have been affecting the information you're getting about your customers. Only then will you know that you're hearing the unvarnished truth.

Back in 1988, market share for spreadsheet software packages was somewhat unevenly divided. Microsoft Excel had 7 percent against Lotus 1-2-3's 70 percent. Those of us in Microsoft marketing who were responsible for Excel couldn't understand it. We knew we had the better product. The focus groups we conducted proved that 1-2-3 users were amazed by Excel, which offered deep menus and the now-standard but at the time stunning new feature called "WYSIWYG" (What You See Is What You Get). Our strategy was to focus on WYSIWYG and use it to "Rock your world."

Some time later, Excel had dropped to 6 percent, 1-2-3 had slipped a few points to 65 percent, and another product, Quattro-Pro, had grabbed 25 percent. What happened?

Two things had conspired against us. One was our zealousness. We knew we had the better, more powerful product. We were so confident about this that it was hard for us to notice anything to the contrary. It turned out that we were so busy listening to what we wanted to hear that we missed the truth of how 1-2-3 users were responding to Excel.

The other was human nature. We had not really accounted for the artificial constraints of environments such as a focus group. Respondents to whom you're giving Cokes and M&Ms don't want to disappoint you—especially when you seem so happy with yourselves and when you ask questions in a way that implies the answers you really want. When they told us, "I guess I'd buy," we thought that was great support for our position. Unfortunately, as we learned from their actual purchase behavior in the market, what they really meant was "No way."

We decided we ought to better understand spreadsheet users— all those people who were busy buying somebody else's product. Get to know them up close and personal. So we hired a 1-2-3 lover into our marketing group. Then we videotaped his first encounter with Excel. We discovered that what we had been taking for awe on the part of the focus group members was simply confusion.

It turned out that the first sixty seconds was what mattered the most. Even though this 1-2-3 user had a number of frustrations with the product, he was very comfortable with it and habituated to how it worked. While Excel seemed interesting and different, he frankly had no idea where to start. He kept hitting the backslash key in hopes that something would happen, as it did in 1-2-3. But Excel didn't use the backslash key; nothing happened. He soon turned the program off and went back to what he already knew.

Wow. No wonder customers were rejecting us. With our new in-house 1-2-3 fanatic calling the signals, we ran tests with a number of other fans of the competing product, which gave us a broader picture but confirmed what that first experience had taught us.

So we embarked on a new strategy. We created "Help for 1-2-3 Users" that allowed them to get started on Excel without changing their behavior. When they hit the familiar backslash, the stuff they expected to happen, happened. And we built working models that made it easy for them to test-drive the product before purchase. This broke the logjam.

You already know the outcome.

Are you getting all the tough-love input you need? If you heard the truth about why many people prefer your competitor's product, would you know what to do about it?

How Does Anybody with a Business to Run Do All This Customer Analysis Without Spending Tons of Time and Money?

How do you do it? You can begin to learn a lot about your customers' playing field—for both current customers and potential ones—without conducting expensive market research and without wasting tons of time in focus groups. You can integrate your research into your daily conduct of business. It's not hard.

First, keep it simple.

Start small. Talk to people you know. Talk to employees, salespeople, colleagues in other companies, your family—whoever is the best representative of your customer. Find out what's up in their world; ask about their problems, their needs, their goals. Drill in on their product experience and their issues with it.

Find a group of individual customers you can talk to. Get more out of your existing sales efforts by making sure you use them as a chance to learn. If you haven't already, go on a few sales calls or handle the phones. It's often best to do this with the most demanding customers or prospects. As Bill Gates once said, "Your most unhappy customers are your greatest source of learning." They will tell you the stuff you need to know. Ask tough questions; be prepared for tough answers. If they seem to be telling you only the good stuff that's nice to hear, don't be satisfied; ask again.

One company we work with targeted teens and found out that talking to them was a sure eye-opener. Adolescents aren't afraid to tell you what they think is cool and what isn't. But how about insurance agents? These guys were used to making sure they said the right thing—they didn't want to let down their listener and chance losing a sale. Trained to be polite and agreeable, they just kept smiling. The company folks really had to push to get them to open up about the problems they had with the company's products.

Second, keep it digestible.

As we've seen, your target customer base can be widely diverse. It really helps if you can narrow or break this discovery process into digestible chunks. There are many, many different ways to do this segmentation: competitive, demographic, psychographic, etc. But two ways seem to be most useful: segmenting by the customer's roles in the purchase process, and by their attitudes toward your category's products or technologies.

The Avogadro and American Express examples illustrate the first steps of segmentation by role in the purchase process. Taking this further, you want to know who is most interested, who holds the pocketbook, whose approval is required, and so on. You're looking for the fulcrum or lever—the person whose approval is most important, whose voice on your topic carries the most weight. At Microsoft we broke this typically into four segments or targets:

- The *general business user,* or GBU, who, although belonging to the majority of users, tended to be a follower and had limited influence or none at all;

- The nontechnical *business decision maker,* or BDM, who owned the budget and whose approval was important;
- The *technical decision maker,* or TDM, who generally did not initiate interest in a new product but who often held a veto based on his or her judgment of whether or not it could be implemented;
- Finally, the *influential end user,* or IEU—the enthusiast or resident expert to whom the GBUs and BDMs turned and whose enthusiasm could often overcome or circumvent the objections of the TDM. When we were at Microsoft, we generally found that it was the influential end users who were the fulcrum.

In terms of segmentation by attitudes, one of the most useful approaches involves understanding how quickly and regularly different people or groups adopt new products—where they fit on the spectrum between bleeding edge and laggards. At Microsoft we called the segments regulars, seekers, doubters, and sleepers.

- *Regulars* were those who always bought;
- *Seekers* were those who needed sufficient information first to make a considered choice;
- *Doubters* were those who needed to see others adopt first before they even considered;
- And *sleepers* were those who only came along last, kicking and screaming all the way.

Each of these types of segmentation determines how you refine and even narrow the customer gap you are trying to fill, and when you should attempt to fill it. Those who spend more money become a higher priority. Those who are most receptive offer the easiest place to start.

Third, keep your customer analysis direct.

Doing scientific market research and analysis can be of immense value. But to really absorb the conclusion, you have to get your hands dirty. It's not just business, it has to get personal.

Of course, you need to meet customers up close and look them in the eye. But you can and should go beyond that. You should be one of them. You should make sure you are your own customer. It will keep you honest and it will teach you things you might not otherwise have found out.

For years we tried to understand and influence the purchasing of Office, Word, and Excel by small-business owners. We tried using the same approach with them as we did with large corporations. We tried including all kinds of fancy new products based on focus groups and primary research. None of it worked. It wasn't until we really experienced for ourselves what the small business customers were experiencing that we realized where we were going wrong and changed our strategy.

While we were running all of our focus groups and surveys, a terrific summer intern, Tony Liano, who didn't know any better went out and had business cards printed, and got a few of us to pretend to be small-business people. We did our own "Secret Shopper" research. We'd go into a store, tell the salesperson we were setting ourselves up in business, and ask for his advice. And we'd make it clear that we were very budget- and time-constrained.

The salesperson would start by selling us a bunch of things like office furniture, phones, and faxes. And even when he got around to selling computer technology, it would be all about the newest computer. When it came to software, he'd usually recommend a bookkeeping program and something like a simple contact manager. Office wouldn't even be mentioned. And when we asked, the sales rep would usually try to sell us something from a Microsoft competitor. Why? Because he made a better margin on it.

The same kinds of issues and priorities were confirmed in our direct discussions with other small-business people—who now would talk to us as colleagues. They didn't think of themselves as running small businesses. They saw themselves foremost as contractors, or florists, or accountants.

What an eye-opener. All along we had been doing "small-business" campaigns and "small-business" products, when our target actually did not think of themselves this way. It took some hard turning, but our response was to adapt to their characteristics. We made sure to target vertical industry-specific partners who provided software solutions to small businesses. And we targeted our packaging and presence to complement new PCs and grant incentives to the channels where small businesses bought their overall computing supplies.

How do your own customers think of themselves? Do they refer to themselves with the same kind of category labels you've been pasting on them?

Finally–Keep It Going

It's one thing to make all these terrific discoveries and take action on them. But your business and your customers keep moving. Conditions keep changing. How can you stay on top of these changes, in between big focus groups, SWAT-team secret shopper missions, deep customer dives, and so forth?

For one thing, you don't have to talk to all your customers all the time. The old 80/20 rule can apply here, too. If you can find a limited group of customers (20 percent) who are real experts and who will "tell it like it is," then you have a great start (getting 80 percent of the input you need). Keep the group small enough so that it's easy to talk to them all regularly.

Intelligent Results has done this to great effect. They have a group of expert customers that they call their "kitchen cabinet." They talk to them frequently, asking hard questions and getting hard answers in return. This group of advanced, influential users also keeps them abreast of trends in the industry and the competition.

Make talks with such a group of people an ongoing part of your planning process. Thank and honor them for helping you. In some cases, you can make them advisors or even board members. You can meet regularly (but not so frequently that you wear out your welcome).

With input from all these friends and customers, you can begin to develop a theory around all you're learning. You can build a conceptual model of your target customer. This is an ideal or archetype of the customer or set of customers you've met, what we call your "canonical buyer"—an amalgam embodied in an imaginary person or character who represents your target customers' characteristics and attitudes.

In the Microsoft Office group, we created just such a simulated personality. We called him Joe Schlabatt, and he became our own personalized embodiment of the average user. Not some abstract job title, for us he represented a mindset, a collection of attitudes and experiences.

In very serious meetings about product usability or to check the simplicity of our messages, we always asked ourselves, "Would Joe Schlabatt get this? Would he use this?"

Sometimes we would also role play with Joe—developing a sort of virtual debating society with different team members taking on different core personalities and attitudes. It was a great way to flesh things out.

Even though he was fictional, Joe was a huge help. And we grew quite fond of him.

Whether you're in a big company needing to be refreshed or a start-up trying to break in, whether you are trying to reach an entirely new set of customers or keep the ones you have happy, doing your customer ABCs will help guide your core strategy or play. It will allow you to truly target your efforts and it will help define your offering to that target.

Take-Aways for Analyzing Your Customers' Playing Field

1. Remember, you probably don't know your customers as well as you think you do. Start by identifying who you think your target is. Be specific.

2. Find out their ABCs. Call one of your toughest customers, meet with them, ask hard questions. Knowing where they stand, what's missing, and what's in the way tells you where the opportunity is.

3. Remember that your customers have alternatives and that they are also being targeted by your competitors. Your customers define your offering. Their critical needs are what you should design your offering around. Understand their motivations and make sure you have what matters to them most.

4. Customers are the ones who pay you. Follow the money, all of it. Ignore at your peril anyone who touches your revenue stream. Put your highest priority on the guys who spend the most. The folks who are most receptive provide the opportunity as the easiest place to start.

5. Make sure you're really listening. Don't just accept at face value everything you hear. Get your hands dirty. Don't wait for market research, but roll up your sleeves and ask your customers what they think about your product. Be one of them. Use your imagination to understand them. Keep it going. Never stop learning more about your customers.

Coming Up

By focusing on your customers, you narrow the field of your homework in some very useful ways. Now go ahead and narrow it some more. The next part of mapping your playing field takes a hard look at the other players running around on it: your competitors.

You have to play this game like someone just hit your mother with a two-by-four.

—DAN BIRDWELL, DEFENSIVE LINEMAN, OAKLAND RAIDERS

10. Your Competitive Playing Field

Want to make your life easier? Go out and find some really stiff opposition.

OK, maybe not easier. But definitely more interesting, in just about every way. Ever notice how a kid will ignore a toy until another kid starts to play with it? Then they begin to fight over it. It's true in business, too. Things get a lot more interesting when a little competition enters the picture.

In some ways, competition is what your Playbook is all about. It's incredibly valuable to spend time learning about your customers and their motivations, issues, and needs. But you and your target customers are not alone on the playing field. Count on your customers to weigh your vision, your mission, and your promises against the alternatives being spread temptingly in front of them by your competition.

Winning means winning relative to competition. Understanding these competitors is the third element of doing your homework.

Some competitors can do all kinds of good things for you. They can warm up the market; they can generate attention and interest.

Serious competitors keep you on your toes. There's nothing like healthy rivalry to motivate action. It's hard to be lazy when someone else is trying to eat your lunch.

If you study them properly, competitors will give you ideas, point out opportunities, and identify pitfalls that you might not find on your own. They will deepen your understanding of your customers and, as you will see later, even of yourself. In other words, they will give you a playing field on which to test and improve all of the analysis you have done so far.

It's not as tough as you might think. But it means you'll have to go behind enemy lines. You'll have to discover their strengths and weaknesses, and find out their plans. Dangerous? Not really. We're not suggesting espionage, we're suggesting homework. And it starts with the same type of handy gap analysis you've done before.

Turning a Great Offering into a Competitive Weapon

A company called Pure Networks illustrates the incredible importance of digging into your competition. Pure had great insight into their industry and a compelling new technology. This technology, the basis for a new approach for home networking, promised to solve many of the problems that users had been struggling with. The company seemed to be the first movers in the market. They were all alone. And then everything changed.

Pure Networks had a lot going for it. But, not unlike in most small companies, even those with tremendous innovation, the founders woke up one morning and discovered they were no longer alone. They found themselves confronting industry giants breathing down their necks. Of course, if you're doing anything worthwhile, this is inevitable—especially in technology. It may be scary, but, if it's unavoidable, you might as well find a way to make the best of it.

The founders had spent decades as leaders in the personal computing business before starting their current company. They specialized in making computers and networks easier for ordinary, everyday humans. By 2003, home networking had dramatically increased in size with the advent of wireless networking. No more complicated cables. Just plug a box into the wall and go.

Home networking routers not only comprised the fastest growing category but also had the highest return rate of any computer product ever. Up to 50 percent of all home network hardware was brought back to the store or sent back to the Internet retailer. There was a huge customer disconnect. The stuff was great as long as it worked. If it didn't, suddenly the average user found himself drowning in a sea of acronyms and complexity.

The Pure Networks team had invented a revolutionary approach to networking to overcome this problem (Fig. 10–1). They developed a new generation of hardware router that came with incredibly easy-to-use software that would make it trivial to set up the equipment and establish security. And they were excited about bringing it to market.

When they went out to show their solution to prospects, they found agreement everywhere that the available products were not cutting the mustard; people agreed that their new approach was unique and timely.

Then, suddenly, almost simultaneously, the major home networking vendors announced products that offered nearly every feature of the Pure Networks systems. The very next week, Cisco acquired Linksys, the 70 percent leader in networking, bringing huge resources to the table. And prices began falling. Home networking routers dropped in price from $250 to $50 in a little more than six months as Linksys, D-link, Netgear, SMC, and a host of others competed mercilessly on price in a Drag Race to the finish.

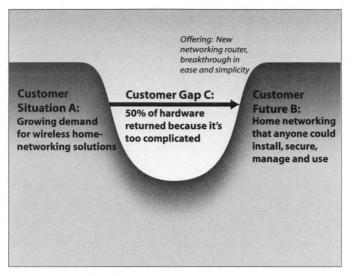

Offering: New networking router, breakthrough in ease and simplicity

Customer Situation A:
Growing demand for wireless home-networking solutions

Customer Gap C:
50% of hardware returned because it's too complicated

Customer Future B:
Home networking that anyone could install, secure, manage and use

Fig. 10–1. Pure Networks' customer ABCs

Some big guys had crashed the party. Disaster for the start-up. Or so you might think.

Pure Networks now faced a big challenge. They had to explain how they were different and why that particular "different" was better. How did they do that? They went back to their homework and took a fresh look at their assessment of the industry, the customers, and their own technology, with an eye toward the competition.

Here's the process.

What Are You Up Against?

Pure dug in deep. They read everything they could about these competitive offerings. They studied all the announcements and advertisements. They asked their prospective customers what they thought and how they had been pitched by Cisco and Netgear. And as soon as each new competitive product became available, they bought and road tested it.

They asked themselves, What is the competition's product line? How does it compare to ours? What are its strengths? What are its weaknesses? Where are the gaps? What claims and promises are they making, what comparisons? How true are they? Again, most importantly, all this had to be assessed through the eyes of the customers.

This investigation generated loads of priceless information. The big guys had done their own homework on the customers and built worthy products. This was going to be tough. Pure accepted the idea that they could not beat the competition on every dimension, but felt confident that they would be able to beat them on several.

The sheer size and clout of Cisco and the other big networking vendors, with their high volumes and their established distribution channels, meant that it would be tough to win with hardware. A start-up like Pure could never match them in those areas.

So Pure abandoned their hardware approach. They didn't go head-to-head, instead focusing on a weak point they recognized in design: poor interaction between the PCs users were trying to connect together in their home network and the network routers manufactured by these big vendors. Rather than forcing customers to replace a Linksys box, Pure decided that they could offer a way of managing any box or combination of boxes from the user's PC. They focused on offering network management software—an add-on for networking hardware rather than an alternative.

They had found a competitive gap. By focusing on this gap they were able to define a sustainable market position worth claiming (Fig. 10–2). Their solution would work across any hardware router in the home. By repositioning Pure into this competitive gap, they again became leaders in a new field, the home network operating system.

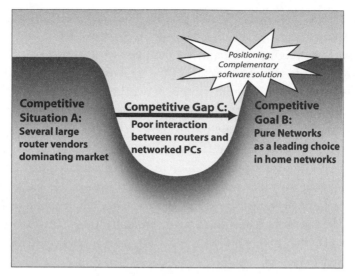

Fig. 10–2. Pure Networks' competitive ABCs

In launching this kind of process for your own company, ask yourself what your competitors' strengths and weaknesses are. Are you positioned correctly to avoid their strengths and exploit their weaknesses?

What Are Your Competitors' Targets and Priorities?

Pure knew that the big competitors were fearsome but also that they were hardware companies focused on selling boxes. They had lots of revenues, but very small profits. They were experts at manufacturing and at quickly integrating new designs from the computer chip manufacturers, but relied on third parties to write their software. This colored their thinking and affected their targeting and positioning. Focused on hardware, they could not really afford to be truly targeted in their offerings—they had to push fast product cycles at low margins to remain competitive.

Pure could ride the coattails of the big guys in terms of PR and awareness for the overall home networking category. Linksys, D-link, and the others were great at preparing the battlefield (remember, they were competing against each other, too). Free from worrying about the awareness issue, Pure could rise above the fray and target its offering as an add-on to the hardware. Within months of realizing this, the company got their software included with a major home networking vendor as a value-added. By being willing to make the radical shift from hardware/software products to software only, they had literally turned a competitor into a distribution partner.

Do you have a good sense of where your competitors are spending their time? Do you know their hot buttons? Can you match these to the map of the customer playing field and find the holes?

How Do Your Competitors Make Money?

Understanding how your competitors make money leads you directly to their priorities and issues. You should look for where their resources are deployed, how many people they have, and in which departments. How do they sell? What are their channels of distribution and the mix of these channels? Across their product lines, which ones are the cash cows and the growth engines, and which are the pet experiments or the backwaters?

Linksys and D-link have very well defined business models. They drive for high-volume sales through high-volume channels. They have relatively low margins, but their goal is to get inexpensive boxes out there and then move on to the next generation.

Pure chose to become the flip side. They focused on the ISPs that connect homes together and so really care about managing support calls. Pure's networking software allowed broadband ISPs like AOL and Comcast to diagnose problems remotely and lower the cost of support. Instead of entering the retail channel and going head-to-head with hardware vendors, Pure found a different channel and exploited it.

In short order, Pure had a multimillion-dollar contract from a major ISP that wanted to extend their service offerings and their consumer products. By complementing the hardware vendors, Pure ended up with a highly lucrative contract that didn't rely on managing inventory and having great retail distribution.

Do you understand your competitors' business models? Do you know how they make money and how this affects their decisions? Does this create any blind spots you can sneak up on?

Thinking Ahead

Anticipate competitive threats and opportunities. Try to predict your competitors' strategies and their next moves.

In order to do this you have to begin to think like them. To understand their customers and products as well as how they think, act, and make money, you need to create hypotheses that help you project into the future.

Assume that your competitors are not stupid. If they have weaknesses that you are exploiting, expect them to work hard to fix the problems. Put yourself in their shoes. What would you do if you were them? What investments would you make? What changes to the product line, positioning, or pricing? What would you be most worried about and what would you do about it? Make sure

you are designing your plans based not just on what your competitors are doing today but on what they might do next.

Don't Be Proud–Use Your Competitors to Look for Good Ideas

A long-time colleague, Dennis Tevlin, recently told us his jungle theory of company behavior. As he sees it, there are three kinds of companies: gorillas, chimps, and monkeys. Gorillas just squash things. Chimps think hard about things. And monkeys follow the old adage, "Monkey see, monkey do." Not every company can be a gorilla. Sometimes knowing the right answers isn't good enough. But even though imitation may be the highest form of flattery, it's often also the most efficient path to product planning. If a competitor is doing something right, you avoid imitation at your peril.

Pure benefited in many ways from having competition enter its category. They found new awareness, new focus, and new differentiation. Based on this, the company was able to stake out a unique and desirable—meaning high-performance—position in the marketplace. That, of course, is the good part. They still have to work like hell to maintain that position. And they can never let down their guard.

For better or worse, competition is a fact of life. You are not alone on the playing field.

So, Who Is Your Competition Anyway? Start by Minding Your Ps and Qs

What does your map look like? Are you the high-priced exclusive offering, battling it out to retain your premium position? Are you the low-cost supplier struggling to maintain your cost advantage?

Or are you duking it out to win the hearts and minds and pocket-books of the great big middle?

How do your customers see this map laid out in terms of their alternatives? Where do they see your competitors relative to you? Where are the gaps?

We've already introduced the concept of the Ps and Qs map in Chapter Two and elsewhere as we looked at the individual plays. The map is a tool you will use over and over again, so let's look at it in greater depth.

A Ps and Qs map shows you not only the layout of the competition but also the choices your customers have to make. So if you lay it out right, it shows you the courses of action available to you.

Fig. 10–3 shows the playing field, which represents your category with quantity (or total volume) on the X axis and price on the Y axis. Now you have to fill it in.

Let's take another look at how useful the Ps and Qs can be by examining the desktop publishing field in terms of the classic Best-of-

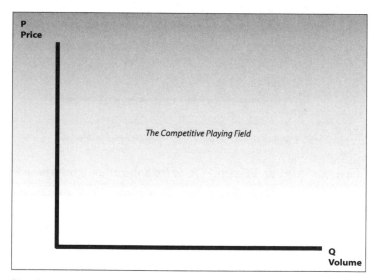

Fig. 10–3. The Ps and Qs playing field

Both Play that happened in that industry segment. It's interesting, because at first, when the category was just getting started, there really was only a high-end offering in the market.

At the time, Interleaf was the main player, offering a really expensive, totally proprietary solution that was hardware-based and sold to publishing companies (Fig. 10–4). No one but professionals used it. But for that matter, at that time no one but professionals did the publishing tasks of layout, paste-up, and so on. And for them, Interleaf was the gold standard.

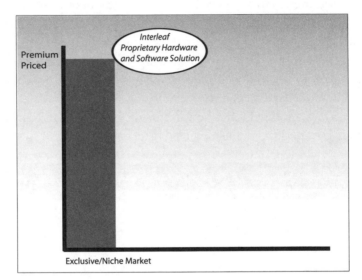

Fig. 10–4. Early desktop publishing—for professionals only

Then along came PCs and GUIs (graphical user interfaces). In particular, along came the Apple Macintosh, and things really changed.

For the comparatively moderate expense of a word processor and an adequate printer, an average person could now make halfway-decent-looking newsletters with relative ease. Publishing was no longer the exclusive preserve of professionals. In this simple form, it had become a mass market (Fig. 10–5).

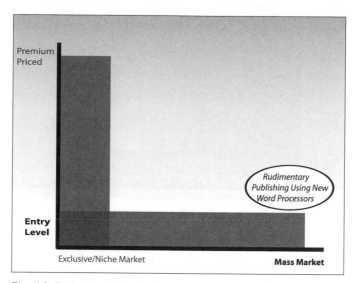

Fig. 10–5. A new entry-level market

But still, a word processor lacked a ton of the functionality of professional publishing. A huge gap remained, waiting to be filled. Along came Aldus with their PageMaker software; when it hit the market, everything changed again.

Aldus targeted PageMaker to this middle ground (Fig. 10–6). They sought to bridge the gap between professional publishing and word processing, bringing the best of both together. Although the price was relatively high compared to other software, it was nothing compared to the professional, proprietary systems. PageMaker had great functionality and it worked at first on any Mac and then on any PC.

This was great. It truly showed a new, middle way. In fact, this middle way was so big and juicy that it attracted a score of con-

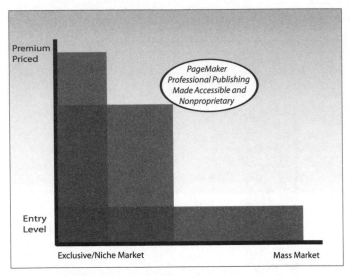

Fig. 10–6. Aldus PageMaker makes the high-end accessible.

tenders. The true battle for desktop publishing had begun. Ventura Publishing, Photo Deluxe, and others began to vie for owning that rich lode in the middle of the market (Fig. 10–7).

Meanwhile word processors were getting better and better. All of this put pressure on the manufacturers to develop greater functional depth and robustness of the products. And it put them under pressure on prices and on margins.

With each of these players trying to get the others' customers to switch, in the end even Aldus had to find a way to compete on price. In addition, a whole host of supporting companies and products cropped up—fonts, font managers, printer managers, and so on—all finding a way to make money from a category that had only just been created.

Eventually the category expanded beyond its container. Most of these companies and products had to combine in order to keep up with the rapidly expanding market expectations as the capabilities

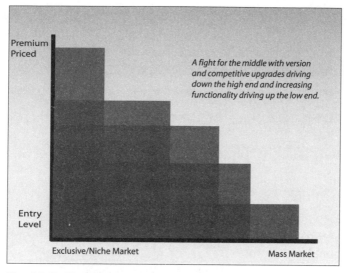

Fig. 10-7. The fight for the middle

and value propositions grew with each more fully integrated software product.

When you construct your own competitive map, what does it look like? Are you the high-priced, exclusive offering, fighting it out to retain your premium position? Are you the low-cost supplier struggling to maintain your cost advantage? Or are you battling it out to win the hearts and minds and pocketbooks of the great big middle?

How do your customers see their alternatives? Where are your competitors relative to you? Where are the gaps?

The Ps and Qs map is a tool you should refer back to regularly—when you look at competition, when you look at customers, and when you look at yourself. If you lay the map out accurately and examine it closely, it will reveal the courses of action available to you, and you'll use the map in choosing your play. If you keep it simple, there are only a few basic possible configurations of the Ps and Qs map; the configuration you find yourself in is a key indicator you'll use in determining which play is best suited to your needs.

Look Everywhere–Just Because You're Paranoid Doesn't Mean That Everyone *Isn't* Out to Get You

You probably already have a good list of competitors to lay out on your Ps and Qs map. But as already noted, some of your biggest threats may not come from the obvious sources. Here's how we like to group competitors:

> Companies that are actually attacking you
> Companies that seem friendly or complementary

Companies That Are Actually Attacking You

Have you ever noticed how we sometimes tend to see our major competitor as inevitable, and spend our efforts on other things? Your major competitors are the companies that directly target you and your customer base. They are the ones claiming that they are better than you and attempting to steal market share from you and everyone else in the game. These are the guys you find confronting you in customer pitches. In this sense, competitors in your category often pose the most serious short-term threat and will be the immediate focus of your play. The fact is that you cannot afford to overlook them or take them for granted.

Companies That Seem Friendly
or Complementary

Trust no one. Sometimes companies that seem friendly or complementary can pose an important long-term threat. They have the same customers as you; they may actually be partnering with you. Watch out!

You need to make sure that your customers are well aware of the value you provide so that your position with them is safe and defensible. Sometimes a complementary product can become perceived as more valuable than the original. If you aren't careful, in the process of reducing your costs or enhancing your offering, seemingly friendly partners can take over mindshare in the market and end up owning the customer relationship. If they do this deeply enough, they may unseat you. The culprit company may not even be in your own category but in a related one.

For example, most insurance carriers rely on big networks of local and regional independent agents to represent them, selling their products and handling a lot of the customer relations. Sound like good partners, right? Well, most of the time. But about two hundred new insurance carriers are formed each year in the United States. Of these, the majority are actually started by these very same independent agents. Having long histories and direct personal experience in their local towns, these agents know who are the best customers in their market, who are the lowest risk, who are the most regular payers. What's more, these agents have been the true face of the insurance company to most of their customers. Not the faceless, remote firm in some distant city represented only by a logo on the form they fill out and the invoice they receive.

With the agent's knowledge and the customer's loyalty, it's relatively easy for an agent to attract the capital required for setting himself up in business and then shaving off the best customers as the initial base for his new, competitive insurance carrier. What's worse (or better, depending on your point of view) is that all this can happen right under the big carrier's nose without their ever recognizing what has gone on.

What Other Things Might Your Customers Spend Their Money On?

Most everybody overlooks this one. Remember what you are ultimately competing for: your customers' money. And they have lots of other things to spend that money on. In this sense you can define your competition as anything that might take precedence over you in your customers' pocketbooks. Add to that the factors of inertia and the choice of saving money rather than spending it. Together, these can add up to one of the strongest forces you have to compete with. These priorities crowd you just as effectively as a strong direct competitor: less of your customers' money lands in your coffers.

This is another thing we learned after we went on a secret shopper mission for Microsoft, claiming that we were starting a small business. Most small businesses at the time cared a lot more about things like office furniture, courting potential clients, and paying their employees than they did about computers or software. In this sense, we had to make sure we were competing effectively for their attention.

Every day, you compete for the privilege of serving your customers' needs. You must make sure you drive a sense of urgency in your customers' minds. Looking at the situation from this perspective reminds you that you need to stay aware of alternative means of serving that need, and stay aware, as well, of new entrants to the market. This is where defining your category broadly enough can matter most. If you thought of yourself in the portable CD player business, you would see the Sony Walkman as your top competition. But if you saw yourself in the portable music business, you would have to look at the emergence of a much broader range including MP3 players, cell phone music, and more.

It's Not Enough to Know Who and Where Your Competitors Are–You Need to Know How to Beat Them

What are the other priorities competing for your customers' attention? Do you consider these the competition?

Back in 1993, in the local area networking (LAN) software market, Microsoft LAN Manager had 3 percent market share, against Novell Netware's 60 percent. We who marketed LAN Manager knew that we had a big task ahead of us. Novell was the industry standard. If we were going to win, we were going to have to chip away at them. We built what we thought was a strong competitive strategy. Unfortunately this strategy was based on a set of assumptions about the products, not a truly deep study of them.

We felt that the Novell product was rigid, that it suffered from requiring network administrators to set up shared file systems over a network, and that it was really only high performance in certain limited applications and "small-I/O" (or limited-capacity) environments. We also thought that their pricing was complicated, with tons of different product options. Based on these assumptions, we felt, we *knew,* that we had the better product. Our strategy was to emphasize the ease and simplicity of our file server, "large I/O," and one low price.

But much like our experience with Excel recounted in the previous chapter, we didn't make a dent in market share; it remained Microsoft, 3 percent, and Novell, 60 percent.

Huh? Why weren't people buying our stuff? Why were they staying with Novell? We must be missing something.

We decided that we ought to get to know the competitive landscape better. First, we talked to distributors, tore apart their financials, and talked to customers and to our own salespeople. We discovered that despite all the supposed complexity in their public product and price sheets, Novell really made most of their money (95 percent revenue per user) on a simple $100, low-functionality "runtime" edition. So much for the huge new advantage coming from one low price.

Next, we became their customer. One of our team members went out and became a "Certified Novell Expert." She took all the classes and tests. One of the things that immediately struck her was language. Novell customers had developed and were used to a specific set of terms associated with the company's products. Because we had built a new product with much improved functionality, we had new words for everything. For example, what we called NetUse, they called MapRoot. At that point we realized our words were confusing the heck out of our targets. Novell had invented the terminology, and we were going to have to live with it.

Then we got to know their organization and people. We sought out and met their VPs at tradeshows. It really helped to see and talk with these guys face to face. It turned out that they had a major culture difference between their teams in Provo, Utah, and San Jose, California. We had always thought the San Jose crowd were the ones to beat. But we learned that the Provo guys held the power. It was critical for us to anticipate their reactions.

Finally, we got to know their customers. It turned out that customers didn't know what a LAN was. They thought of it as the network. Eighty percent of them stored everything on one server. Because most of them thought of this as one big blob, they never needed to understand where all the nodes were. And they never really had any use for our hot feature NetUse. Oh, yeah, and 95 percent of the applications that they ran were only "small-I/O" anyway. So much for our vaunted, robust "large-I/O" advantage.

What a wake-up call. There's nothing like knowing that the advantages you think you have over your competitors don't really matter to customers. So we repositioned ourselves. NT Server (evolving out of LAN Manager) became a "multipurpose" server operating system that combined the abilities of NetWare with the advantages of the UNIX operating system. In addition, we made it easier to set up and administer than either NetWare or UNIX. Rather than continuing to tout our newness, we took a much more grounded approach, showing how we outperformed on common tasks like file and print.

This strategy made a huge difference and really helped Microsoft NT for the first time gain a strong foothold in the network world.

How You'll Do It

Remember what Don Vito Corleone said in *The Godfather?* "Keep your friends close and your enemies closer."

Just as you have learned how to keep track of your customers and your competitor's customers, you also have to get to know your competition—and get to know them well. As much as you may think you know your competition, they are always moving and changing. If you respond and make changes, you can expect them to, as well. It takes real work to keep on top of what they're doing. It pays to make tracking them a disciplined process—one that's a normal course of business.

Here are some basic outlines of how to make that happen effectively and without making yourself any more paranoid than you need to be.

FIRST, CONDUCT ACTIVE RECONNAISSANCE.

Make understanding and tracking the competition part of people's jobs. You can spread such reconnaissance tasks across your team or, even better, break them into specific roles, or take on the job yourself of playing these roles.

Deploy scouts. You can recruit the business expert, who's equipped to understand all elements of the competition's organization and business. And the product wonk, who's a real user and knows their products upside down and sideways. The Web site surfer, who keeps scouring their sites and other related sites for any changes or hints of breaking news. In addition, it's great if you can find the gone-native sales rep or channel partner who really understands what you're up against in sales situations.

Remember the kitchen cabinet. Gather your best candidates—inside the company and outside—into a group you can keep going back to.

Keep your eyes open in your recruiting efforts. Sometimes your best source of competitive information comes from new hires or folks you interview, as long as you aren't asking for anything that crosses the line. It doesn't hurt to find retired competitive company execs and get them to be advisors or board members.

One firm we know found that their chief competitor had acquired a company a year or so earlier, an acquisition that was not the friendliest. Plenty of the top execs and key employees of the newly acquired firm were mucho displeased, in part because their new CEO had very different ideas and a very different culture than what they were used to. The new folks felt they didn't fit in. And many of them didn't last. There was no love lost between the newly jobless and the folks they had left behind, but those who had left took with them great insights on their former company's priorities and operating methods. The man who had been CEO of the acquired company became a valued advisor to our portfolio company, and several of their formerly discontented salespeople became among their top performers. It's easy to find out whom your competitors have acquired. Just look up the company's financial disclosures on the Web. There are lots of good, easy sources of facts. So . . .

IDENTIFY AND SCOUR THE RIGHT INFORMATION SOURCES.

If you're not already aware of it, you'll be dazzled by the amount of information about companies that's readily available. The Web has done nothing but make this easier. In fact, there is often so much information that it's overwhelming to comb through it all. Here are some places to start.

Of course, you've already looked at analyst reports, some of which are very, very good. If it's a public company, you're certainly already looking at their quarterly and annual reports. Not just the numbers but the commentary. What they say about themselves and how they say it can be incredibly revealing. They often tell you about things like painful organizational changes and failing research projects, if you read between the lines.

Also, make it a point to listen to the conference calls that the execs give—the ones that used to be just for the Wall Street community but are now required to be open to all. These calls cover tough questions and can yield highly valuable insight into how the company execs think.

Follow the news. Most good financial Web sites allow you to set up newsflashes on all the announcements and new coverage of companies you select. We used to set up an e-mail alias for the teams that followed each competitor. Now it's even easier to share all this information and chat about it, with tools like Instant Messaging (IM) and internal blogs (Web logs) where everyone can post revealing tidbits they've come across.

Watch your competitor's marketing, which will tell you a lot about the company and how they perceive themselves. Do they want to be cool? Are they aggressive? Are they Mister Rogers?

Look at Oracle. Most of its ads are designed to attack someone, even in categories where they lead; it's apparently ingrained in the corporate culture—they just can't help it. This gives you a hint of what their knee-jerk responses might be. Look at Coke and Pepsi. If one launches something new, the other will follow. IBM, on the other hand, doesn't run ads making comparisons, no matter what.

Try to understand the image your competition has in the market, which will tell you a lot about their strengths and their constraints. If they really own that image in the market, don't try to own it as well. If they are perceived as safe and reliable, it will be hard for them to win on revolutionary innovation. If they are seen as super-aggressive, it will be difficult for them to win on being a good partner. For good or for bad, companies, like people, have a hard time overcoming their reputations.

KEEP IT DIRECT. GET YOUR HANDS DIRTY.

Remember that talking directly to your competitors' customers is an absolutely essential part of understanding their strengths and weaknesses, in the terms that matter the most. But, beyond this, there is nothing like actually *being* a customer of your competitors' products or services to understand the true situation. There are several things you can and should do to make this happen.

First and foremost, buy their products, especially advanced releases. Use them like crazy and evaluate them relative to your own.

At Microsoft, Lotus Notes was another competitive product we really needed to understand. We had built this great e-mail and collaboration product called Exchange. It was doing pretty well, but we couldn't understand why it was continuing to lose in competitive situations with Notes, especially at the departmental level (versus IT purchases across the whole enterprise). In fact, there was a large number of accounts where we were selling some Exchange but running into roadblocks because people were using both Exchange and Notes. That just didn't seem to make any sense.

So we tagged our own resident Exchange bigot to figure it out. Scott Gode was the product manager on Exchange and he loved it with a passion. We told him that he had to buy Notes and use it to build and run an internal application for our group. This was not without controversy. At Microsoft we had a strong philosophy of "eating our own dog food." We could not rip out our core e-mail infrastructure of Exchange. So this would have to be a mixed environment with both products—just like those installations that had confounded us. We picked an important but not mission-critical application—project management for a marketing campaign. You guessed it—our competitive Exchange vs. Notes campaign. We contracted a Lotus Notes solution provider to help us. We installed the product. And then we used it.

And a funny thing happened. Lo and behold, it worked. And it worked well. Scott discovered that the little departmental application was great. It was easy to build. It didn't take too long to get it running, and it was easy to learn and use. Now we understood why so many customers used both Exchange and Notes together. And we were able to respond in our product plan. We made sure to add this flexibility and programmability into the product. It made Exchange a much more attractive product, across the whole enterprise.

We mentioned earlier how being a secret shopper can help you understand customers. Doing the same thing can really help you understand the competitors. Here again, act as if you were comparison shopping. Go to the store, the Web sites; call the salespeople and go through the process of evaluating and purchasing. See what salespeople and partners recommend, how and why.

You've seen how much value you can gain out of having one of your people become a certified expert in the competitive product. You can get similar insight by joining their user groups and going to their presentations, seminars, Webinars, and so on. All these things will help you better understand how your customers think of both of you. And it will keep you humble.

FINALLY, MAKE IT RELEVANT AND ACTIONABLE . . . AND THEN KEEP IT GOING.

Remember, competitors will respond. Make sure you anticipate their next moves. One easy and fun way to do this is with an exercise called Playing the Red Flag.

It's a simple simulation where you put together all you have learned into a kind of game. You think through core differences and plans between you and your competitor. What are the most important gaps? What would you do about them now if you were on the other side? You play out your own plans and then you think like the other side. Imagine their thrust and parry.

Thrust: What would their frontal response be? Given the nature of their organization, how would they reposition against anything you do? What would their forty-eight-hour response be?

Parry: Understand which acts serve as a mere distraction and which are an attempt to hurt you where it counts the most.

Putting It All Together

Whether you are in a big company needing to be refreshed or a start-up trying to break in, whether you are attempting to enter a new market against entrenched competitors or to defend yourself against pesky newcomers, doing your competitive ABCs and learning your Ps and Qs will help you talk to your customers in their own language, and respond to competitors in terms that will be effective.

Take-Aways for Analyzing Your Competitive Playing Field

1. Face the music. Remember, having strong competition keeps you on your toes. Embrace the challenge of understanding them incredibly well.

2. Do your competitive ABCs. Your competitors define your differentiation. It is in comparison to them that your offering will be evaluated. Knowing where your competition stands, their strengths and weaknesses, and what to anticipate from them tells you what position is worth shooting for and how hard it will be to get. Understand their motivations and anticipate their next moves and responses to your actions.

3. Leave no stone unturned. Your enemies won't always declare themselves. Make sure to look for them everywhere. Most importantly, look for them through your customers' eyes. Whatever competes for your customers' attention competes with you.

4. Use the simple Ps and Qs to map where the money is made. Look for the gaps. This is a key input to choosing your play.

5. Never stop. Make sure you take what you learn to heart. Make it a part of your job and that of your team. Be your competitors' customers. Use their products. Think like them. Imagine what they would do. Be ready.

Coming Up

Focusing on your competition heats things up. Next we turn the spotlight on the one element you ought to have the most control over: yourself.

If you know the enemy and yourself, you need not fear a hundred battles. If you know yourself but not the enemy, for every victory you will also suffer a defeat. If you know neither the enemy nor yourself, you will succumb in every battle.

—SUN TZU

11. Assessing Your Own Capabilities

What's the most entrenched obstacle on your playing field? Look in the mirror.

Meet your most tenacious opponent. No matter what you do, he or she can always undo all of your best plans. This formidable opponent can invalidate all of the intelligence and analysis you have done and turn it against you.

Who is this most fearsome adversary? You, of course.

No matter how much homework you do on the industry, on your customers, and on your competitors, none of it matters if you aren't honest with yourself. Honest about the real needs of your customers and how well or poorly you are serving them. Honest about the strengths and weaknesses of your rivals, the threats they pose, and your readiness to meet them.

Most importantly, all this homework is squandered if you aren't truly honest about your own abilities and your shortcomings.

Even when companies understand the opportunity fully, they will fail to successfully achieve if they don't know what they need to invest in to make it possible. Even with the best intelligence, companies succumb to competitive threats when they don't spend the right amount of energy arming themselves to meet the threats. And even with everything else in place, companies unwittingly surrender their position in the market when they don't admit their failures in meeting customer expectations and don't learn what they need to do to overcome them.

Winning means being in shape for the game. And you can't get in shape if you aren't willing to get on the scale and weigh yourself once in a while. Then it's time to exercise. No pain, no gain.

Before you choose a play that may make sense for your market situation but doesn't match your own capabilities and competencies, take a good long look in the mirror. And then get started doing what you need to do to enhance those abilities or offset your shortcomings.

The ABCs of Self-Discovery–Turning Vision and Competitive Spirit into a Real Ability to Succeed

McCaw Cellular, a truly successful, truly driven company, was inspired by a great vision: people communicating anywhere, anytime they wanted, no longer tethered by the length of their telephone cord. They were pioneers in using wireless technology to offer mobile telephony service to tons of customers and in creating what amounted to a whole new industry. They developed a leading position in this industry against mounting competition.

Back in 1990, they seemed to have it all wrapped up—great vision, great offering, strong position in the marketplace. Or did they? The challenge they faced, and the steps they took to meet that challenge, provide a textbook case of assessing your own capabilities and using that understanding to shape your product strategy (Fig. 11–1).

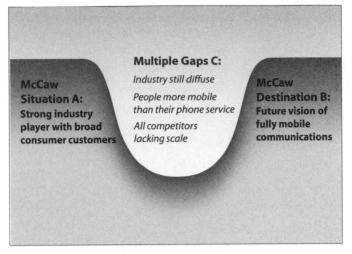

Multiple Gaps C:

Industry still diffuse

People more mobile than their phone service

All competitors lacking scale

McCaw Situation A: Strong industry player with broad consumer customers

McCaw Destination B: Future vision of fully mobile communications

Fig. 11–1. McCaw Cellular's overall ABCs

First, make sure that you really know where you are.

The company leadership—Craig McCaw, Nick Kauser, Rob Mechaley, and Steve Hooper—were not complacent or easily satisfied. They took a step back and realized that they were still far off from reaching their true vision.

Sure, McCaw customers (or the customers of any wireless carrier, for that matter) could use their cell phones in the car, walking around, even out on the boat—so long as they were in the network's coverage area. Sure, McCaw had built the leading network with arguably the best coverage. But these guys knew their customers. They knew because they had walked in their customers' shoes. All that any one of these McCaw execs had to do was hop on a plane to see how far they were from fully reaching their goal. Just land in a city where McCaw hadn't yet built a network and try to make a call. Nothing. Nada. So much for the promise of truly mobile communications.

And most of their customers actually did travel, all over the country. The result: grumpy customers—customers whose expectations had been heightened by the mobile experience, but who had had those expectations frustrated because of the shortcomings of the providers.

Well, that just would not do. These guys had to find an answer.

Second, look closely for what's missing and what's in the way.

The McCaw team took a close look at their own capabilities. And they made a hard-nosed assessment of their own gaps—the gaps between what they themselves could do in the near term and what they wanted to achieve for their customers.

The costs of building out a network were very high. It was already tough to build and maintain all the infrastructure required to serve their customers at a reasonable cost. But everyone else in the industry was struggling downfield toward the same goal line. Craig McCaw and his team had studied their competitors and knew that the other guys were struggling with the same problem. The gap was the same for everyone.

The McCaw folks were honest about their own shortcomings. Here's where their insight came into play. Alone, all any one of these carriers could offer was coverage within their own network, which, regardless of how aggressively they were investing, would continue to be severely limited. It was a simple function of time, resources, and geography. But if you wove all these networks together, they made a patchwork quilt of coverage that would allow true mobile communications for the user almost no matter where in the U.S. they traveled.

Third, be honest about what you can and cannot do about it.

The resources of even the greatest companies have limits. Even the most powerful companies cannot achieve all their goals immediately. McCaw was following one of the most important lessons: mapping out what's needed to solve a problem and being realistic about how long it will take you to get a solution in place.

If only they could find a way to connect these networks and allow their customers to get access to them as they traveled. Driven, passionate, highly competitive, but also pragmatic and honest with themselves, the McCaw leaders figured out the way. They put themselves in their competitors' shoes. They knew the only practical solution would have to overcome a number of constraints. Because they understood all these, deeply, they knew what action plan was needed (Fig. 11-2).

Fourth, understand your own stakes and economics.

The solution would have to be win–win. All the cellular companies would have to continue to make money from their own customers regardless of which network was providing them service. And vice versa: the carriers needed to know that their networks would not get barraged by other carriers' customers without at least enough compensation to cover their costs. And all this had to happen while weaving together these competing networks.

It must have taken a horrendous amount of convincing and cajoling, but McCaw managed to corral the key players, who came to-

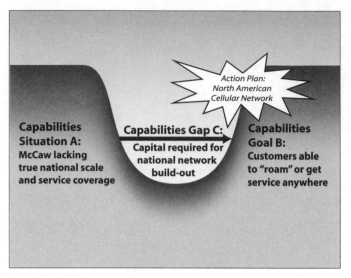

Fig. 11–2. McCaw's action plan to fill the capabilities gap

gether as the North American Cellular Network (NACN), dedicated to bringing seamless nationwide roaming to life.

The NACN was basically a giant clearinghouse for managing and reconciling all the traffic of one carrier's customers as they migrated on and off other carriers' networks. But it was much more complicated than that. There was a lot of technology involved to make sure these transitions and hand-offs were seamless and made sense (and the McCaw guys like Rob Mechaley and Nick Kauser happened to have invented the technology that made this possible). Complex money matters (rates, payment settlements, reconciliation) had to be worked out, too; all this needed mechanisms and processes. Oh, yeah, and they had to get most of their competitors to sign up for it to get off the ground.

Whole books could be written about this story, but suffice it to say, their plan worked. And the result is one we still benefit from today every time we travel outside the coverage area of our carrier and roam. Last but definitely not least, the other result was that McCaw was in the driver's seat when it came to roaming charges and ability to attract national customers most quickly.

Fifth, think ahead.

What does the future hold? Given the likely next moves of your competitors and the changing expectations of your customers, what do you need to be investing in?

Because of their honest assessment of their own gaps and their practical determination to overcome them, these leaders of McCaw were able to conceive and deliver a real plan and solution for achieving their vision. They still had to strive continuously to improve service and grow their coverage profitably. They still had to compete like crazy to win out over the other carriers. But across all these efforts, their honest and practical self-assessment continued to be critical. This same approach led to the eventual multibillion-dollar acquisition of McCaw by AT&T, bringing the scale, branding clout, and leverage they really needed.

The same kind of hard-nosed self-assessment not only gives you the critical advantage of being able to choose the right play but also reveals what you need to do to execute it successfully. It gives you the advantage of making sure all of your assessment has been as accurate and unbiased as possible. And it gives you one other advantage, as well: it makes clear the ingredients needed in your action plan and the set of priorities you need to follow for conquering your most important shortcomings in a way that is actually doable.

Who Are You? No, This Is Not Existentialism, This Is Business. And Yes, It's a Really Important Question.

Sounds funny, but before you go off and start your self-help program, you've got to make sure you know just who that self is.

We were recently working with one of our firm's portfolio companies as they prepared for their public launch. Like a lot of our other start-ups, they had great technology, a true breakthrough in the field of mathematics, but they didn't know how to achieve a breakthrough to the minds of their targets. We brought in a colleague, Christopher Ireland of Cheskin Research, as a fresh set of eyes. A very experienced and seasoned practitioner, she started by asking some very basic questions:

1. Who do you think you are?
2. Who do other people think you are?
3. Who do you want to be? What is the point B of your own identity?

1. Who do you think you are?

Like a lot of technology companies we work with, this company had several different personalities within it—superstrong math genius founders, a disciplined engineering team, and hard-boiled business leaders. Each of these folks gave different answers to what they thought the company actually was, defaulting to their own comfort zones. The math geniuses saw the company as one offering revolutionary science, the engineering guys saw it as a products company, and the business folks scratched their heads and worried because they knew that it had to be a *business*-business. OK. If they couldn't agree, then maybe there was another angle.

2. Who do other people think you are?

Truth be told, the customer is always the deciding factor. How they think of you matters a lot more than how you think of yourself. How many times have you seen some kind of brand advertising that was really wishful thinking? Companies declaring to their audience, "Hey, look at me, I'm customer friendly," or "Hey, look at me, I'm really innovative," or, worst of all, "Trust me"—when deep in their hearts they know that their customers think of them in just the opposite terms. Don't delude yourself. And don't try too hard to prove the opposite of your customers' impressions—not unless you've done the hard work first.

When that start-up was getting ready to launch, they looked at how their customers, their partners, and others in the industry perceived them, and the picture quickly came into sharper focus. Most of these folks would not describe them as "a products company"— because they had only just shipped their first product. They wouldn't describe them as a hard-core, make-your-numbers business company, because they weren't yet big enough. But most who responded did recognize the power of their math as pretty darn promising and potentially revolutionary.

Seeing this, it made sense for Christopher to ask the final question.

3. Who do you want to be? What is the point B of your own identity?

Those annoying ads we all scoff at do tell us something about the companies—if not about what the company is, then about what they want to be. In the firm we were working with, the desires were obvious. It was legitimate and important that the company truly become what each one of the various groups within it originally saw it as. For it to be successful, it had to hold onto its strong identity as a breakthrough math company, while adding enough legitimacy as an engineering and product company to drive real adoption, and showing enough down-to-earth business acumen to be trusted and taken seriously.

This is an important thing to remember: In the midst of self-criticism and the strong desire to improve or adapt to your challenges and goals, you should always be true to yourself, to what the company is, and what it stands for. Stray too far from that and you are likely to misstep.

With all that in mind, the company went right back and reexamined the gap analysis they had done that led them to hire Christopher in the first place. They asked what the distance was that they needed to cover to go from who they then were to who they wanted to be in the future.

Make sure that the point B you choose is realistic. Take a good look at the distance you have to cover to get there and make sure you set your sights on what is achievable in a reasonable timeframe. Companies cannot go overnight from being operationally inept to customer-service machines, from paranoid laggards to innovative leaders, or from industry pariahs to trusted partners. You need to have a plan. You need to know what to work on.

If you're going to choose a play or make key decisions based on a real assessment of where you are and where you can get, you need to dig deep. If you

want to be ready for any of these, you need to understand more about what
makes your company tick.

Getting to the Bottom of It–Not Just Who You Are but What Makes You That Way

Facing up to your shortcomings is healthy. But only if you're going to do something about them. And you can't do anything about them unless you really understand what makes your company the way it is.

This means putting yourself under the same detailed scrutiny you did for your competition. Just as when you analyzed them, you need to dig into only three key dimensions: your products and services, your business—that is, how you make money—and your organization—its people, processes, and culture.

You have to understand the strengths and weaknesses of your products and/or services. There's no better way to do this than firsthand. We've talked about how to do this: be your own customer.

When Gordon Bethune became CEO of Continental Airlines back in the mid-1990s, there wasn't much he needed to know in terms of what the company was. It was the worst. Employees thought so, customers thought so. But he knew he wanted it to be the best.

So one of the first things he did was to fly it. A lot. And, boy, did it make him mad. The planes were late, the employees were grumpy, the baggage got lost—the list of problems went on and on.

But instead of just getting angry, he really dug into all of the problem areas. What were the things that made his customers mad? Finding these things out gave him key ammunition for making change.

At Ignition, we use the products of almost all our portfolio companies to the degree that we actually are their target customers (or in some cases, like phones for teens, our kids become the customers). This makes us a useful test bed and source of feedback. This is another role for your kitchen cabinet; ask those friends, family, board members, and the like to use your products and give you honest feedback.

At Microsoft, that rule about "eating our own dog food" meant that we were all testers of each of the alpha and beta versions of our own products. We experienced how these products affected our lives and work, and we used even early, raw software for truly mission-critical tasks. This could be exciting—seeing and working with the coolest new products before anyone else. It could also be annoying, when your day got longer because of bugs or performance issues. It wasn't enough to just experience these issues. You had to write them down and report them. This experience made our marketing a lot smarter and it made the products a lot better, a lot sooner.

At American Express this same kind of philosophy was a far cry from dog food. Even as a brand-new junior executive, you had to use the card, which was great. AmEx was a travel and leisure company, so you had to travel and stay and eat at great places, showing others how prestigious carrying the card could be. Not necessarily the most cost-efficient method, but delightful fun.

You can take all this a bit too far. We've heard stories that Coke folks won't go to restaurants where they serve Pepsi. A friend who works at Starbucks corporate simply cannot stand the sight of people drinking other brands of coffee. And as good as their french fries are, could you imagine never eating anywhere but Mc-Donald's?

Once you know your products or services, you need to know how you make money from them. This is the second aspect of your company that you have to understand deeply: the economics of your business.

At Continental, Bethune identified some of the key problems in the way the company thought about making money. They had already filed for bankruptcy—not once but several times. Continental's management had a long history of cutting costs. Everywhere. He looked closely at this and saw that cutting costs in so many areas—like cleaning the planes, painting them, and hiring people to service them faster—wasn't really saving money, it was costing them business. He saw a direct relationship between this kind of lowest common denominator mentality and the level of service and satisfaction he found when flying the airline as a customer.

How do you spend money? What makes up the lion's share of costs? Are you investing in the right new programs or products? How do your products sell? What are their channels of distribution and the mix of those channels? Are there core areas that are almost too hard for you to abandon? Which are your cash cows? Are they sacred cows that you have an emotional attachment to beyond economic rationale?

Lots of companies have any number of huge existing businesses; while these can be an advantage, the desire not to cannibalize them may lead managers to close their eyes on the possibility of investing in alternatives. Does your business model cause you to have blind spots? Don't just stare in the rear-view mirror. Turn your head and look to make sure.

Finally, remember that your company is not made up of just inventory, accounts receivable and payable, and assets and liabilities. All those things come from somewhere. Your company is first and foremost made up of people. If you really care about an honest assessment of your strengths and weaknesses, dig in and take a hard look about how your people are organized, what motivates them, and what formal processes and informal culture they operate in.

The best way to understand this? Walk around. Talk to people. Ask questions. Again, get your hands dirty.

On one of his first jobs, co-author John Zagula worked as a laborer in a paint factory. The other laborers, a very tough, grizzled crowd, looked on young college types with suspicion if not contempt. The newest manager of the factory, exactly such a smart, young college type, started off his new position by personally working every job in production, side by side with the laborers, humbly asking for help and for hints on the tricks of each assembly-line station or process. From then on, the old hands still teased him, but they did it in front of him and with a kind of respect.

This sort of hands-on exposure isn't always possible, and may be more suitable to some aspects of a business than others, but the philosophy is illuminating. Try to understand the situations and motivations of the various different groups of people in your company.

Gordon Bethune certainly made a point of doing that at Continental. He spent time with employees, he watched them as a customer and then as a manager. What he found was upsetting but not surprising. No wonder they were demoralized, frustrated, and poorly performing: They weren't proud to be Continental employees. They wouldn't even own up to it. And they sure didn't feel secure, what with the constant cost cuts and the threat of bankruptcy ever looming.

Bethune also found that their organization and processes were a big part of the problem. The various departments communicated little with one another, cooperated less, and spent a lot of time fighting over scarcer and scarcer resources. By getting to the root of Continental's problems, he was able to make the changes needed to turn his ship around.

Don't be afraid to make changes frequently in order to keep your organization nimble. When we were at Microsoft, one of the company's biggest strengths was its organization—or lack thereof. Reorgs happened frequently, people were always changing jobs. Still, you always knew that someone's title mattered a lot less than what they were good at. The underlying culture was just as important as the formal organization and processes, if not even more important.

No matter where you were, even if you weren't on the main Redmond campus, you always knew that everyone was just an e-mail away. In a company full of overachievers who think of themselves as underachievers, such an informal culture was essential to retaining innovation and flexibility.

In your own company, make sure to be realistic about your people, their strengths and weaknesses, and the type of organization that will bring out the best in them.

Remember that example of asking employees what they thought the company was? Your company, too, is almost certainly made up of several different groups that all contribute to its culture. Before you go too far in trying to move that culture, make sure you know what each of these groups is up to and what they're thinking.

Bethune took what he learned and worked wonders on Continental (see his terrific book, *From Worst to First*, for the details and lessons of how). The math-oriented company described earlier took what they learned to arrive at a clearer vision and plan for themselves. You can do the same, taking what you learn about your own company and using it to guide your strategy but also to bound your decisions in realism.

Keep Everything in Balance So the Scales You Weighed Yourself On Don't Tip in Someone Else's Favor

Studying yourself will teach you one thing above all else: you still have a lot of work to do. And, as well, that you can't do everything. At least not all at once.

Winning is a matter of trade-offs, of priorities. The balance between driving ambition and realistic goals is critical, especially when it comes to affecting change in the one player on your playing field over which you should have the most control—yourself. If you don't find this balance, watch out. Overshoot and you lose; undershoot and you miss the mark, letting some weaker contender grow stronger.

There are a million things you can do to improve your company and to improve your chances in the marketplace. How do you scrutinize them all? One helpful tool that our colleague Jon Anderson came up with was to think of all of these choices as a portfolio of options. Ask yourself how many different deployments of your resource you can manage and how concentrated or diversified you need to be.

Lay these out as in Fig. 11–3. You routinely evaluate investments on the basis of risk and return. Why should investments in your own company be any different—whether those investments be in dollars, people, time, or effort?

Use a chart like this as a template for laying out the options you want to consider. Ask yourself, Which areas of improvement will

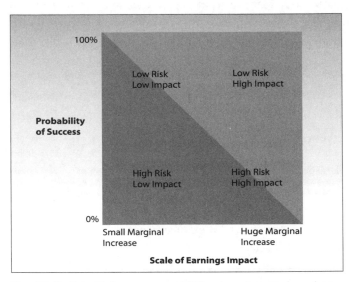

Fig. 11–3. Prioritizing your capabilities investments based on their potential impact

have the biggest payout? Which will be the easiest to accomplish? At our own venture capital firm, we always like to start by making sure that before we move on to other investments, we have put all the effort we can into the lowest-hanging, juiciest fruit—in other words, the areas where the benefits of improvement are highest, the likelihood of success most secure, and the level of effort required the smallest. Depending on your own appetites, you can then move on to either those efforts that are smaller, with less at risk and less effort required, or to those that are huge in potential but higher up in the tree.

Making choices that fit your profile gives you the greatest likelihood of successfully executing the play you choose. It doesn't pay to be right; it only pays to be right and then take advantage of it.

One company that took this idea to heart is called RadioFrame Networks. To be honest, they succeeded in this against some of the authors' initial instincts.

RadioFrame has a solution for dramatically improving the reception of wireless devices inside buildings that are usually unreached by cellular signals, and their solution is much more cost effective, simple, and reliable than previous technologies. It makes cell phone users happier because their phones still work in tall buildings, elevators, and so on. It makes wireless telephone carriers happier because they can serve customers better and generate more payable minutes of call time.

When we saw the technology, we were pumped. It was superbly designed. It could do great things. Beyond the pure impact on cell phone service, it worked with wireless data networks as well. We thought, *Wow, these guys have a tiger by the tail. Let's go for it. Let's trumpet all these features and own the biggest vision we can.*

Well, sounder minds prevailed. And good for them. The founders and leaders of RadioFrame knew themselves well. They had a strong vision and big ambitions, but they were also realistic about what it was going to take to get there. They chose to take achievable steps first.

The company team had all come from the world of wireless carriers. They understood their language and how the telecom carriers operated. This knowledge gave them a strong playing card, which they were wise enough to recognize and use, so they elected to focus on the carriers and their problems. Since they were a small company, this was a digestible goal and one they were particularly well suited to tackle. But beyond that, they also decided to focus initially on one specific carrier. They knew that getting that relationship in the bag would give them the legitimacy to go after others.

Smart. Rather than overreaching, they reached just right and made terrific progress, earning a name for themselves in their market. They understood the trade-offs and they knew themselves well enough to make those trade-offs intelligently.

The Four Trade-offs

Four key dimensions—your resources, your timeframes, your risk appetite, and your ambition and motivation—will guide your choices in understanding the key trade-offs and your appetites and abilities to accept them.

YOUR RESOURCES

A true, realistic assessment of how strong you are relative to the others on the playing field will make all the difference between securing a clear foothold and getting wiped out.

YOUR TIMEFRAMES

Knowing the overall market, the state of the competition, and the mood of your customer well enough will let you gauge how much time you have to execute a play as well as how much time you have to conquer your shortcomings. In some of these cases, patience is the key. It can make all the difference between being starved out or accepting the de facto surrender of your tired competitor. In other cases, if you aren't fast, you aren't around anymore.

YOUR RISK APPETITE

No matter what path you choose, there is no sure thing. As you run down the playing field, things will often change unexpectedly. How strong is your stomach in the face of sturdy opposition? How firm are your nerves as bad news and curveballs come your way? Knowing how much risk you are really willing to take can mean the difference between making the touchdown or getting tackled.

YOUR AMBITION AND MOTIVATION

In business, the stakes are high. How big is the prize you're after? And how much is it worth to you? Many times you have no choice— you are in it for your survival. Remember, that prize you're after is in someone else's sights, too. Whatever your choice, make it and stick to it like crazy. Commitment counts. Big time. It can do a lot to overcome those risks.

Assess yourself on these four key dimensions before you choose your play, and you will have a lot better shot of seeing it through.

Take-Aways for Assessing Your Own Capabilities

1. All the work you have done on understanding the market, customers, and competition will only mislead you if you aren't totally honest and willing to face hard facts.

2. Knowing your own limitations is key to setting your sights on realistic goals. It's the final step in getting to the point B of your future vision, your attractive offering, and your differentiated position. Doing the ABC gap analysis on your own strengths and weaknesses leads to the action plan you need to make all of these a reality.

3. The first step in doing this is making sure you really know who you are today, whom others perceive you as, who you want to be, and the distance between these.

4. The best way to learn about your own strengths and weaknesses is through direct experience. Be a customer of your own products. Dig into your numbers. Do your own Ps and Qs. Understand your people, their motivations, their relationships, and their needs.

5. Finally, think ahead. Plan out how you're going to overcome your gaps. Prioritize your investment of resources. Pick the low-hanging fruit first and go from there. Make sure to prioritize based on your real abilities and appetites. Specifically, be sure your choices match your real resource level, your true time horizons, your stomach for risk, and the size of the prize you are committed to.

Coming Up

Next up, running your play as a great, on-the-field, marketing/sales campaign.

PART III

Running the Play as
a Killer Campaign

The key elements for executing successful campaigns on the real market playing
field:

- Teams
- Timing
- Tactics

Coaches who can outline plays on a blackboard are a dime a dozen. The ones who win get inside their players and motivate.

—VINCE LOMBARDI

12. Pulling the Campaign Team Together

You've chosen your play, you've mapped the field, now you have to choose your players.

Whether you're in a Fortune 500 company or a five-person non-profit, the best strategy in the world isn't worth the paper it's printed on if you can't execute it. And, other than pulling out of your driveway and into the parking lot, you can't execute much of anything in the market all by yourself. You need people. You need a team. And not just any team. You need the right team. You need a kick-ass campaign team that can take your play and run with it.

But just what should this team look and work like? What actually makes an effective team?

Recently, one of our portfolio companies, Nth Orbit, found an answer in a big way. This start-up company develops and markets software for risk assessment and compliance, and they had taken on the challenge of repositioning and relaunching themselves in the marketplace. They had already built a great product of very broad appeal, but they found that in a down market, technology sales cycles had become abnormally long—a tough situation for anybody, but especially tough for a new, small company.

Luckily, their savvy CEO, Vani Kola, never stopped doing her homework. She found that the Nth Orbit core technology had great applicability to a newly urgent customer issue, one with big dollars attached to it. Shifting to focus on this opportunity was a make-or-break-the-company bet. The opportunity was waiting, but they had to jump to and come out swinging. It would take the coordinated efforts of a cohesive team to pull this off.

And pull it off they did. Seamlessly. Under Vani's leadership and inspiration and the team's dedication, they successfully put the company on a strong footing in its new marketplace.

How?

First, for this team to create and deliver a unified campaign, they had to be unified themselves. They needed a single purpose, a common inspiration to guide them. They had to care, they had to believe in what they were all trying to accomplish together. A new play itself can provide the spark to revitalize and refocus a team.

The Nth Orbit relaunch campaign team—and all great teams that we've been on or seen execute really effectively—have always been smart about one particular essential element: they have matched the right people with the right process.

People

Vani knew that they had a myriad of tasks to check off before they would be ready to successfully relaunch the company. It would take leadership to pull off all this. It would also take good management. She had to get the right people assigned to all of these tasks. Inputs, decisions, and actions would be required from the people in charge of Sales, Product, Finance, Marketing, and Operations. And to avoid confusion and unnecessary loss of time, roles and responsibilities had to be clear and consistent for each member.

Process

She understood that this group of people had to function cohesively as a team. For the campaign to avoid contradictions, they had to be coordinated in their efforts. They had to communicate effectively. They had to identify and resolve issues efficiently. And they would need basic processes to help them make all this happen, processes that would enhance their sense of ownership, the value of their contribution, and their accountability. Not processes that would get in the way of doing the job effectively.

As you go out and turn your play into results, as you drive your planning into real marketing campaigns, you need the kind of disciplined, synchronized group that makes it all happen in the heat of action. You need to make sure that you have nailed the Who, How, and Why of your team. That's what driving a great, effective campaign and running your play successfully are all about.

So How Do You Assemble and Organize This Wonder Team?

As venture capitalists we have a lot of mottos, but one of the most powerful and lasting is "Solve people, not problems." If you are passionate and deeply engaged, you will always be tempted to get your hands dirty and to personally stay on top of every detail. But in great campaigns, there are so many different tasks, so many different problems to solve, that there is no way that one person can drive them all. The real way to make sure that all the details are handled and all the problems are solved is to assign the right person to handle each.

And whether big team or small, for each task and each problem, every member of the team needs to know his or her role clearly, and also know those of their teammates. Some people may wear lots of different hats across a campaign, but they had better know which hat they are wearing when. Otherwise things get horribly confused.

There may be lots of ways to delineate such roles and responsibilities, but there's one method for categorizing them we have seen work over and over again. It's simple. For any task a person can only play one of three roles:

Owner, or
Decision maker, or
Contributor

Owners: Making sure everything gets done

As we're using the term here, whoever is accountable for making sure something gets done is the "owner" of that effort. Many people may be involved in the task, but the owner drives the process forward and ensures its timely completion.

What do owners own? They own the schedule for a task, communicating what's happening with it and the relationships of all the people involved in making the thing happen—whether those people report to them or not.

At the highest level, even though no single person can do everything, there also needs to be a single owner for the whole campaign. This role is not the same as the inspirational leader or cheerleader but rather the day-to-day, hold-it-all-together, buck-stops-here project driver. Sound straightforward? It's not simple. This person has to be the facilitator and monitor for all communications between owners of individual project elements, decision makers, and contributors and must be the manager of all the processes and the ultimate traffic cop on the project.

In the case of the Nth Orbit relaunch/repositioning campaign, the task was critical enough, and the mission central enough, that the CEO took on the role of project owner herself—no one else would do. Even in a midsize company, that's not practical for every campaign. In fact, within one company, often several different campaigns or projects are running at the same time, making it unrealistic for the leader to head each one, even if she or he wanted to. Instead, the overall management is delegated to individual project leaders.

It doesn't matter so much how senior this person is or what her reporting relationships are if she truly is anointed and supported by management as the project owner. What matters most is how organized, reliable, and responsible she is and how well she manages relationships inside and outside of the group. If everyone knows they have been anointed by top management, then they're armed with ample authority to match their massive responsibility.

With many of the product launches we've been involved in, the project owner was not the obvious person at all. In one major product launch at Microsoft, we had teams of seasoned marketing experts working for us, each with gobs of experience and seniority. But when push came to shove, the person who cracked the whip, the person who kicked butt and took names, was Erin O'Melia, our administrative assistant. She had the initiative, drive, and raw organizational talent to become the de facto launch project owner. And she did a great job of it. (And you won't be surprised to learn that she went on to become a terrific marketing and product professional in her own right.)

Decision Makers

With judgment and authority, decision makers take all the inputs, break logjams, and give the go-ahead. Being a project or task owner doesn't necessarily carry the title of decision maker on any given campaign element. The owner makes sure that everything gets done. The decision maker is the person who has been assigned the authority to determine which is the right way for jobs to get done, and approves specific actions and selections. This distinction is critical to avoid confusion and delays.

In a PR-driven campaign, for example, the owner of the press release may be one person, the decision maker on the text may be another—or even several others if there are a lot of quotes to be gathered and approved. Other times the same person wears both hats, as process owner and output approver. This can speed the process, but you have to watch out for bottlenecks if the decision makers get overloaded and some important items never reach the top of their To Do list.

You need to be disciplined about identifying required decisions and matching the right decision maker to each. And for making sure the decision makers are provided with the information they need, and the timeframe within which they have to make the decision. You also need to ensure that decision makers' decisions don't get unmade or their authority taken away. Any assignment you make has to be for real. Its parameters have to be clear—otherwise you "demotivate" everyone and slow everything down.

Everyone wants to be a decision maker. But beware of blurring ownership and decision-making authority or of setting false expectations about the extent of people's roles just to keep someone happy. That never works out.

One other thing: never, never, never assign more than one decision maker to any problem. Missteps like this are pretty well guaranteed to bring the whole effort to a screaming, messy halt.

Contributors

Drawing on the combined expertise and hard work of all the contributors, the project actually moves ahead and gets done.

The third role of individual contributor or project participant can in some ways be the most important. Every task requires numerous inputs that shape the decisions and ensure the outcomes. Getting these inputs from the right people and to the right decision makers can spell the difference between superb execution and embarrassing failure.

Make sure you include all the right participants and contributors—first because you want the advice and input, but also because with so much going on, things can fall through the cracks. Missing even something simple can set you up for a disaster. In one of the very first direct mail campaigns we were ever involved with, the whole outcome was saved by one person. It wasn't a marketing person, it wasn't a salesperson, it wasn't a strategy person, it was simply a person who answered the phones. She had the sense to check the phone number. Duh. We were just about to print millions of mailers with a catchy 1-800-phrase but through sheer oversight we were off one digit from a number we actually owned. Luckily we included her on the launch team. And luckily we made her a contributor on reviewing the creative marketing and sales support.

So, three roles: owner, decision maker, and contributors. All critical. All different. Make sure the right people are in the right roles and they know when they're playing which. For the owner of the effort, what matters is drive and organization. For the decision makers, what matters is judgment and authority. For the contributors, what matters is expertise and hard work.

How Do You Pick Players for Your Campaign Team? And Where Do You Find Them?

Typically you will want to draw from all parts of your organization to ensure that all the tasks and outputs come together seamlessly. In many cases, a number of the participants may be outside of your organization or company—for example, advertising and PR agencies, outsourced fulfillment houses, channel partners. But every group that will play a role has to be included. Also, you don't want to forget your kitchen cabinet people. The opinions and inputs of the very same people whom you looked to for guidance on understanding the situation of the customer and competitive playing field will be even more valuable as you hit that field running with actual tactics.

Fig. 12–1 shows a prototypical launch project matrix that designates who should carry the responsibility for each of the key efforts. It

	Executive Management	Product Development	Marketing	Sales	Business Development	Fulfillment/ Operations
Launch calendar	Decision maker	Participant	Owner	Participant	Participant	Participant
Event coordination	Participant	Participant	Decision maker/ Owner	Participant	Participant	Participant
Press tour	Decision maker/Participant	Participant	Owner	Participant	Participant	Participant
Demand creation (ads, direct mail, etc.)	Participant	Participant	Decision maker/ Owner	Participant	—	Participant
Sales collateral	—	Participant	Owner	Decision maker	Participant	Participant
Channel readiness	Decision maker/Participant	—	Participant	Participant	Owner	Participant
Customer service	Decision maker	Participant	Participant	Participant	—	Owner

Fig. 12–1. Typical campaign roles and responsibilities

also indicates each of the core tasks that need to be managed. In your own project matrix, the roles and responsibilities assignments will vary more and will need to be more detailed, with each box listing the name of a person and details of her or his specific responsibilities. Even this generalized version, though, illustrates the difference between owning, deciding, and participating. Let's walk through it.

Different Plays Require Different Tactics

Synchronized campaigns demand powerful, integrated teams across disciplines. But each play has its own unique pros and cons, rewards and risks, strengths and weaknesses. And as such, each play draws uniquely on certain skills. Depending on the play you have chosen, some types of players are likely to be more critical to its success than others. Center the team around them.

THE DRAG RACE

The true hero of this play is *the salesperson*. This play is all about convincing people that you are better, faster, and/or cheaper than one other competitor. Of course, the product has to keep up with the claims being made, and the financial wherewithal has to be maintained to support the contest. But the real deciding factor of this play is the pitch. That's why the players who make it or break it are the people who deliver the pitch compellingly (and maybe also the communications people who craft it).

THE PLATFORM

For this play, the hero is *the business manager*, since this play is all about using success to build an ecosystem, one that is powerful and profitable. Sure, marketing has to make membership in this ecosystem seem exclusive and inclusive at the same time. Sure, the product/technology has to create an evolving standard that binds the ecosystem's members. All true. But the real genius of the Platform Play comes from creating and maintaining a business model that minimizes the costs and maximizes the profits of being the category leader, while sharing the benefits with tons of others.

THE STEALTH

In a Stealth Play, the hero is *the CEO.* In many ways this play asks more of the whole team than any of the others. This one defers the fun of the chase and the rewards of market leadership in exchange for survival. It requires great stores of humility, patience, and responsiveness in the short term, great dedication to the goal, and conviction of long-term success. It takes insight and cunning to find footholds while struggling to hold on for dear life—to find opportunity where others see danger. It takes true leadership to keep a team nimble and motivated in such circumstances. And it takes some of the crazy ambition and ego we love to see in CEOs in order to stay passionate, committed, and utterly convinced of ultimate victory.

THE BEST-OF-BOTH

The true hero of the Best-of-Both Play is *the product person.* This play is all about delivering a new combination of value that people did not previously think possible. Of course, when you have a winning combination like this, you need marketing people to make the most hay out of it. And, of course, you need salespeople to drive the momentum for change. But whatever the product, service, or other offering, none of this is possible without real innovation. The engineering, operations, or service innovator who sees the future and captures it makes this play possible, and makes it so exciting.

THE HIGH-LOW

When you run a High-Low Play, your hero is *the marketing person.* The High-Low is hard. Splitting a category and maintaining ownership of both parts is a task not for the faint of heart. You do have to have credible products or offerings on both ends of the spectrum. And you do have to have channels that somehow support both of these. But pulling off this kind of story is the biggest challenge. Making very different, even opposing, targets feel equally satisfied is a task of great diplomacy, finesse, and persuasion. You face the daunting challenge of addressing all their needs, leaving no one behind, and giving each a migration path between extremes. Only a true marketing veteran—someone already tested in the other plays—would be eager to embrace this Olympics-level challenge.

As you gather and organize your campaign team, make sure to have the right player (the right hero) for the play you're launching. Choose wrong on any key player, and your play is a lot less likely to succeed. But choose right, and you can rely on them. So choose the right player, get out of the way, and depend on them heavily in driving the campaign and deciding its direction.

Making Sure the Team Stays Focused

Identifying all the right players is one thing. Getting them to work together, get stuff done, and get it done on time is another. There are tons of good books on management techniques and team motivation. But for the purposes of this little treatise on how to kick butt and take names in a play-driven campaign, we'll boil it down to the essentials. Three things matter in turning your collection of owners, decision makers, and contributors into a cohesive cadre of capable campaigners.

Those three things (to continue the excessive alliteration) are calendar, consistency, and communication.

Calendar: The heartbeat of the campaign

Timing is everything in a campaign. Deadlines do a lot to light a fire under people (we know—as we write, this book's deadline is fast approaching). There's a reason that symphony orchestras have a conductor to keep the beat and make sure everyone reaches the final note together. There's a reason that paratroopers synchronize their watches. No matter how smart the play, if the players aren't all acting on the same schedule, no one will be there to catch the ball when you throw it.

The campaign calendar is the most central feature of any operation. Items without dates aren't deliverables; they're no more than items on a wish list.

And the most important date of all is D-Day, the drop-dead date for everything to be ready. The day that you go live. Even if you've chosen strategically to do a soft launch or to deemphasize "the big event"—as might often be the case for a Stealth or even a Platform Play—it really helps to have one central date that everyone can focus on. And can celebrate once it has been successfully reached.

The calendar is the focal point around which many of the most important decisions have to be made. Timing is the central fulcrum for almost all the critical trade-offs—being fully ready versus missing a window of opportunity, speed to market versus strength of advantage, and all the others.

But, as always happens when plans meet reality, things slip. People overpromise. They miss dates. Slips that are big enough to put D-Day and the whole campaign in jeopardy will sometimes happen. You need to be prepared with fall-back plans for dealing with big problems if they do arise. "Smart" schedules make allowances for these problems.

Consistency: Staying in sync even when things change

This is where the final element of consistency comes in—consistency of project standards and management. Nobody is going to hand you a crystal ball that shows you in advance all the possible issues and snags in a project. But one simple methodology can really help you stay on top of all of these things and prioritize them consistently: the familiar red/yellow/green charts that show at a glance the status of every element of the project.

You put together a chart with a master list of every task to be done, every input and deliverable, every owner, participant, and decision maker. Each of these is assigned a color for every meeting or reporting period. In our own version of this system, a green light means everything for that element is on track or completed. Yellow means that the item needs to be monitored and that additional resources may need to be provided. And red means "Houston, we have a problem."

Focus the attention of your teams on these issues, constantly driving to make every red a yellow, if not a green. Make sure that you and the players involved report accurately and that you always know what tasks have yellow or red status.

Communication: The glue that holds it all together

But how do you make certain all the different parts of your effort stay in sync under all these varying conditions? By ensuring that your teams communicate well. Easy to say; harder to do. Your team will be multidisciplinary and often virtual from a reporting standpoint. You'll need to ensure that they have places to gather and at-a-click ways to communicate as well as the right forums and tools to exchange information and get problems solved quickly, efficiently, and securely. We've found several ways of doing this. The steps are incredibly simple—so much that they'll seem obvious. But don't underrate them; they can be surprisingly effective.

GIVE THE TEAM A NAME.

People wear lots of hats. Giving the campaign team a name helps them know which one they're wearing when a project item pops up. When co-author John Zagula first joined Microsoft, he was plunked into a classic job filled with lots of responsibility and hardly any authority. His first task was to organize the direct marketing launch for Microsoft Windows 3.1. There were all kinds of players involved from various groups across Manufacturing, Operations, Product, the ad agency, Database, Sales, and so on. Each of these groups knew that crap flows downhill and they would have to do a lot of the shoveling if they didn't stay in touch with what everybody else was doing.

To make sure they were all in sync, John asked them to become a team for this effort. They all got together and named it VOLT, an acronym for Virtual Operations Leadership Team. People were proud to be included. It worked so well that every time afterward that the company launched a product, it became a standing requirement to constitute this kind of team. And the name stuck. In fact, that name became an institution of sorts—long after John had moved on to other roles, a VOLT team was formed every time a new product was coming up for launch. You cannot overestimate the impact that a powerful team name can bestow.

SET UP REGULAR TEAM MEETINGS.

Part of what made the VOLT team work was that the members all came together in a way that reminded them of why they were a team. They had weekly meetings, at exactly the same time every week. The agenda for these meetings was always the same: the project task list, where they were, how they were going to get to the next step. As things heated up, they met more frequently, as often as every day—at least by phone. There is no substitute for direct contact to maintain accountability. And at the end of all of it, they met at the usual time and place to celebrate their success.

GIVE MEMBERS MEANS TO COMMUNICATE AND TRACK PROGRESS BETWEEN MEETINGS.

Sure, meetings are important, but we've all discovered the inverse relationship between the number and length of meetings you attend and the amount of actual work you get done. Communicating between meetings is critical; providing a means to do it is easy. One of the first things we always did after setting up a VOLT team was to create an e-mail alias for it so that any member could always simply e-mail the whole team with any updates and issues.

These days, tools for collaborating come in a lot more shapes and sizes. Many of our portfolio companies now use blogs (Web logs) or Intranet sites for posting information and discussing issues. Tools like Groove, Microsoft Project, BaseCamp, and others offer more structure and guidance than your own freeform site. Whatever the tool, just make sure that every member of the team actually uses it.

A Well-Honed Team: Ready for Their Marching Orders

If every person on the team knows what their roles are, when and where to meet, and how to communicate, if you all live off the same calendar, and if you all consistently follow the traffic lights, you are well on your way to a smoothly functioning, crack campaign team that can execute whatever play you picked for your business.

Take-Aways for Pulling the Campaign Team Together

1. **The Who and How of the Campaign Team.** You can't run a play by yourself. You need a team. Make it a good one and arm it for success. Without a team, you can't execute any play at all.

2. **Right People/Right Roles: owner, decision maker, and contributor.** These are the only three roles that matter. And they cut across org charts. Your team will be multidisciplinary and often virtual from a reporting standpoint. Don't let there be any confusion between the three basic roles. Remember that the owner makes sure that everything gets done, while the decision maker determines which is the right way for jobs to get done, and approves specific actions and selections. And never underestimate the role of the contributors. But most importantly, make sure to put overall project ownership in the hands of someone who knows how to drive deadlines, kick butt, and take names.

3. **Different Heroes for Different Plays.** You chose your play to match both your goals and the conditions you assessed. Make sure you stay true to that assessment in pulling together your team. The various players will have a more central role in some plays, less central in others. Often the central person will be the sales guy for a Drag Race, the product guy for a Best-of-Both, the marketing guy for a High–Low Play. For this key person, make sure you select a star and that his input and involvement are central to the team.

4. **Team Cohesion.** A team only functions well if the members know they're actually working as a team. Never overlook the power of giving the team a name. A team name reinforces the fact of team membership and provides an anchor for its activities and communications.

5. **Calendar, Consistency, Communication.** Give the team the right means to communicate to one another. Prioritize all the tasks and identify them consistently as Red, Yellow, or Green. Drive regular but not oppressive team meetings to assess, reset, and acknowledge progress on these priorities. Finally, center all this around a single calendar that drives the campaign to D-Day.

Coming Up

Assembling and organizing a team and inspiring it with a strong mission is absolutely essential to success on the playing field. But beyond that, when the team is ready to go on the road, every member needs to hit the highway with the same set of instructions. The next chapter provides a guide to creating those instructions—the campaign brief.

Everything should be made as simple as possible, but not one bit simpler.

—ALBERT EINSTEIN

13. The Campaign Brief

To keep your team and your campaign on track, keep them on the same page. And keep that page complete, but short.

A sixty-page marketing plan. A two-hundred–page business plan. A two-hundred–page research report. A lot of noble effort, yes—but do they really get people to move in the right direction?

Maybe yes, maybe no. We know from experience that a single, well–put-together input document can make all the difference between a mediocre campaign coming in disparate parts and an awesome integrated campaign with real impact.

Whether your campaign is launching a product or a whole company, whether it's attacking a competitor or just covering your butt, it needs to be consistent, synchronous, and well orchestrated if it's to have any impact. You may have pulled together the right team and resources to drive this campaign, but even the best hand-picked campaign team is not going to make anything but noise unless they are all working off the same page.

Two campaigns launched at about the same time underscore the importance of this warning. One was for Microsoft Office, by far the bigger product with a bigger budget, the other for a newer, less proven product, FrontPage, with a lot fewer dollars in the kitty. Other than that, they had just about everything in common—similar teams, same company, same marketing mix (PR, event, advertising, Web, direct mail, sales pitches, etc). Everything except for the strength and consistency of the input document, otherwise known as the campaign brief.

In the first campaign, the Microsoft Office team felt so confident about the product that they didn't take enough time on the brief and they didn't stick to it religiously. The second product (Front-Page) was newer, so the campaign lead, Ted Bremer, and the whole team worked harder to make sure they understood how it worked and what its value was. And this showed in the brief. The outcome: despite differences in budget and product history, the first campaign had inconsistent messages and initially disappointing results; the second campaign hung together tightly and was much more impactful, generating a very high volume of new product trials and conversions to paid product, not to mention target audience awareness and industry buzz.

So What's in a Campaign Brief and How Do You Write One?

First, your campaign brief will be the single document you'll follow for the campaign, so you need to cover pretty much everything. The campaign will involve all the members of your team—employees, managers, outside vendors, salespeople, and others—so the brief needs to set out compelling reasons about why anyone should care in the first place about this company, product, or offering you are launching. It needs to explain your mission and vision. It needs to share the realities of the market you face and the reasons behind the strategy you've chosen. And it needs to provide the implications and campaign guidelines that result from that strategy.

Well, wasn't that kind of what this whole Playbook thing was supposed to do? Haven't you just spent all this time carefully and intelligently figuring out all these things as part of composing your own Playbook? Shouldn't that be enough?

Yes, of course, that's exactly what the Playbook is all about. On the other hand, there's no way you want to share all this with your campaign team. Not unless you want to put them to sleep. It would take too long, and most of them wouldn't have the patience to read it all, anyway. Although this brief is for internal (or virtually internal) consumption and doesn't have to be superpolished, your song sheet cannot be a lullaby. It must be a drumline.

If you want any of these various independent inside and outside players to understand or remember what the heck the campaign is supposed to be about, the message has got to be crisp. That's why we call it a "brief." Your homework, customer, competitor, and market analysis led you to this point; now you have to synthesize it.

You find the key points, the essence, of all the analysis, strategy, and guidance you've come up with so far—and cram it all onto a single page. That's right, onto *one* single page. And you have to make it really easy to understand and remember. But don't despair, you already have all the data, you just need to put it in a supersimple form. To make the process easier, what follows is a handy template to guide you through this process.

On the one page, you're going to put three core paragraphs that lay out the whole rationale of your strategy, each paragraph no longer than three sentences:

> *The case*—the rationale behind the business, product, or offering.
> *The story*—the inspiration of vision, mission, and values.

The positioning—the core claim you are planning to stake in the market.

And there are two other important paragraphs, also critical to the success of the campaign, that you will include:

Key support—the evidence and data about your product or offering that makes it possible to sustain your case, story, and claims.

Objectives, goals, and metrics—what you hope to accomplish with the campaign and how you will know when you've gotten there.

Those are the elements. Now let's get to work.

Paragraph One—The Case: Turning your homework into a pitch everyone can understand

You started this whole Playbook undertaking by doing some focused homework on your industry, your customer and prospect base, your competitive playing field, and your own competencies. You found some gaps, some opportunities that you can exploit. Now you'll convert that full situation analysis into one simple, compelling case for why you are proposing this whole effort in the first place.

To prevent yourself from getting lost and tangled up in the minutiae in doing all this complex analysis, you followed our simple ABCs method—with *A* representing the summary current situation, *B* representing the better way or possible future, and *C*, the gap or path from point A to point B. For conveying your summary case in your campaign brief (and, in fact, for holding people's attention when you are making just about any argument you will ever need to make), there is an equally simple method to match the ABCs.

This wondrously magical technique is called . . . *Yes, But, So.*

These three little words are the only ones you really need to kick off any logical argument. And they will help you keep it down to three sentences.

Here's an example. We started out Part II's coverage of the situation analysis and homework with the story of Henry Ford and the Model T. Behind all the momentous business and technology dynamics and historic industry forces was a very simple three-sentence case:

> *Yes,* cars remain the domain of elites and aficionados, not regular people.
> *But,* the underlying auto technology and manufacturing techniques are becoming more efficient.
> *So,* we should now be able to make a reliable car that the mass market can afford.

Another example updates the Ford story with similar challenges and opportunities in the modern time—the Volkswagen approach, especially since the company relaunched with its more daring line of cars like the Jetta and the new Bug.

> *Yes,* there are terrific, German-engineered cars available on the market for driving enthusiasts.
> *But,* they are very expensive and appeal only to those who can afford them.
> *So,* let's offer a high performance German car for average enthusiasts.

Sounds simple, but frankly, we think it's profound. Why? It's the psychology of getting someone to agree with you. Follow the logic of how it works:

Yes. Of course, your case starts with "Yes." However often it's actually used, *yes* has got to be one of the most popular words in the English language. It's what we all want to hear most. And there's a reason. Finding a way to empathize, to identify with someone, is the most important starting point to any interaction. That's the purpose of the "Yes" in our little Yes, But, So formula. "Yes" shows that you understand and acknowledge the facts of the situation—market situation, customer responses and desires, competitive strengths and responses, and the immediate feedback of your audience.

But. "Yes" is not enough. Nothing does, can, or should stay the same. That's where "But" comes in. Only when you understand the gap between the current situation and the desired or potential situations can you make any progress. The "But" statement forces you into a position of being open minded and critical, taking things from a different perspective. It is questioning, challenging; it's what keeps things fresh. In this context, "But" drives you to recognize the opening, the potential break in the situation, the kernel of change.

So. What's next? It's pretty dissatisfying to leave a conversation on a negative note, focusing on just the problems. Once you know your limitations and challenges, you have to decide what to do about them. That's what "So" is all about—taking all this analysis and converting it into a call to action. It's about embracing the possible. It addresses the need to find some resolution, hope, goals, or motivation in a tough situation. "So" is your way of taking all this analysis and hypothesizing and converting it into recommended action, into resolve and commitment. "So" means "Let's go!"

If you hadn't already noticed, the Yes, But, So formula conforms pretty neatly to the ABCs. But it helps make them believable and interesting. The "Yes" step lets your listeners know that you've heard their position and you understand. "But" announces that you know there can be a better way. "So" presents your idea for how to get there.

What were your ABCs? How do you translate them into a three-sentence case with "Yes," "But," and "So"?

Paragraph Two—The Story: Inspiration with the Three "We's"

It's one thing to get people to understand why you're doing what you're doing. That's necessary and important. But getting them motivated, getting them to care—hey, that's another story. And not just care, but care deeply enough to work really hard on it.

One-time presidential candidate Adlai Stevenson once said, "When Cicero spoke, men marveled. When Caesar spoke, men marched." You have to evoke the emotion of a Cicero and the conviction of a Caesar.

What will you use for a rallying cry? What can you say that will inspire your team to action—not just the eager young members but also the cynical old campaigners who think they've heard it all before? What story can you hammer out that not only sets your team on the march but also makes them feel proud and privileged to do so?

How the heck should we know? We can't give you the answer—only the guidance. You and your team alone know your real motivation. But we can help you make sure that the way you convey this story is crisp, concise, and complete. Here again we have a simple technique to guide you. And again it aims to limit you to only three sentences or phrases. For us, this simple method goes by the name of *the Three "We's."* It works basically like this:

> **"We believe . . ."** This is your short summary statement of your vision—your view of the desired future that could be and should be possible.

"We will . . ." This is your mission statement or the role you assign yourself in helping to realize the vision.
"We are . . ." This statement summarizes your values—the ideals or attributes that you will adhere to as you work toward fulfilling your mission.

Taking the Volkswagen example to the next level, the company might have presented the statements something like this (italics are added for emphasis—you won't use them in your own version):

> At Volkswagen, *we believe* that everyone should really enjoy their driving experience.
> At Volkswagen, *we will* help make this possible by building the very best performing cars at prices buyers in our market can afford.
> At Volkswagen, *we are* dedicated to a great combination of value, performance, and personality in all our cars.

Or take another example of a company you're familiar with from earlier in these pages—Extend America, the inspired rural wireless carrier. Their story can be summed up neatly as:

> At Extend America, *we believe* that everyone in this country should have access to quality wireless communications.
> At Extend America, *we will* bring quality wireless coverage to all areas of rural America where such service has previously been unavailable.
> At Extend America, *we are* dedicated to delivering wireless services with quality, affordability, and availability.

Let's look at Microsoft, where they motivated lots of partners and thousands of employees (your co-authors included) to bust their behinds and burn the midnight oil with their incredibly simple but honestly inspiring story:

> At Microsoft, *we believe* in a future where there is "A Computer on Every Desktop and in Every Home."
>
> At Microsoft, *we will* build the software that makes computing easy and accessible enough for everyone in the world to take advantage of.
>
> At Microsoft, *we are* dedicated to delivering ever greater ease of use, power, and affordability in all our products.

What do you believe, what are you dedicated to? What story are you marching to? Is it simple and strong enough to get others to march with you?

Paragraph Three—The Positioning: The XYZs of your advantage

This is the heart of the brief. And honestly, it's the heart of your marketing strategy. If *the story* tells about owning the future, *the positioning* tells about staking a legitimate claim in the present. It takes all your vision and mission background, and points it directly at the reality of the market and how you are going to meet it.

Sound positioning provides the foundation for creating specific demand. This positioning underlies all successful marketing messages. What's positioning? There are as many definitions as there are marketing people, but for us, positioning lays out the core claim you are planning to make in the market.

At its heart, great positioning is a great argument for how you win. It articulates the bet you are making.

Your positioning statement encompasses the essence of the play you've chosen in terms your people can understand. And, once again, in our rulebook it can't be any longer than three sentences.

But believe it or not, there's a handy shortcut for this critical task, as well. It's called the **XYZs.**

(Sorry for all the alphabet soup—the ABCs, the Ps and Qs, and now the XYZs. We know at first glance it sounds confusing, but we promise that once you start using these shorthand formulas, they will really simplify your strategy efforts and discussions.)

This one gives you another simple formula, one that will provide the skeleton for any successful positioning. The XYZ variables translate like this:

> X is the category of company, product, service, or other offering you've chosen to win—perhaps broadly, perhaps narrowly, as called for by your play.
> Y is the target audience with their unmet need.
> Z is the differentiation, advantage, or key positive distinction you have over your competition.

XYZ works out as a statement like this: "We are the only X that solves Y problem in Z unique way."

Back to Volkswagen again to extend the illustration. Using this formula, their positioning looks straightforward but turns out to be very powerful:

> Volkswagen makes the only German cars (X)
> . . . that the target customers (Y) can afford
> . . . and enjoy driving as much as the highest-priced alternatives (Z).

Each one of these elements is critical. And each draws deeply on the work you've already done in your Playbook.

X—THE CATEGORY DEFINITION

One of the positioning decisions you will make stands out in importance above all the rest. It's the one we've arrived at now: deciding where you are competing. "What's your category?" in other words. Category matters because if you define it well enough, you have in essence chosen your playing field.

Make sure to define your category in such a way that your solution/product/offering can win. Remember how Southwest Airlines did their XYZs—the "only short-haul, low-fare, high-frequency, point-to-point carrier in America." This is a great example of constraining your category so that you are best positioned within it. They kept their X as a short-haul carrier so they could be the only ones to offer Y American commuters Z flights with low fares and high frequency.

Make sure you articulate this category definition in a way that your targets can understand. It may be tempting to believe that your offering is so innovative that it constitutes an entirely new category, but introducing and having to explain something unfamiliar sets up an immediate roadblock to further consideration—a roadblock that is almost always unnecessary.

Take an existing category and effectively modify it. Remember the company Intelligent Results from Chapter Nine. They were a start-up with a dramatic technical breakthrough in the analysis and use of unstructured or text data. But they did not call themselves the unstructured data company. No one would have understood what that was. Instead they called themselves an analytics company "powered by unstructured data" (we'll have more to say about differentiation later).

Finally, you need to be sure you place yourself in a category that your target buyers see as a priority. It will do you no good to place yourself in a category that is clearly understood and where you have clear advantages over others, if that category ranks as a low priority to those with the checkbooks. Remember how Nth Orbit re-launched themselves as a company by focusing on a newly urgent customer issue. That urgency allowed them to reposition themselves with a bang, not a whimper.

Y—THE CUSTOMER NEED

This leads to the second element, the customer problem, or Y. You need to decide how narrowly or broadly you want to define the target customer and how this definition may change in what time-frame. This decision will be bound by how specific vs. how general your claims can and should be. Once the customer set has been clearly defined, the next step for solving Y is to figure out the customers' problem and shape the criteria for successfully solving that problem in such a way that brings the greatest advantages to you and your strategy.

Z—THE DISTINCTIVENESS OF YOUR OFFERING

This leads to your differentiation, or Z. You need to cement the whole argument in a strong claim of differentiation. Your claim of uniqueness must be one that you can support by the truth of the current offering as well as by the long-term abilities of the company to deliver. It must be defendable. In addition, it must pass the same litmus tests as those applied to the X of this formula in terms of clarity, comprehension, and relevance.

This differentiation binds the whole argument and defines the terms by which you plan to win in the hearts and minds of your targets. It's a statement of the primary bet you must make in order to win in the market, and is a direct outcropping of the play you choose to run.

Is your positioning true to your assessment of your playing field? Is the category well defined enough and within your reach? Is the customer problem urgent and interesting enough? And are you advantaged enough against the competitors you face in the market?

Is your positioning true to the play you've chosen? Fig. 13–1 presents a quick guide to help you make sure.

	X Category	Y Customer Problem	Z Differentiation
Drag Race	Already established by others	Current alternatives not good enough	Better than the best alternative in every way
Platform	A whole industry	Peace of mind, variety	The accepted standard
Stealth	A niche	Very specific unmet needs	Works well with other players
Best-of-Both	Two categories or extremes	Having to choose	Makes paradox possible
High–Low	One large default	Facing a compromise	Flexibility, room to grow

Fig. 13–1. Basic XYZ positioning for each play

Fleshing Out the Brief–Two Rules for Stating Your Case, Story, and Positioning

Your campaign brief is not just a document. It is a vital tool for your campaign. It needs to be a tool that everyone on the campaign team can easily use. As such it needs to communicate simply and clearly. Here are two basic principles or rules of thumb that will help keep the information and guidance you provide in the brief—and the target audience facing communications themselves—clear and on target.

The Rule of Three

You've seen with each element of the brief that you've been forced to keep things simple by constraining yourself to just three sentences. Well, nowhere is this limitation more important than when it comes to supporting your claims. Even if, based on your play, you choose tactically to load up your story with piles of features to win a product comparison list, here you still need to focus on just three areas of support. More than that and no one will remember them. It's no wonder McDonald's had the line "Food, Folks and Fun." Who would have responded to "Food, Folks, Fun, Filling, Fortifying, and Fast"?

The three elements you choose to focus on need to be in sync with one another and to flow from one to the next—which leads to yet another of our shortcut techniques:

The Rule of P>B>F

P>B>F is shorthand for "Proof is stronger than Benefits, which are stronger than Features."

You say you're the cheapest? Prove it. You say you're the easiest to maintain? Show it. You're going to need some ammunition to back up all your claims.

That's the point of the final section of the brief. It will fill in the essential details, building on the bald argument you've assembled so far. As your team now prepares to turn all this thinking and argument into real communications that will hit the market, they need some ammunition to back up all their claims.

This supporting data falls into three categories; from least to most impactful, the categories are:

Functionality and features: what you have. These are the things that your company, product, or service actually does. And what the product elements or service programs are that you use to deliver this functionality.

Needs and benefits: why they should care. This is all about answering the customer's question "What's in it for me?"—the aspects of your offering your customer actually cares about, and how their lot is bettered by what you have to sell them.

Evidence or proof: why they should believe you. Here is the data you draw on to truly show that you aren't just making idle claims but can back up what you say.

Features and functionality are great. They are clearly what you internally spend a lot of your time on. And, similar to the way you think about your category (that is, your X), you should list the ones that only you have.

But cool features are not enough, at least not for most customers. Most people are like you and me—they have to believe that they are actually going to get some benefit before they fork over their hard-earned cash.

Benefits are essential. When pulling this ammunition together, you need to make sure you think benefit, benefit, benefit. As in your positioning, when you think about your Y customer, you need to put all of these nice features in the context of your customers' needs. Why should they care about a category of features and functionality? What do those features and functions actually do for them?

Finally, proof speaks a lot louder than all this other stuff. It's one thing to say that you do something and even to get people to care. But they aren't going to act unless they believe you. The stronger the facts you have at your disposal to support your claims, the better. Match the evidence to each category of feature and benefit. And always lead with the strongest you have.

Clearly the most powerful kind of proof of your claims is market acceptance. If you have a lot of market power and you've gained significant customer traction, you should be able to find a way to claim actual leadership (Fig. 13–2). You should find a way to say that you are the number one in your category. Anyone who is in a position to say "number-one best-selling" and doesn't use it is a fool. That claim is your best—in fact, your *only*—way to capture the market as a whole.

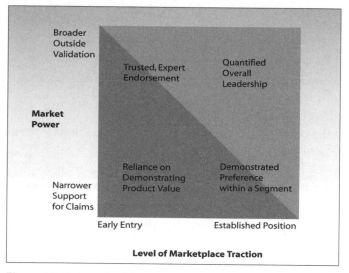

Figure 13–2. How best to prove your claims

If you aren't quite there yet but you've made some good traction, you can approximate a number-one kind of claim. You can be number one among a subset of the market, preferably one that other customers can relate or aspire to. "Choosy mothers choose Jif" is a classic example. You're not exactly sure who those choosy mothers they surveyed are, but you know that you would rather be one of them than a totally negligent, lackadaisical mom.

Another great example was Microsoft Word with its Word vs. WordPerfect challenge. Focusing on those who were part of the blind "taste test," Word was able to claim that more WordPerfect users actually chose Word over WordPerfect itself. This is a great method for getting the early majority to begin to convert. They will remain part of the group they respect or envy.

If you have had the time and effort to prove your product or offering to more people than just you, even if the results are small you should still make as much hay out of them as possible. Anyone, *anyone* who likes you and is willing to talk about it is evidence. This can take many forms ranging from early customer testimonials, to favorable reviews, to recognized expert endorsements. Market laggards and economic buyers will want statistically significant data of some sort, but a big chunk of the market that is more aggressive will feel sufficient comfort from knowing that they aren't the first to stick their necks out and try something new.

On the other hand, if you're just starting and don't have much customer or expert evidence, you'll just have to rely on the product or offering itself. You'll need to show as much of what you have as possible. While a lot of your target audiences won't be swayed by this, if you can target the early adopters correctly with the right kind of show-and-tell, you may get them excited enough to buy. Early adopters don't really care if it's number one or not—in fact, for them number one can mean passé.

Always lead with your strongest proof. But remember that each piece of your evidence matters to different targets.

Here's one last look at the Volkswagen example to see how all this support might hang together: Sales data underscored the affordability of Volkswagen cars. Reviews from the likes of *Road and Track* and *JD Powers* underscored performance of their product. And the actual car and test drive underscored how fun their cars were.

The benefits derive from a set of features and functionality. They are the punch line, why the features are there. The Volkswagen range of product line allows for all kinds of buyers. You may not know or care what MPG, MPH, or double overhead cam are. But, the benefits are clear. You don't need to spend a lot on gas—the car accelerates quickly. It isn't noisy. And the little flower vase in the Bug poetically demonstrates that the company is dedicated to fun.

Complete, but Short and Sweet: Those Are the Best Marching Orders.

Pulling the campaign team together is one thing. But getting them to run down the field with a single purpose is another. Summarizing your whole strategy—your advantage, your goals, and the support they will need along the way, and doing it in a manner that is easily translated into messages that the campaign's targets can easily understand—is the essence of the campaign brief. Armed with this very crisp brief, your campaign team is ready to charge off toward the end zone.

Take-Aways for Planning the Campaign Brief

The campaign brief is the single document that ensures unity and consistency among all the members of your campaign team and all the elements of your actual campaign. You create it as a *one-page* document summarizing the entire Playbook you have created thus far. The brief will have these elements:

1. **The Case.** For the team to buy into the campaign and its strategy, they need to understand the rationale behind it. The Yes, But, So approach offers a simple formula for making this clear in three sentences that acknowledge the situation, challenge the status quo, and propose an alternative.

2. **The Story.** This part provides the motivation. You need to put forth your shared mission, vision, and values with great clarity. The Three "We's"—We believe, We will, and We are—give you a great method for doing this simply and consistently.

3. **The Positioning (XYZs).** This is the heart of the brief and the fulcrum of the campaign. Your positioning is the central claim that you will stake in the market. Turning this positioning claim into an accepted market reality is the key bet behind your play. Following the XYZ formula—"the only X company (or product) that solves Y customer problem in Z unique way"—ensures that this argument is both complete and concise.

4. **The Support.** Finally, the campaign brief needs to include the ammunition that all of your team and all of the campaign deliverables will draw upon to sustain your case, story, and claims. Remember the Rule of Three and focus on no more categories of support than that. Also remember the Rule of P>B>F: lead with your strongest proof first, then explain what you do in terms of real benefits to the customer, and organize all the features that make these possible.

Coming Up

Now that you have your team and a brief to guide them, you can move into action. How do you go from strategy and positioning to reaching people and persuading them? You're now faced with a whole other set of choices, decisions, and judgments you will have to render as you and your team begin generating the campaign deliverables and placing them out in the market.

We look at these deliverables next and provide some helpful tips and tricks to make sure they do a good job for you out there in the real world of supply and demand.

Think like a wise man but communicate in the language of the people.

—WILLIAM BUTLER YEATS

14. Campaign Deliverables

At the end of all your planning and preparing, you gotta get your message out there in the market and see if it sticks.

No matter what your strategy, no matter what your play, it all comes down to this: do customers and prospects listen, do they believe, and do they open up their checkbooks and start signing?

Up to now, everything we've been dealing with has been about inputs—strategy inputs, team inputs, campaign inputs. Now it's time for outputs. It's no longer about planning, it's about doing—getting out there in the market and making it happen. It's about generating interest and motivating action. If you can't do that well, what good is all the rest?

How do you make this happen? Simple: effective communications. Your messages need to grab people, hold their attention and interest, and get them to do something.

Easier said than done, of course. Every one of these situations is different—different audiences, different levels of receptivity, different delivery vehicles. But all of them have some basic things in common. We start with an inventory of the key messages you will need to craft, along with some tips on how to craft them, for making each of them more powerful and more effective. From there, you'll improvise to adapt them to your own situation. But that's the fun part.

Campaign Messaging: Turning Positioning XYZs into Words People Read and Relate To

Marketing people like to throw around the term *messaging* all the time. It helps them feel important. But it's straightforward enough: messaging is the stuff you say, the messages you convey into the market.

Isn't that what you just did with your positioning, all that work that went into the campaign brief about Yes, But, So and XYZs? People sometimes fall into the trap of using the terms *positioning* and *messaging* interchangeably. They are not the same.

Positioning is the logic that guides everything. You use it inside the organization to help you make sure all of your messaging flows from a consistent theme and is in sync with your strategy. Great positioning does not have to be eloquent or catchy. It just has to be right.

Messaging is all the various public expressions of that positioning in the activities you conduct to persuade people to become customers, and to persuade customers to pay you more. Messaging is the actual words you use to communicate with your target audience. These words and how you put them together really matter.

Because so many people misuse these terms in ways that confuse their efforts, it will help to take a look at some familiar examples to identify the basic positioning and the core messaging derived from it.

To begin with, we look at some of the differences in one of the most widely advertised categories—athletic apparel.

Think of a company whose positioning is all about being the leader in personal empowerment for everyone in every sport, for making everyone feel that they can and they just should get out there and give it a try. Can you guess who it is?

Nike. Their familiar messaging "Just do it" serves as a call to action for you to feel such empowerment.

In contrast, one of Nike's rivals positions themselves as the specialized, high-performance provider for the serious amateur. Any ideas? If you use them, you'll know.

The company is called Mizuno. And their messaging of "Serious Performance" reinforces their differentiation as premier, exacting, quality, professional-level.

Given the amount of traffic that fast food companies need to generate, they recognize competitive messaging as a vital focus.

Think of a company that gained the enviable situation of simply being able to focus positioning on category leadership. Their name *equals* fast food.

McDonald's, of course. The messaging of "You deserve a break today" helped establish the whole notion of affordable fast food, liberating you from the drudgery of cooking or the time and expense of sitting in a restaurant when you really wanted to be getting other things done.

On the other hand, one rival company set out to differentiate themselves from the leader by focusing on *customized* fast food.

Burger King's "Have it your way" message helped it establish a foothold in the market with its position of offering choice.

And from the automotive segment, one of the companies we looked at earlier established and maintained its position as the premier source of exclusive German performance engineering.

BMW punctuated this positioning and its focus on superior mechanics with the bold claim of "The Ultimate Driving Machine."

But, as we have observed in some depth, one of BMW's rival countrymen rode the coattails of this great positioning to offer a Best-of-Both alternative.

Volkswagen's messaging of "Drivers Wanted" offers an open, accessible invitation to anyone who loves to drive.

Making Your Own Message Compelling

You're the one to know what's really unique and exciting about your company; we can give you some guidelines to get you started. We have a simple formula (we sure do like formulas, don't we?) that can act as both your checklist and your litmus test to complete and judge whether your messaging is going to stand up.

This formula is called MUST. It's simple. See Fig. 14–1 for how it works.

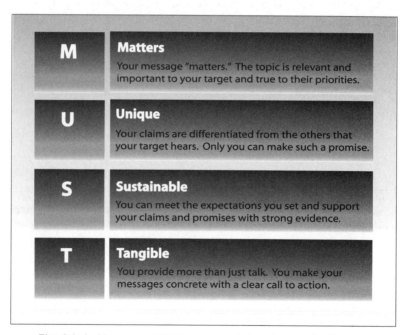

M — Matters
Your message "matters." The topic is relevant and important to your target and true to their priorities.

U — Unique
Your claims are differentiated from the others that your target hears. Only you can make such a promise.

S — Sustainable
You can meet the expectations you set and support your claims and promises with strong evidence.

T — Tangible
You provide more than just talk. You make your messages concrete with a clear call to action.

Fig. 14–1. Messages MUST do these things to be effective.

Let's go back to the preceding messaging examples to see how they stand up with this litmus test in mind, starting again with the sports case.

	MIZUNO	**NIKE**
Matters	Mizuno establishes its relevance by focusing on a specialized slice of the market: serious amateurs. And that gives such people what they care about: serious equipment.	Nike appeals to the athlete in everyone. By offering the common person the same equipment as the pros, they appeal by association to the desire to be cool, strong, and fit.
Unique	Mizuno differentiates itself by focusing on the highest quality and design, and using performance-tested materials.	Nike maintains its position by focusing on coolness, innovative designs, and powerful imagery.
Sustainable	Mizuno supports its claims with ongoing investments in research and technology.	Nike supports its coolness appeal with a continuous stream of new designs.
Tangible	Mizuno makes this all tangible by giving product specifications, ratings, and reviews.	Nike relies on the likes of Tiger Woods as proof enough.

Very different but both powerful, and both complete.

How about fast food?

	McDONALD'S	BURGER KING
Matters	With its emphasis on consistent, fast food on the go, McDonald's appeals to everyone who doesn't have enough time.	Burger King appeals to those who want choices and so want their fast food made to order.
Unique	Only McDonald's has the huge number of nearly identical locations.	Burger King emphasizes the difference in its product—flame-broiled burgers, for example.
Sustainable	McDonald's relies on its ubiquity and leading sales to support its claim as the default choice.	Burger King hopes that being a more custom alternative will keep you coming.
Tangible	The perfect example of their appeal is the happy meal, complete with toy.	What better way to tell that the food is hot and made to order than . . . burn marks?

And the car category—

	BMW	VOLKSWAGEN
Matters	BMW focuses on yuppies' need for prestige—people who want a fast car they can show off.	VW focuses on a broader audience of regular people who want an affordable, reliable car that is also fun and fast.

	BMW	**VOLKSWAGEN**
Unique	BMW puts its focus on the quality and perfection of German engineering.	The focus is on German engineering . . . for everyone.
Sustainable	The guys at BMW defined the category of luxury performance.	These guys established themselves as a Best-of-Both alternative.
Tangible	Hey, your choice. Do you fancy a slick BMW Z4 Roadster?	. . . Or how about a new bright yellow VW Beetle?

Talking the Way That Your Audiences Want to Hear

Speaking in a voice that your target customers find appealing can be critical to the success of conveying your messages. No matter what your message, this *tone and manner* can mean the difference between a warm reception and a cold shoulder.

What makes the right tone and manner for your campaign depends on a wide variety of factors including the tone and manner of the competition, how aggressive your play is designed to be, and the purpose of the communication piece itself. But the most important factor is the situation of your target audience and whether they're inclined to be receptive.

In order for your message to be well received, you will need to tune your communications style differently depending on how the audience already knows you, what their attitude is about you, and how well informed they are. Pick the style as shown by Fig. 14–2.

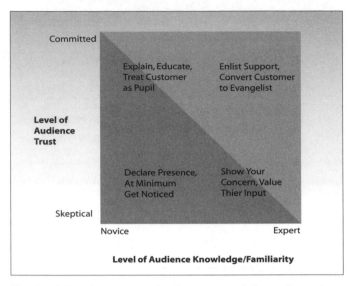

Fig. 14–2. Varying communications approach by audience type

High-Trust/High-Knowledge Targets

The customer situation also maps roughly to the plays. If your target already knows you and loves you *and* they are a very sophisticated, well-informed group, then make sure to treat them with the utmost respect. Make them feel that they are part of the team. There are other circumstances where this applies, but this is clearly what you want to do when you are running the Platform Play. As the leader you want to build the biggest ecosystem of allies possible. You need to make sure that your communications invite and incent them to help. If you are a Platform, you want to be the trusted standard. But do not be overbearing in your leadership position; you want to maintain and deepen their respect and trust in you. Even if you're not a Platform, treating loyal, knowledgeable audiences well can do a lot for powerful, positive word of mouth.

Low-Trust/High-Knowledge Targets

As is often the case when you're running a Drag Race where you are entering an established market as the challenger, your audience can be very sophisticated and well informed. Because you are new and they don't trust you yet, you need to make sure you overcome their concerns with information. They will understand how to digest it. The stronger your proof, the more quickly you will gain their respect.

This same dynamic may be true in starting a Stealth Play, where your targets are very knowledgeable about the niche you're entering but you are still new to them. In this case, make sure you show that you respect and understand their concerns. Speak their language. Make sure they feel that you can listen to them and that you respond. Recognize their input in your communications. What you learn, speak back to them and show your gratitude; if they are people in a niche market, they'll appreciate the attention.

High-Trust/Low-Knowledge Targets

If your audience is not sophisticated on your topic but predisposed to listen to you, because of either experience or your reputation, then be helpful. This can sometimes be the case with the High–Low Play where you already have customers using your entry-level product and you now offer a migration path to a more sophisticated premium edition. Make it easy for them. Invite them in and take the time to give them the information and guidance they need to make their decisions. Give them guides. Provide step-by-step instructions. Walk them through, all the way over to your cash register. One of

Merrill Lynch's best-selling tools was a basic guide to understanding financial statements. It was easier to use and understand than most business school finance textbooks.

Low-Trust/Low-Knowledge Targets

The final audience group neither understands the topic nor knows and trusts you. What the heck can you do to grab them with something provocative? Try this: make a declaration that might at least start them thinking. This is sometimes the case with the Best-of-Both Play where you are aiming at the big middle of the market and proposing a combination of things that they would previously not have thought of together. Go for it. The effort can be really worthwhile.

The Components of Effective Messaging

The components of your message will depend on whether you are doing an ad, sponsorship, press release, pitch, or some other form of communication. Sometimes all you will need is one sentence. How do you navigate through all this? There are a few key types of messages that you really need to pay attention to. These are the promise, the content, and the close.

1. The Promise

You open with your promise. This is where you pledge to make something good happen for your customer. Whatever you are selling costs something or you wouldn't be in business. And people get kind of emotional about their money. So your target's life had better be better after they buy your stuff or they are going to get mad. The beating heart of your message is your offering. And you only have about one second to get their attention. So, right—sometimes your headline states your promise.

Everything we have talked about thus far in terms of MUST and positioning should have prepared you from the standpoint of what you have to promise. But how you promise it also has to be intriguing.

Here too there is no magic. But there is a technique that is pretty powerful if you can make it work for your offering.

IT'S CALLED THE *RULE OF PARADOX*

As we saw in the Best-of-Both Play, people like to have their cake and eat it, too. But even if you are not running that play, if you ever want to capture people's attention, promise them two things in one, two things that they don't normally expect to come together. Such promises are intriguing and, if they are true, they are memorable and exciting.

A classic example: when Miller launched the entire light-beer category with its promise of "Tastes Great, Less Filling." A paradox— how could it be both? Sounds hard to believe but maybe I'll try it.

This kind of promise also works well in more complex categories. Such a promise formed the cornerstone of Apple's marketing with the memorable and lasting "Power made easy."

Similarly, Microsoft Office launched the application suite category with the promise of "Four Full-Featured Applications That Work Together Like One."

Whatever you do with your promise, keep it short and powerful. One promise only. But, as we've seen, it's great if you can include two things within the one that your customers wouldn't normally expect together. Compare each of the above paradox promises with their stand-alone alternatives. Read them and see what you think.

"Less Filling." Now there's a boring promise for you. Air is less filling. So what? But the strength in that combination, "Tastes Great, Less Filling," is intriguing enough to make you want to give it a try.

"Power." Sounds a bit better. But what kind of power? Unbridled power? Extreme power? Could be a bit intimidating or even dangerous in the wrong hand. "Power Made Easy" sure feels a lot more comfortable, doesn't it?

"Four Full-Featured Applications." How many? Four? That seems like a lot. Actually, sounds kind of fat. Could be a bit cumbersome just carrying around all the manuals. "Four Full-Featured Applications That Work Together Like One." Now *that* maybe I can handle.

You be the judge. But the way we see it, the short promises on their own, even though they have the virtue of being more brief, leave us wondering what's so special. Yet bonded together into a synthesis, each seems a lot more unique and enticing.

2. The Content

This is where you support your promise. The body copy, the backup, the core content. You thought a lot about support as you were pulling together the elements of the campaign brief. Now it's time to move from an inventory of all your good stuff, however well organized, into a select set of gems that interest and persuade.

By following the Rule of Three, you've already done a lot of the work to make simple what could be copious and confusing supporting evidence. You've also done your best to make it compelling by focusing on proof first, benefits second, and finally on the features from which both come. But there are a few more things you can do to make your supporting evidence work harder for you.

YOUR SECRET SAUCE

Across the three categories of features, benefits, and proof, you can bind it all together with one special ingredient. This ingredient is your "Secret Sauce," a technology, method, or innovation that only you have and that sits behind or is the source of all your offering's features. If you have one, touting that "secret sauce" not only binds together your detailed features and functionality into one memorable handle but also reinforces it and makes concrete your differentiation. Remember, it's not just the thing but also the name of the thing that makes it a compelling part of your message. If you don't name your unique element, you're not taking full advantage of it, and you invite easier imitation.

This notion first came from the food industry where special formulas and recipes were highly guarded secrets. Just think of Heinz ketchup. The idea of fifty-seven different kinds of tomatoes in its ketchup was memorable, but the name of the secret formula remained even more so, after we had all forgotten where the number fifty-seven came from. Of course, after you ate a burger with Heinz 57, you could always reach for a Certs breath mint with Retsin™. What's Retsin? Who knows. But whatever it was, it was intriguing and they were the only ones who had it.

Secret sauces can play a role in any category. In technology, with Microsoft Office, across all those "Four Full-Featured Applications" was one source of special goodness. The company called it Intellisense® Technology. No one really knew what the heck it was, but it sounded good and it seemed to make sense with all the features that were being demoed.

We've talked a lot about different cars in our examples. Chevron gas supposedly makes them go faster and cleaner because it has Techron®. And the ride should be smoother and safer with

Bridgestone Tires because they have something called UNI-T® or "Ultimate Tire Technology."

Secret sauces even follow you into the bathroom. Schick razors are supposedly better because they have ComfortStrip™ technology. And Crest toothpaste doesn't just have fluoride to keep away cavities no matter how many sugar bugs your kids invite into their mouths; Crest and only Crest has Floristat®.

Finally, to help you lead your customer down the right path and clear it a bit for them, we offer one last formula to guide you.

AWESOME, AWESOME, NOT SCREWED UP

This offers a simple way to make sure that your three categories of benefits, features, and proof are working hardest for you to persuade your target to go your way:

> Step One—Entice them with an aspect of your offering you know is highly appealing; that is, "awesome."
>
> Step Two—But then highlight one more superattractive thing to make sure you've really captured their attention. Emphasize "awesome" again.
>
> Step Three—Don't let anything stand in their way; anticipate their worries and doubts, and clear a way past them. In other words, finally assure them that your offering is "not screwed up."

With this approach, you motivate and excite your audience using one powerful promise, then another, and then you reduce their final barriers to movement by preempting their biggest concern or obstacle to purchase. All with just three statements. How you do this depends on what you have to offer and your target audience—what they are motivated by and what they are concerned about.

In our automotive cases, it was pretty simple. Volkswagen had performance, which is awesome, they had fun and they had style, which are also awesome. But the obvious question in the minds of their targets—average, economy-minded people—was, *Fine, but I wonder, if it's so good, am I going to have to pay the price of a BMW to get all that?* As the Best-of-Both Player, Volkswagen gave a loud NO in answer. Their offering was not screwed up by the high costs that otherwise make such cars unaffordable for most drivers.

Volvo's variant on this was that its new turbo wagons were fast (awesome) and sleek (awesome), but for the company's target—families with kids—the question was whether all that speed came at the sacrifice of safety. For them, too, the answer was no—all that speed and design are not screwed up by being as dangerous to drive as a Porsche or Lamborghini on a track.

Southwest Airlines could be proud that it could claim that its flights were frequent and on time. But did their tickets cost as much as the big guys'? No, again.

Technical audiences have their own hot buttons. In the case of Microsoft BackOffice, which sold to IT professionals, customers were happy that the products interoperated and were scalable, but they wanted to know that they were also secure. They were, and of course we featured that fact in our messages.

Whatever you do, remember—as you pull together your supporting content, as you pile on feature after feature, benefit after benefit, and proof after proof—when you heat people up and get them excited, you also have to address their concerns. You have to reduce any friction that might stand between them and the action you want them to take.

3. The Close

Finally, you come to the last part of your message, the offer or call to action. No special advice here, no formulas. Just the simple reminder—always ask. If you don't, they can't say yes. Sure, you have to give them a concrete step to take, a number to call, a form to fill out, a button to press. But the main thing is to ask them to do it.

Every communication is an opportunity. Not just to persuade people to think of you differently but to get them to act. This may seem like such an obvious step, but it's surprising, even shocking, how often otherwise great communications miss the final step—the chance for intelligence gathering, the opportunity for lead generation, even the chance to make a sale—because the message crafters simply overlooked the most important part, the close.

Convincing others that you are great may make you proud, but it doesn't make you rich. If you grabbed 'em with all the stuff above, you've got to keep 'em by getting some sort of commitment. Whether it's to ask a question, to make a complaint, or to place an order, the call to action is the part of the message that makes this happen. It's the invitation to your target to "come on down" and join you. Make sure they hear that invitation and have a chance to RSVP.

And whether it's a URL, a phone number, or an e-mail address, you need to give your target the information for getting in touch. All of these vehicles are messages themselves. Make sure to include them. Prominently. And try to have them synchronize with your other messages.

Ultimately, you had better be there when consumers respond. Answer the phone, support your Web site, return their e-mails. Take them to the next step and keep them coming. Track what happens. In addition to driving action, these calls, e-mails, and Web site hits are the pulse of your campaign. They are a great way to gauge its impact. Listen to what they tell you, and use the information to adapt as is appropriate.

Getting Heard, Getting Response, and Responding in Kind: That Is What It's All About.

The sales, profits, and market share your messages generate are the true measure of your whole Playbook. Play, playing field, and the campaign to run down it are not academic exercises. They are only useful tools if they have an impact, if they help you make money, and if they help you win and defend your place in the market. Now that you've delivered your messages and seen their impact, keep it going. Adapt, improve, reassess, and deliver again, not only the messages themselves, but also the whole of your Playbook. Remember, it is a living thing.

Take-Aways for Campaign Deliverables

1. **Positioning vs. messaging.** Messaging is a key marketing discipline. It's not complicated. It's the concrete words that you use to persuade your target audience to do what you want them to. Positioning is the statement of the theme that the messaging needs to convey. Messaging is derived from sound positioning, but is distinct from it. Where positioning is internal, messaging is external; it has to speak in a way people understand.

2. **MUST.** Getting your messaging right varies with every situation. But there are some basic guidelines. Your messages need to Matter, be Unique, be Sustainable, and be Tangible. If your messages pass this litmus test, you are well on your way.

3. **The right tone.** Just like conversation, marketing communications require a different touch for different target groups and in different situations. Adjust your tone to the level of trust in which you are held and the level of knowledge your target has about the topic of your effort. Where there's less knowledge, use more guidance; where there's less trust, use more facts.

4. **Rule of Paradox.** The heart of your messaging is your promise. Make it worth listening to. One of the best ways to do that is to offer an oxymoron—an otherwise unlikely combination of two into one. (If you can back up this promise with an exclusive secret sauce that sits behind it all, so much the better.)

5. **"Awesome, Awesome, Not Screwed Up."** But remember, no matter how powerful your promise, people may hesitate to act. Things that seem too good to be true often are. Take your target's concerns head on. Convincing them that you have addressed their concerns will help remove a barrier to action.

Coming Up

Following the logic of keeping it brief and providing a few simple pages of marching orders, the final chapter sends you on your way with just that: a brief summary of the whole Playbook system, the most important concepts to remember, and the inputs to apply to your own Playbook, complete with some simple forms for you to use to make the whole process easier.

Take time to deliberate, but when the time for action has arrived, stop thinking and go in.

—NAPOLEON BONAPARTE

15. Conclusion and Call to Action

Enough thinking. Enough planning. Enough wordsmithing. Time to suit up. Time to turn plans into action. Time to play ball.

In the preceding chapters, we've shared all the tools, tips, and techniques you need to pick your play, to understand the terrain you'll be running it on, and to get your team charging hard with the best tactics they can muster.

Now it's your turn. Now you get to use the Marketing Playbook you have developed for yourself. Now you get to test and improve it in the real world of customers and competition. Now you get to face the challenge of winning and retaining your rightful industry position. Now the real work and the real fun of marketing begins.

But before you go off on your exciting way, we want to leave you with two final things: a quick refresher on the tools you will take with you, and some last words of advice.

A Quick Refresher

We've crammed a lot of ideas and techniques and many years of learning and experience into these pages. But across this whole exercise, if you remember anything, remember just these three concepts:

> Your strategy options—picking one of just five plays;
> Your playing field—doing the ABC gap analysis;
> Your campaign—driving home your positioning XYZs.

Here is a quick summary and set of cheat sheets to each of them.

Your Menu of Strategy Options: The Five Plays

Fig. 15–1 presents a short summary menu of the play options—the conditions each is most appropriate for, the conditions required for

	Conditions	Requirement	Rewards	Risks	Response
Drag Race	Fragmented market	Superior offering	Clear focus, simplicity	Wherewithal, profitability	+ Platform - Drag Race
Platform	Won Drag Race	Partner business model	Security, lowest costs	Envy, complacence	+ Stealth - Drag Race
Stealth	Lost Drag Race	Winnable niche(s)	Survival, costs/margins	Irrelevance, take-over	+ Platform - Drag Race
Best-of-Both	High–Low trade-offs	Winning combination	Big market, split competition	Arrogance, rejection	+ High–Low - 2 Drag Races
High–Low	Generic incumbent	Premium *and* entry editions	Retained profit, migration path	Resources, complexity	+ Best-of-Both - 2 Drag Races

Fig. 15–1. Summary menu of the five plays

each, the reasons to choose or avoid each one, and the responses you can expect and should be prepared for once you've chosen.

In assessing and reassessing your choice, take a hard look at your own relative position and assets. For the conditions you see and foresee, do you have the right weapons? Have your resources outgrown your current strategy, or is it proving too much of a struggle? Are you capable of entering new businesses that require new thinking?

Also make sure the rewards and risks make sense. Are the incentives that enticed you into choosing your play still enticing? Are they out of your reach or are there bigger fish to fry? Have you avoided the pitfalls or fallen in?

Finally, make sure you understand the likely response of other players. Try to understand and anticipate the play that your competitors are running against you and choose the very best response yourself.

Most importantly, keep your analysis of the playing field fresh. Do the same gaps exist as when you first chose the play? If not, what are the new opportunities and challenges, and which play best suits them?

Many Gaps, One Map: The ABCs of Your Playing Field

Make sure you have a total picture of the *A* (current situation), *B* (future goals), and *C* (path for moving from one to the other). You've looked at the ABCs of your industry, customers, competition, and yourself. But try to prioritize the most important findings across them all. What is the most critical feature of your current situation, the one that requires the most attention? With that in mind, what are the best, most exciting yet realistic goals? Can this be summarized into one "point B"? Finally, what are the most important things you have to do to bridge between them? Across customers, competition, and yourself, what changes make most sense to focus on?

Each of your specific gap analyses yields specific findings. Your industry gap analysis yields a vision of the future worth shooting for. Your customer gap analysis yields the kind of offer that could be compelling. Your competitive analysis yields the relative position that needs to be differentiated. And your self-assessment yields the key action steps you need to take to deliver on any of these goals. Make sure these multiple gap analyses also come together into one fundamental picture and set of priorities that can guide you overall, as illustrated in Fig. 15–2.

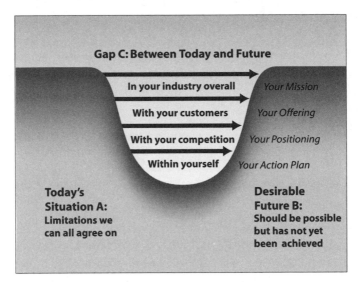

Fig. 15–2. Your playing field: summary ABCs

Remember to go back to this analysis often as you are in the thick of choosing and running your play. Things change; being in action gives you new intelligence. Make sure you are ready to digest and respond to these inputs as they come. Fig. 15–3 provides a shorthand review of what you need to know.

	Know Your Industry	Know Your Customer	Know Your Competition	Know Yourself
State of Things	Its economics and politics	What and how they buy	How they make money	How you operate
Places to Look	Gaps and opportunities	Concerns and priorities	Threats and vulnerabilities	Strengths and weaknesses
Bets to Make	Key trends	Critical needs	Next moves	Investment futures

Fig. 15–3. Assessing your playing field: the key things to know

In looking at your industry, focus on the economics and politics that make it tick. Look for the gaps and opportunities that are worth exploiting or avoiding. And make sure to have a keen sense of the direction things are going and which direction makes sense to bet on.

In looking at your customers, understand how they tick. What is their purchase behavior today? See if you can find the opening for change in what they are concerned about and what they care about most. And as a result, make sure you are always perceived as addressing a truly critical need.

In looking at and comparing yourself to the competition, try to understand their modus operandi. Use the Ps and Qs to map how you and they make money. How does this influence their decisions? Try to secure yourself against the biggest threats they pose and try to find ways to exploit their most nagging vulnerabilities. And make sure you use this knowledge to anticipate their responses to your own actions.

Finally, in looking at your own company, take a long, clear look at your own operations. How do you make money, how do you communicate and make decisions? Be honest about your strengths and weaknesses. And build a rational plan for investing in future improvement.

Do these things and not only will you know the contours of your market landscape, you will be able to navigate them effectively as you run down the field. That is where you pull it all together and finally drive for victory, with your marketing and sales campaigns.

Killer Marketing Campaigns: Driving Home Your Positioning XYZs

The real moment of truth and the true test of all your strategy and analysis comes in the heat of real battle, in the action of your marketing campaign. Pulling off a great, successful campaign centers around three key elements.

First, you cannot run a great campaign by yourself. You are the coach, but you need a team. Make sure to assign each player the right role, and keep them all together with a single campaign calendar.

Second, you have to motivate this team with a single, inspiring set of marching orders—your campaign brief. At the heart of this (and, for that matter, the heart of your whole campaign) is your positioning. The formula for this positioning argument or claim is simple: people have to believe that you are the only X (category) of offering that solves their Y (customer problem) in Z (differentiation) unique way.

Finally, you have to communicate to your targets in a way that grabs them, that they believe, and that motivates them to give you (instead of someone else) their money. Remember to keep your messages simple, offer them something that is surprising, and support your claims with the most compelling evidence you have. And, no matter what you are trying to tell them, don't leave them hanging. Give them something to do: leave them with a clear, specific action step.

Here is a short set of forms that can help you guide your campaign through all of these elements. Fig. 15–4 lays out the concepts; Fig. 15–5 is filled in with an example; and Fig. 15–6 is a blank form for you to fill out for your own play and your own campaign.

Project		
The campaign	*Name*	*Objective*	*Time Line*
	Your campaign	To win *your* play	Soon
The team	*Owners*	*Decision Makers*	*Participants*
	Your most organized doer	*You* and maybe your boss	*Your* whole virtual team
The temperature	*Red*	*Yellow*	*Green*
	Hopefully, other people's stuff	The stuff *your* direct reports are doing	With luck, *your* stuff
Case		
Yes. Situation	*Your* assessment		
But. Gap	*Your* concern		
So. **Insight to fill gap**	*Your* ambition		
Story		
Vision: Desired future (based on insight)	What *you* believe		
Mission: Role in realizing vision	What *you* commit to		
Values: Criteria for fulfilling mission	What *you* stand for	What *you* stand for	What *you* stand for

Fig. 15–4. Basic outline for your own campaign worksheet

Positioning		
X category	The category *you can win in*	
Y target	The low-hanging fruit *you will win*	
Z differentiation	The key thing *you have over the other guy*	
Message		
Promise	*Your* paradox, the cake and eat it too *you* have to offer	
Tagline	*Your* invitation	
Secret sauce	*Your* trademarked coolness	
Argument		
	Rule of three		
Benefits	*You're* "awesome"	*You're* "awesome"	*You're* "not screwed up"
Proof	*Your* best evidence of awesome	*Your* best evidence of awesome	*Your* best evidence of not screwed up
Features, functionality	Name of *your* awesome stuff	Name of *your* awesome stuff	Name of *your* stuff that keeps working
Voice Tone and manner	The level of familiarity and info warranted by *your* target's level of trust and knowledge		
Offer Call to action	*Your* most attractive next step		

Project			
The campaign	*Name*	*Objective*	*Time Line*
	Drivers wanted	Relaunch VW image	December
The team	*Owners*	*Decision Makers*	*Participants*
	Marketing, ad agency	Germany	Sales, dealers, engineering
The temperature	*Red*	*Yellow*	*Green*
	Product inventory	Local ads	Tagline
Case			
Yes. Situation	Yes, there are terrific, German-engineered cars available on the market for driving enthusiasts.		
But. Gap	But they are very, very expensive and appeal only to snobs.		
So. Insight to fill gap	So, why can't there be a high-performance car for average enthusiasts?		
Story			
Vision: Desired future (based on insight)	We believe everyone should really enjoy their driving experience.		
Mission: Role in realizing vision	We help make this possible by building the very best performing cars at prices average people can afford.		
Values: Criteria for fulfilling mission	Value	Performance	Personality

Fig. 15–5. Hypothetical Volkswagen campaign worksheet

Positioning			
X category	We make the only high-performance cars		
Y target	That average people can afford		
Z differentiation	And enjoy driving as much as the highest-priced alternatives.		
Message			
Promise	German engineering for everyone		
Tagline	Drivers wanted		
Secret sauce	Fahrvergnugen		
Argument			
	Rule of three		
Benefits	Performance	Fun	Affordability
Proof	Great reviews	Customer testimonials	Number-one–selling
Features, functionality	X Horsepower, MPH, etc.	Flower vase	Product line
Voice Tone and manner	Warm, familiar, inviting, fun, playful		
Offer Call to action	Test drive one today, no money down, 0% financing		

Project		
Name	**Objective**	**Time Line**
Owners	**Decision Makers**	**Participants**
Red	**Yellow**	**Green**

Row labels: **The campaign**, **The team**, **The temperature**

Case		
Yes. Situation		
But. Gap		
So. Insight to fill gap		

Story		
Vision: Desired future (based on insight)		
Mission: Role in realizing vision		
Values: Criteria for fulfilling mission		

Figure 15–6. Blank campaign worksheet for you to copy and fill in

Positioning		
X category		
Y target		
Z differentiation		

Message		
Promise		
Tagline		
Secret sauce		

Argument		
	Fill in your three	
Benefits		
Proof		
Features, functionality		
Voice Tone and manner		
Offer Call to action		

Last Words of Advice:
Keep Doing, Keep Learning.

Marketing is a living thing. All these theories and techniques don't amount to a hill of beans in the abstract; they only come to life if you use them.

So go out there and try things.

And whatever comes, never, never give up. Learn from every victory and every defeat. If you're open to them, each will bring with it another chapter in your own personal Playbook.

And that Playbook, your own Playbook, is the only one that matters.

So what are you waiting for?

Go get 'em!

Index